TRENDS IN COGNITIVE AND BEHAVIOURAL THERAPIES

TRENDS IN COGNITIVE AND BEHAVIOURAL THERAPIES

Edited by

Paul M. Salkovskis
University of Oxford, Department of Psychiatry, Warneford Hospital, Oxford, UK

JOHN WILEY & SONS
Chichester · New York · Brisbane · Toronto · Singapore

Copyright © 1996 by John Wiley & Sons Ltd,
Baffins Lane, Chichester,
West Sussex PO19 1UD, England

National   01243 779777
International   (+44) 1243 779777

Other Wiley Editorial Offices

John Wiley & Sons, Inc., 605 Third Avenue,
New York, NY 10158-0012, USA

Jacaranda Wiley Ltd, 33 Park Road, Milton,
Queensland 4064, Australia

John Wiley & Sons (Canada) Ltd, 22 Worcester Road,
Rexdale, Ontario M9W 1L1, Canada

John Wiley & Sons (Asia) Pte Ltd, 2 Clementi Loop #02-01,
Jin Xing Distripark, Singapore 0512

Library of Congress Cataloging-in-Publication Data

Trends in cognitive and behavioural therapies / edited by Paul M.
   Salkovskis.
      Includes bibliographical references and index.
      ISBN 0-471-96172-8 (hardcover). — ISBN 0-471-95788-7 (paper)
      1. Cognitive therapy.   I. Salkovskis, Paul M.
   RC489.C63T74   1996
   616.89'142—dc20   95–31227
                                                             CIP

British Library Cataloguing in Publication Data

A catalogue record for this book is available from the British Library

ISBN 0-471-96172-8 (cased)
ISBN 0-471-95788-7 (paper)

Typeset in 10/12pt Times by Dorwyn Ltd, Rowlands Castle, Hants
Printed and bound in Great Britain by Biddles Ltd, Guildford

This book is printed on acid-free paper responsibly manufactured from
sustainable forestation, for which at least two trees are planted for each one
used for paper production.

CONTENTS

About the Editor   vii
List of Contributors   viii
Preface   x

Chapter One   Trends in Cognitive and Behavioural Therapies   1
                   S.J. Rachman

Chapter Two   Avoidance Behaviour is Motivated by Threat Beliefs:
                   A Possible Resolution of the Cognition-Behaviour
                   Debate   25
                   Paul M. Salkovskis

Chapter Three   Social Phobia, Avoidant Personality Disorder and
                   the Multiaxial Conceptualization of Interpersonal
                   Anxiety   43
                   Richard G. Heimberg

Chapter Four   Personality Disorder and the Will: A Cognitive
                   Neuropsychological Approach to Schizotypal
                   Personality   63
                   J.M.G. Williams

Chapter Five   Control as a Pathway to Recovery from Alcohol
                   Problems   77
                   Mark B. Sobell and Linda C. Sobell

Chapter Six   A Cognitive Perspective on Gambling   89
                   Robert Ladouceur and Michael Walker

Chapter Seven   Emotion in Cognitive–Behavioral Theory
                   and Treatment   121
                   Jeremy D. Safran

Chapter Eight   Cognitive–Behavioural Therapy for Hallucinations
                  and Delusions: Current Practices and Future
                  Trends   133
                  *Lawrence Yusupoff, Gillian Haddock, William Sellwood
                  and Nicholas Tarrier*

Chapter Nine   Post-Traumatic Stress Disorder in Children   147
                  William Yule

Index   163

ABOUT THE EDITOR

Paul Salkovskis is currently Wellcome Trust Senior Research Fellow in Basic Biomedical Science at the University of Oxford Department of Psychiatry. He received his clinical training at the Institute of Psychiatry before moving to work in full-time clinical practice in Yorkshire. Having worked for seven years as a clinician with a strong interest in research work he moved to the University of Oxford where he became a researcher with a strong interest in clinical treatment. He worked with David M. Clark on the development of the cognitive theory and treatment for panic and agoraphobia. He has also played a key role in the development of the cognitive-behavioural approach to Obsessive-Compulsive Disorder, Obsessional Ruminations and Hypochondriasis. Since 1988 he has been editor of the journal of the British Association for Behavioural and Cognitive Psychotherapies, *Behavioural and Cognitive Psychotherapy*. He is on the editorial boards of numerous journals and has published around one hundred journal articles and book chapters. He is known nationally and internationally as a researcher and teacher in the area of cognitive and behavioural psychotherapy.

CONTRIBUTORS

Gillian Haddock   School of Psychiatry and Behavioural Sciences, Department of Clinical Psychology, Withington Hospital, West Didsbury, Manchester M20 8LR, UK

Richard G. Heimburg   Department of Psychology, State University of New York at Albany, New York 12222, USA

Robert Ladouceur,   Laboratoire de thérapies behaviorales, Ecole de psychologie, Université Laval, Québec, Canada G1K 7P4

S.J. Rachman   Department of Psychology, University of British Columbia, 2136 West Mall, Vancouver, British Columbia, Canada V6T 1Y7

Paul M. Salkovskis   University of Oxford, Department of Psychiatry, Warneford Hospital, Oxford OX3 7JX, UK

Jeremy D. Safran   Graduate Faculty, Clinical Psychology Program, The New School for Social Research, 65 Fifth Avenue, New York, NY 10003, USA

William Sellwood   School of Psychiatry and Behavioural Sciences, Department of Clinical Psychology, Withington Hospital, West Didsbury, Manchester M20 8LR, UK

Mark B. Sobell   Department of Family and Community Medicine, Psychology and Behavioural Science, University of Toronto, 33 Russell Street, Toronto, Ontario, Canada M5S 2S1

Linda C. Sobell   Department of Family and Community Medicine, Psychology and Behavioural Science, University of Toronto, 33 Russell Street, Toronto, Ontario, Canada M5S 2S1

Nicholas Tarrier   School of Psychiatry and Behavioural Sciences, Department of Clinical Psychology, Withington Hospital, West Didsbury, Manchester M20 8LR, UK

Michael Walker — Department of Psychology, University of Sydney, NSW, Australia 2006

J.M.G. Williams — Department of Psychology, University College of North Wales, Bangor, Gwynnedd, LL57 2DG, UK

William Yule — Institute of Psychiatry, De Crespigny Park, London SE5 8AF, UK

Lawrence Yusupoff — School of Psychiatry and Behavioural Sciences, Department of Clinical Psychology, Withington Hospital, West Didsbury, Manchester M20 8LR, UK

PREFACE

The success of cognitive-behavioural approaches to treatment has primarily been due to the emphasis on sensitive and thoughtful clinical work on the one hand and a focus on basic and applied research on the other. The resulting scientist-practitioner model is, of course, an abiding legacy from behaviour therapy (Salkovskis, 1984, 1986). Inevitably, practitioners and clinicians have become victims of the success of the field. An exponential increase in published articles, books and journals has made it impossible to encompass the entire field. The sheer volume of material tends to obscure the key trends.

This book is the first of an occasional series which seeks to identify key trends in cognitive-behavioural approaches to the understanding and treatment of psychological problems. The aim is to offer a platform to people working in the field in order that they might identify such trends and make informed judgements as to whether they are good or bad. Each author has been asked to distil knowledge from their own field. Where detailed information about research and/or treatment strategies is required, this is provided, but no atempt has been made to exhaustively review the literature. The authors have been encouraged to express their opinions and make explicit value judgements and opinions (their own or those which are implicit in current work). In addition, authors have been asked to offer suggestions concerning future directions, to criticize existing trends and generally to attempt to influence the reader and the field.

In this first volume, Jack Rachman identifies and discusses developments in cognitive-behavioural approaches as a whole. Few are as well qualified as Jack to identify and influence trends in this area. His analysis of present trends is optimistic; more specifically, he highlights the important contribution of cognitive approaches and their likely importance in treatments formerly considered to be primarily behavioural in effect. In my own chapter, I consider cognition–behaviour links and highlight problems with exposure 'theories'. In particular, it is suggested that the eclectic combination of cognitive and behavioural treatments can be replaced by a view in which threat beliefs are key in motivating avoidant behaviour whilst avoidant behaviour can play a key role in maintaining threat beliefs.

The last five years have seen a growing interest in more complex and longer-term problems. Much has been written about their cognitive treatment, although there is little research on treatment. Unfortunately, most clinicians and researchers have chosen to adopt the label 'personality disorder' to describe problems such as chronic low self-esteem, difficulties in coping with relationships and so on. The use of this unsatisfactory diagnostic label clearly reflects the influence of the DSM III (now DSM IV) on those concerned with psychological treatment. Formerly, the diagnosis of 'personality disorder' tended to be correlated with value judgements made by the clinician (almost never with the agreement or even knowledge of the patient). In many instances, such a diagnosis reflected the clinician's dislike or even a sense of superiority. The revival of what was a previously discredited concept carries with it the danger of the recurrence of such misuses of the term. Two thoughtful chapters confront the issue of personality disorder. Rick Heimberg identifies some of the difficulties involved in the specific diagnosis of avoidant personality disorder and its relationship with social phobia. This paper highlights the elusiveness of personality disorder concepts. Mark Williams adopts a bold approach, suggesting that the more direct investigation of psychological processes will repay effort. This is a most encouraging development; it makes it possible to relate measurable psychological processes to the type of symptoms which people complain of. The possibility of experimental studies promises a more systematic and less psychiatric approach of the type which Jack Rachman highlights as being crucial to future developments in cognitive-behavioural treatments.

Similar considerations are raised by Mark and Linda Sobell. Advocates of disease models of alcohol abuse have tended to have an overwhelming influence on clinical practice without any real reference to research findings. The Sobells have long advocated a less evangelistic approach, and have at times been heavily criticized as a result. Their chapter is a model of the type of balanced approach which is so clearly needed if progress is to be made in the area of addiction. By the same token, Bob Ladouceur and Michael Walker have provided a thoughtful and clear analysis of gambling from a cognitive perspective. This is an area which has, in the past, tended to be the preserve of the more behaviourally oriented, given the obvious relevance of principles of learning theory, particularly reinforcement schedules. However, modern learning theory is part of cognitive science, and issues of expectancy and perceived causality are elegantly laid out by Ladouceur and Walker in this timely analysis. The huge impact of the national lottery in the UK is a microcosm of a worrying worldwide increase in all types of gambling and in the number of people experiencing problems with it.

Cognitive-behavioural approaches to the understanding and treatment of psychological problems have tended to be hampered by the way in which the role of emotion is specified (or not, as the case may be). Jeremy Safran highlights some clinical and theoretical insights which have tended to elude cognitive-behavioural theorists and therapists. He identifies generic principles which could provide theoretical foundations for those interested in applying the cognitive-behavioural approach to emotion, considering emotion as an important and rich aspect of human experience. Some echo of these broader humanistic concerns are to be found in Yusupoff, Haddock, Sellwood and Tarrier's consideration of the treatment for delusions and hallucinations. A hallmark of this rapidly developing area is the way in which the cognitive-behavioural approach allows clinicians to consider people suffering from psychotic symptoms as people suffering from psychotic symptoms rather than as psychotics or schizophrenics. The emotional impact of psychotic symptoms (or psychosis) can be seen as a qualitatively similar reaction to that of a person who has asthmatic symptoms and who receives a diagnosis of asthma. Such symptoms are one facet of the person's life rather than necessarily being a defining feature.

Finally, problems which begin in childhood *can* become a defining feature of the child's later adult life. Bill Yule considers Post-Traumatic Stress Disorder in Children in terms of its effects and treatment. The systematic way in which cognitive-behavioural approaches can consider such problems without resorting to rigid disease concepts is the hallmark not only of this chapter but of all the chapters in this volume. This has always been a key trend in cognitive and behavioural approaches; long may it continue.

Paul M. Salkovskis
September 1995

REFERENCES

Salkovskis, P.M. (1984)   Psychological research by NHS clinical psychologists: an analysis and some suggestions, *Bulletin of the British Psychological Society*, **37**, 375–377.

Salkovskis, P.M. (1986)   The cognitive revolution: new way forward, backward somersault or full circle? *Behavioural Psychotherapy*, **14**, 278–282.

Chapter One

S.J. RACHMAN

Trends in Cognitive and Behavioural Therapies

Behaviour therapy (BT) and cognitive therapy (CT) are well into the process of merging and the resulting combination, cognitive-behavioural therapy (CBT), now dominates clinical research and practice. The background to this fusion will be described and the likely outcome of the merger needs to be considered. Thus far, most attention has been given to depression and latterly to the anxiety disorders, but an expansion into medical and health problems beyond the topics of 'Psychiatric psychology' can be anticipated.

In the first decade of BT there was a good deal of theorizing and grand designs were offered, but the emphasis then shifted to technical topics, notably to the assessment of therapeutic efficacy. Fresh theoretical analyses only emerged with the introduction of cognitive concepts; nevertheless, we remain stronger on efficacy than on understanding. This chapter deals mainly with trends in theory.

The future of CBT will also be shaped by external forces that are less benign than the competition between scientists. As is common knowledge, the cost of providing health care has risen sharply in most industrial countries and now threatens to cause economic difficulties for many of them. The need to contain these costs will affect the provision of psychological therapy, as with all other health care services, and our procedures will have to become increasingly refined and increasingly economic. In the longer term we will have to transform many of our psychological techniques into self-help procedures, which will not only be considerably cheaper but will also help to return to

Trends in Cognitive and Behavioural Therapies. Edited by P.M. Salkovskis.
© 1996 John Wiley & Sons Ltd.

people the main responsibility for protecting and promoting their own health. Another challenge, and one of greater intellectual interest, comes from the current embrace of biological theories by a majority of psychiatrists. Although there is no necessary clash between psychological and biological explanations of problems such as panic disorder or obsessional compulsive disorders (OCD), in practice the theories and procedures often are in competition, particularly as the biological theories are used as justification for using medication as the main or only form of treatment. For a variety of reasons, including the costs and the dominant influence of medicine, drug treatments for psychological problems tend to be the norm (remarkable comparative figures were provided by Barlow, 1993). By comparison, psychological treatments are provided sparingly, despite their acknowledged efficacy [see the NIH consensus conference] (Wolfe and Maser, 1994). This comparative failure to adopt reasonably well established psychological procedures is also documented in the handbook compiled by Giles (1993).

However reluctantly, we also have to take into account all manner of extra-scientific matters. Who will provide the services? Who will pay for them? Can CBT co-exist with biological models? What do we think about, and do about, the massive shift towards treatment by medication? How should the future relations between physician and other health care professionals be shaped and improved?

HISTORY

In order to analyse current trends they need to be considered against the events from which they have emerged. Psychological science has lagged behind other sciences in the accumulation of new knowledge, but once empiricism took its firm hold, essential methodological advances followed. In abnormal psychology, the movement towards adopting empirical methods and standards was slowed by the enticing sophistication of psychoanalysis, until the demand to 'show me' became irresistible. The adoption of empiricism, one of the 'inward workings of the age', transformed the methods of clinical psychology, and behaviour therapy became one of its 'outward facts'. The attractions of, and reasons for establishing, behaviour therapy included the legitimacy of its foundations in academic–scientific psychology, and its advocates' insistence on empirical standards (partly as a reaction to the frustrations of an elusive psychoanalysis).

LEARNING THEORY

Curiously, the specific connections with academic psychology, notably the dominating learning theories of the time, fell away, and now few seem to know and even fewer to care about those connections and their loss. Learning theory played a critical role in the launch of behaviour therapy but then faded out of sight. This left the field open for the development of an empirical and energetic behaviour therapy, which made valuable practical progress, but manifested a declining interest in theory building. It shifted from science to technology (Wolpert, 1992). The recent introduction of cognitive concepts has gone some way to filling the gap between technology and science, and the rapid acceptance of these ideas is, I believe, a reflection of dissatisfaction with an uncritical and undemanding form of empiricism.

PSYCHOTHERAPY

What has been learnt, both positive and negative, about psychotherapy over the past 40 years? How can these conclusions guide future work? What do we need to learn now? And how should we set about finding the necessary answers?

We have developed some plausibly effective therapeutic methods and learnt how to recognize the pitfalls involved in the study of psychotherapy. This recognition has promoted greatly improved standards and methods of investigation. As a result of errors made along the journey, all modern evaluations of psychotherapeutic procedures include some form of (temporarily) non-treated subjects/patients, the assessments are blind, or preferably double-blind, repeated checks on the integrity of the treatment procedures are carried out, the credibility of the comparison treatments is determined, and so forth. The automatic inclusion of a variety of safeguards and controls is a reflection of errors made and lessons learnt. We have also learnt that a number of innovative methods failed to produce useful results, and that the scanty evidence pertaining to the efficacy of psychoanalytic treatment fails to support the therapeutic claims made by proponents of this method. One of the most disappointing psychotherapeutic failures was recorded for Rogerian client-centered psychotherapy, a plausible and well-specified ambitious theory and practice of psychotherapy. Essentially, it was argued that for therapeutic improvement to occur constructive personality change must take place, and that this will happen when three necessary and sufficient therapeutic conditions are provided: warmth, empathy and genuineness. Rogers argued that 'if one or more of these conditions is not present, constructive personality change will not occur' (Rogers, 1957). Considerable effort and time was put into testing the theory, and the final outcome, that the three necessary and sufficient conditions are neither necessary nor sufficient, was a serious disappointment (see Mitchell, Bozarth and Krauft, 1977; Lambert, de Julio and Stein, 1978; Rachman and Wilson, 1980). In the face of reams of negative results [e.g. in one study involving 75 therapists and 120 clients, only 52 of the 1600 hypotheses produced a significant result! – see Mitchell et al. (1977)], most clinicians abandoned Rogerian psychotherapy. However, by some unexplained quirk, the Rogerian theory and methods appear to be widely accepted and practised in counselling of various sorts. Despite the painful disappointment of this ambitious research effort, important lessons were learned about how to conduct research into the mechanisms and effects of psychotherapy, and several methodological safeguards, such as testing for the integrity of the procedures, can be traced to the research on the Rogerian therapy. [Regrettably, therapy-process research continues to present formidable problems; in a recent re-analysis of a significant body of data, Shapiro et al. (1994) found that therapist intervention variables accounted for less than 2% of the variance.]

Before turning to a consideration of current ideas and practices, some remarks about the social context in which psychotherapy is practised are in order. In 1961, Jerome Frank observed that 'we should not forget that, at least in the United States, psychiatrists and psychologists combined, treat far fewer persons than chiropractors and religious healers' (p. 39). Those figures, or some comparable figures, probably are still applicable. In addition, practitioners of psychotherapy, whether psychologists or psychiatrists, increasingly find themselves in competition with physicians who prescribe psychotropic drugs. Even when the evidence for the therapeutic efficacy of psychotherapy is as good as or exceeds that of drug treatment, as in the treatment of panic disorder, patients are far more likely to receive drug treatment than psychotherapy (Barlow, 1993). It is no longer sufficient to demonstrate that psychotherapy is effective, it must also be shown to be economical. Instead of following that uncomfortable path, however, let us consider how the lessons of the past can be put to good use in the theory, research and practice of psychotherapy.

PSYCHOTHERAPY RESEARCH

In historical review, two types of psychotherapy research can be discerned: research into efficacy, usually the comparative efficacy of one or more types of therapy (e.g. desensitization versus pure relaxation) and the other type is investigative research designed to test a specific hypothesis (e.g. is the relief of tension headache pain contingent on a reduction in local muscle tension?). Both types of research are necessary but they serve different functions, and in the long term the investigative research is the most significant. Nevertheless, comparative efficacy research is essential, particularly in the early stages of developing a psychotherapeutic technique. Is this new method effective? Is it more effective than existing techniques? It is pointless to frame scientifically acute questions about a useless treatment procedure. The hypothesis about the need to reduce muscle tension in order to relieve headaches became a good and possible question only after confirmation of the therapeutic effects of biofeedback and relaxation techniques.

It can be argued that progress in acquiring a truly scientific understanding of psychotherapy depends on the design and execution of the second type of research, the investigation of specific hypotheses. The comparative efficacy research enables us to make technological advances but seldom and incidentally adds to our scientific understanding. The distinction between the science and the technology of psychotherapy was lucidly analysed by Eysenck (1994) in the recent update of his classic 1952 paper. He replies to the question, 'What separates science from technology?' (p. 479) with a quotation from Poincaré – 'the collection of facts is no more a science than a heap of stones is a home'.

INVESTIGATIONS

The need for comparative efficacy research is acknowledged, and the technical steps of sample selection, refinement of assessment techniques, ensuring the integrity of treatment, are well understood and constantly under improvement. We are therefore in a position to devote more thought and effort to the rationale and style of investigative hypothesis testing research. I have chosen some examples to illustrate the rationale and the style.

By 1954, Wolpe had developed and tested his fear-reducing technique, systematic desensitization. In his landmark book on psychotherapy, published in 1958, Wolpe set out his theory of psychotherapy (reciprocal inhibition theory) to explain specific techniques such as desensitization. The work was admirably timed, providing the first coherent, clinically centred behavioural therapy. The initial therapeutic results appeared to be impressive, but all of the patients had been assessed and treated by Wolpe himself, and it was already clear that enthusiastic therapists with a strong belief in the value of their ideas and techniques are capable of producing well-satisfied patients. Some critics argued that Wolpe's results probably were achieved by the establishment of a strong therapeutic relationship, and were dependent on his enthusiasm and general therapeutic skills. It was argued that the attribution of his clinical results to the specific techniques, such as desensitization, was misleading.

In a series of experimental investigations that launched the systematic scientific investigation of desensitization, and which provided a model for hundreds of subsequent experiments, Peter Lang (1969) and his colleagues tackled various aspects of the desensitization technique, including the central claim made by Wolpe that the desensitization *technique* was responsible for the reduction of fear.

In his first test of this hypothesis, Lang found that those fearful subjects who completed a course of desensitization showed significant reductions in fear, but comparable subjects who had equivalent amounts of therapeutic time, and who welcomed and valued the non-specific therapeutic relationship that was established, failed to show any reduction in their fears. The provision of a satisfactory therapeutic relationship was not sufficient to shift the fear. In a subsequent and even more telling investigation, Lang, Melamed and Hart (1970) tested the hypothesis by providing a group of fearful subjects with an automated mechanically driven form of desensitization. Each of these experimental investigations, plus additional evidence of other studies, provided strong support for the hypothesis that desensitization produces reductions in fear because of the procedures that are carried out (imaginal rehearsals of fear that occurred during deep relaxation) and are not simply a by-product of the formation of a therapeutic relationship.

The next set of questions focused on the ingredients of the desensitization procedure, and the theoretical explanation for their effects. The desensitization procedure consists of two main elements: graded imaginal rehearsals of the fear-producing stimuli after the induction of a state of deep relaxation. This combination was not incidental, but in keeping with Wolpe's (1958) theory of reciprocal inhibition, according to which the repeated imposition of relaxation over the fear evoked by the images leads to a growing inhibition of fear. In order to achieve enduring inhibition of fear, it is necessary to evoke controlled amounts of fear in a systematic fashion and then to ensure that the fear is suppressed by the imposition of an inhibitory, opposing state, relaxation (or some other opposing state).

In order to investigate these therapeutic hypotheses, it became necessary to introduce a technique for dismantling the elements in desensitization. Is it correct, as the theory proposed, that in order to achieve enduring reductions in fear it is necessary repeatedly to evoke and then suppress (by relaxation) the fear? In 1965 and 1966, investigations of these questions, introducing the dismantling technique, were carried out (Rachman, 1965, 1966) on spider-phobic subjects. They were given one of three forms of therapy: relaxation alone, imaginal rehearsals of the fear stimulus, or the combination of relaxation and imaginal rehearsal (i.e. systematic desensitization). The results of these preliminary studies appeared to support the reciprocal inhibition theory, in that significant fear reduction followed the combination of both elements, and rehearsal alone produced only slight changes. Relaxation alone produced no significant improvement.

The results of the dismantling experiments were consistent with Wolpe's theory, as were the findings from a larger and more closely controlled experiment reported by Davison in 1968. In both of the experiments, as in some others, significant fear reduction was accomplished only when the imaginal rehearsals were followed by relaxation, seemingly because of the repeated occasions in which the fear was inhibited by the relaxation response. However, subsequent research produced numerous examples in which fear was reduced by imaginal rehearsals even in the absence of relaxation; even more convincingly, repeated exposures to the actual fear stimulus, again without accompanying relaxation, proved to be a particularly powerful means of reducing fear. These later findings did not disconfirm Wolpe's theory, but they did show that procedures other than those based on the theory of reciprocal inhibition are capable of reducing fear. Hence, Wolpe's theory could not provide a comprehensive account of fear reduction. A critical test of the theory remains elusive, despite the fact that the theory is stated in a clear and testable form. A variety of technical problems have prevented researchers from coming up with an acid test.

NEGATIVE AFFECT

The absence of theoretical advances in behaviour therapy gradually became a source of scientific discontent. There was a second and more practical need to expand the search beyond the essentially behavioural techniques that characterized the first stage of this new type of psychological therapy. The early and considerable successes in reducing anxiety and overcoming unadaptive avoidance behaviour, as in agoraphobia for example, were not accompanied by successes in dealing with depression, the other major component of 'negative affect' (most adult patients complain of a mixture of anxiety and depression). The early attempts to treat depression, by rearranging the reinforcement contingencies for depressive *behaviour*, made scant progress. (Oddly, a renewed attempt at modifying such contingencies may now prove to be more successful than it was during the original attempt — particularly, as the earlier unwillingness to provide verbal support, advice, analysis and explanation, has disappeared.) The cognitive element in depression is large and obvious, and given the lack of behavioural success, it became the first target of cognitive therapy.

Beck (1967, 1976) was one of several therapists moving in this direction and his pioneering contribution to the cognitive therapy of depression is unmatched. In the rush to understand and explore his ideas and methods, the important role of 'behavioural exercises' was initially overlooked, only to resurface a decade later. The adoption of more specific, specifiable and detailed cognitive ideas and methods, such as Beck's, was facilitated, indeed promoted, by the major shift towards cognitive psychology that was taking place in psychology in general. Previously suspect cognitive concepts and language became allowable, even necessary, and steadily replaced such yawn-inducing concepts as fractional anticipatory goal responses. I suspect that a significant prompt to the shift from pure learning theory to cognitive science was a dissatisfaction with the overwhelming efforts devoted to laboratory animal research, especially the obliging white rate, and the priority assigned to this work; it became increasingly remote from the original object of our scientific curiosity–human behaviour and experience.

The time was ripe for a cognitive clinical psychology and Beck's work was gradually absorbed into behaviour therapy, first in the modification of depression and more recently in the treatment of anxiety. Despite some understandable grumbling, cognitive therapy and behaviour therapy have now merged into cognitive-behavioural therapy.

THE MERGING

The merging of behaviour therapy and cognitive therapy is already well advanced. In the process, the behavioural emphasis on empiricism has been absorbed into cognitive therapy, as has the continuing search for increasingly dependable methods of measurement. The behavioural style of conducting outcome research has similarly been adopted, with its demands for rigorous controls, statistical designs, treatment integrity and credibility, and the rest. The merging of the old (BT), with the new (CT), is not free of problems, and we have already discovered that behavioural changes are more accessible and easier to measure than evanescent cognitions and their fluctuations. Leaving these complexities aside for the moment, it is possible to discern an exchange, in which cognitive concepts are absorbed into behaviour therapy, and cognitive therapists attach increasing emphasis to behavioural experiments and exercises. Researchers and therapists are acutely interested in, and attuned to, the patients'/clients' explanations, understanding, wishes and fears, as never before. *Cognitive therapy is supplying content to behaviour therapy.* This development confirms the historical connection, seldom acknowledged, between phenomenological psychopathology (e.g. Jaspers, 1963) and cognitive therapy.

Long before the infusion of cognitive ideas into this field, obsessions were regarded, indeed *defined*, as unwanted, intrusive thoughts (plus, of course, images and impulses). But the precise content of these unwanted thoughts was of little interest. Thanks to the influence of CT, we now are intensely interested in this content, and can begin to hope that eventually we will be able to follow the content of these thoughts closer and closer to the true nature (and functions) of obsessions. (See below.)

This is a specific and telling example, but the influence of CT goes further and wider. It also offers the promise of greater explanatory power and deeper under-standing of abnormal behaviour and its springs. The outstanding example here is, of course, the newly introduced psychological theory of panic (theories actually, but for present purposes Dr D. Clark's theory (1986; 1988) will be used in exposition). Despite the difficulties it has encountered, some of which are dis-cussed below, Clark's theory has increased our understanding, removed some blurs, and made explicable many facets of panic. The phenomenon now is seen to be coherent, to be psychologically understandable. In many cases, studies and experiments, we are able to make good sense of the person's thoughts and fears, and how they connect. A person whose father died suddenly from cardiac failure becomes highly sensitive to chest discomfort, and is inclined to misinterpret chest pains as signifying an impending heart attack. When he interprets these signs as lift-threatening, he panics. It all makes sense, as do his elaborate schemes to avoid future threats and his safety-seeking behaviour. In numerous instances, this type of cognitive analysis has introduced coherence and understanding. If anything, the danger now is that cognitive explanations are being fashioned too readily and that their evident plausibility can become a trap.

In short, cognitive concepts have widened the explanatory range of BT and helped to fill in the picture. The most solid advances have been achieved in understanding and treating panic disorder, and these advances have spilled over and enlivened research and thinking on OCD and on hypochondriasis, better now regarded as excessive health-anxiety (Salkovskis and Warwick, 1986). We can anticipate important developments in understanding these disorders, and indeed in the full range of anxiety disorders.

The psychology of depression is a separate and troublesome exception, de-spite its early position as the primary target of CT. It may be coincidental that depression never featured prominently in the deliberate merging of CT and BT, but the fact is that the combination of the two types of therapy has so far been most successful in tackling the anxiety disorders.

The nature and the treatment of depression are exceedingly complex subjects and will not be pursued here in any depth. Retrospectively, it has to be said that the early optimism has not been borne out. Beck's (1967, 1976) ambitious, complex and many-layered theory has a broad plausibility but is marred by internal problems (Teasdale and Barnard, 1993), some unlikely assumptions and the unmanageability that often flows from complex and complicated explanations. Progress in coming to grips with this grand scheme has been slow, and the failure of the large-scale collaborative study to produce evidence of the superiority of CT (Elkin et al., 1989; Shea and Elkin, 1992) was a blow, notwithstanding some flaws in that study. The elusiveness of evidence to support the claim that there are exclusive connections between specific cognitive changes and reductions in depression is also troubling, and there is an echo of this problem even in the most resent research on panic (see below).

Why has progress in unravelling Beck's theory of depression been so slow, and why is it so difficult to demonstrate the superiority of cognitive therapy over other treatments? And if the particular value of the therapy is in doubt, how and why should it be expected to bolster or justify the grand theroetical scheme? Does a weak therapy warrant so grand a theory? There are no simple answers available, but it seems intemperate and premature to contemplate the harsh possibility that the therapy lacks power and the theory is unmanageable. Even though the theory is cumbersome, it can be refined and simplified in a way that will make it more easily testable and modifiable. Progress in that enterprise should in turn lead to sharper, more precise treatment tactics. In testing the effects of a refined therapy, greater attention needs to be paid to the causal, sequential connections between cognitive shifts and declines in depression. This is a formidable set of requirements, as has become evident even in the more successful application of CT to panic disorder. For example, it seems probable that a session of CT may initiate cognitive changes which do not become apparent until days or weeks later. Moreover, the complex psychological state that we call 'depression' follows an unknown time course; it certainly does not decline to a measurable degree as you watch it. So we are left with the task of trying to unravel a putative causal connection between two events that have uncertain time courses. A comparable problem arises in trying to determine the causal connection between cognitive changes and episodes of panic.

There has been no shortage of attempts to explain depression. For example, aspects of Lewinsohn's behavioural theory of depression (Lewinsohn, 1974; Lewinsohn, Biglan and Zeiss, 1976) were incorporated into Rehm's (1977) CBT approach (self-control theory), and the resulting therapy shares some features with Beck's methods. Seligman's influential theory of depression as learned helplessness spawned a large volume of research and he also prepared a set of therapeutic guidelines (Seligman, 1981). They are plausible and, like

Rehm's approach, share some features with Beck's therapy, but Seligman's ideas for therapy remain to be evaluated. Interest in testing the value of learned helplessness as an explanation for depression has overshadowed the potential therapeutic applications of Seligman's work. This theory may indeed prove to be more valuable as a means of preventing depression (Jaycox et al., 1994). Recently, Teasdale (1993) made a stimulating attempt to re-attach cognitive theories of depression to the roots of modern cognitive psychology in a model that is bound to provoke a good deal of thought and research.

Overall, work on CT approaches to depression would do well to aspire to the bold simplicity of the cognitive theory of panic. That may not be attainable because of the greater complexity of depression, but the panic theory remains a useful model and can act as a beacon.

As far as anxiety disorders are concerned, the greatest theoretical and clinical progress has been made in applying CBT to the explanation and treatment of panic (Margraf et al., 1993) and consequently, the greatest attention will be devoted to these developments. Promising progress has also been made in tackling other anxiety disorders with CBT, notably specific phobias, claustrophobia, obsessional compulsive disorders and hypochondriasis (approached as a disorder of anxiety).

PANIC: COGNITIVE EXPLANATIONS AND DEDUCTIONS

The leading proponents of a cognitive approach to the treatment of panic are Barlow (1988), who empahsizes the internal as well as the external cues for panic, Beck (1988) and Clark (1986, 1988). According to Clark, 'panic attacks result from the catastrophic misinterpretation of certain bodily sensations' (1986, p. 462). It follows that (1) a reduction in catastrophic cognitions should reduce the episodes of panic, and (1a) that the elimination of the catastrophic cognitions should lead to the cessation of panic. (2) The substitution of non-catastrophic interpretations of these bodily sensations should reduce episodes of panic. (3) There is another, less obvious, deduction, namely that a reduction in the relevant bodily sensations should reduce the opportunities for catastrophic misinterpretations and hence should be followed by a decline in the episodes of panic. (4) Reduction/elimination of the catastrophic cognitions should be followed by a generalized reduction in fear and panics. (5) The enduring reduction of these cognitions should be accompanied by a lasting reduction in the occurrence/intensity of episodes of panic. (5a) A return of these cognitions, or a restoration of their high believability, will be followed by a return of fear and a recurrence of episodes of panic.

1. There is evidence that after successful treatment of panic disorder, patients do report significantly fewer negative cognitions than they did prior to treatment (e.g. Clark, Salkovskis, Hackmann, and Gelder, 1992; Margraf and Schneider, 1991).

2. There is also some indirect evidence to support the second deduction. An encouragingly high percentage of patients are free of panics at the conclusion of treatment. In the most recent controlled studies, 90, 86, 71, 86 and 75% of patients who received cognitive therapy were panic-free at the end of treatment (Margraf et al., 1993). However, we do not have specific information about the nature and number of the remaining cognitions, if any, of the panic-free patients.

3. There is, so far, no quantitative evidence that pertains directly to the third deduction, that is, the extent to which successfully treated patients made fresh but benign interpretations of their bodily sensations. Clinical reports suggest that this change does take place.

4. After successful treatment of panic disorder, patients reported fewer bodily sensations than they did prior to treatment (Clark et al., 1991; Margraf and Schneider, 1991).

The evidence pertaining to the first three deductions is positive but limited in quantity and derived mainly from the clinical experiment on claustrophobics referred to below (Booth and Rachman, 1992). There is also a growing body of support for elements of the underlying theory (Clark, 1991; Ehlers, 1993; McNally, 1994; Rapee, 1993).

5. There are indications that the improvements in reducing panic are stable, and that there is a positive correlation between reduction of the negative cognitions during treatment and the maintenance of improvements (see Clark et al., 1991; Craske and Rodriguez, 1993; Margraf and Schneider, 1991). Similarly, Shafran, Booth and Rachman (1993) found a correlation of 0.47 (p = 0.05) between cognitions at post-test and fear at follow-up in a group of treated claustrophic subjects. Teasdale (1994) discerned a similar possibility in considering the CBT of depression: the therapeutic improvements appear to be enduring. [Unfortunately, the results of the follow-up study of patients in the collaborative study (Shea and Elkin, 1992) provide no support.] It is possible that cognitions predict the stability of change even though they are not the vehicle of change; for example, Margraf also found other predictors of stability, such as the patient–therapist relationship.

CRITICAL COGNITIONS?

Even after successful therapy, a number of patients continue to report some negative cognitions (e.g. Margraf and Schneider, 1991); presumably these are non-critical, or if they are critical, they are no longer strongly believed. The patients also continue to report bodily sensations, and these remaining sensations too, must be non-critical, or now interpreted in a benign manner. From this, one can deduce that some cognitions are critical (the so-called key cognitions; see later) and some bodily sensations too may be critical. In testing the major therapeutic deductions it will be necessary to identify the critical cognitions and bodily sensations in advance. If the *critical* cognitions, identified in this way prior to treatment, persist even after fully successful treatment has been completed, the cognitive theory will be embarrassed.

ALTERNATIVE INTERPRETATIONS; CAUSE, CONSEQUENCE OR CORRELATE?

The decline in cognitions and/or in bodily sensations observed after successful treatment is, of course, open to more than a single interpretation. The decline in cognitions and/or in bodily sensations may produce the reduction of the panics. But it is possible that the decline in cognitions and/or in bodily sensations is a consequence of the reduced episodes of panic, and not the cause. It is also possible that the decline of cognitions is a correlate of the reduction in the episodes of panic [some critics have suggested that the cognitions and their decline may be mere epiphenomena (e.g. Seligman, 1988; Wolpe and Rowan, 1988)]. Wolpe and Rowan argued that the first episode of panic is an unconditioned anxiety response, and the panic *disorder* arises from fear conditioned to stimuli associated with the initial episode.

One reason for giving serious consideration to these alternative explanations arises from the fact that in Margraf and Schneider's (1991) study the patients who received pure exposure treatment without cognitive manipulations showed improvements as large as the patients receiving pure cognitive therapy in which exposures were excluded. Moreover, the cognitions declined to the same extent in both groups. In similar vein, Booth and Rachman (1992) found that the fears and negative cognitions of claustrophobics showed large declines, regardless of whether they received exposure treatment or pure cognitive treatment without any exposure. Van Oppen et al. (1995) recently reported comparably declining cognitions in OCD patients treated by exposure or by CT, and Ost and Westling (1995) reported decreases in negative cognitions after successful treatment of panic by applied relaxation. It appears that negative cognitions can decline after a direct attack or after an indirect attack.

EFFECTS OF INDIRECT TREATMENT ON COGNITIONS

A satisfactory cognitive explanation needs to account for the declining cognitions that occur after a non-direct treatment, such as exposure. The most obvious possibility is that with each exposure, the patient acquires fresh, disconfirmatory evidence (e.g. no heart attack, did not lose control). The accumulation of this personal, direct, disconfirmatory evidence weakens the catastrophic cognitions. However, one is nevertheless left to ponder why the direct assault on cognitions is not *more* effective than the indirect, incidental effects of exposure, as seen in the studies by Margraf and by Ost.

There is an even more difficult problem. It is desirable to accommodate the therapeutic effects of drugs such as imipramine, and the fact that after this treatment, as well, negative cognitions show a small but significant decline (Clark et al., 1991).

CONDITIONS FOR CHANGE

No satisfactory evaluation of the effects of cognitive therapy can ignore the context from which the theory emerges and the evidence pertaining to the validity of the cognitive explanation of the nature and the causes of panic disorder (see Clark, 1988; Craske and Rodriguez, 1993; McNally, 1994; Rachman, 1990; Rachman and Maser, 1988; Rapee, 1993; Seligman, 1988; Teasdale, 1988), but for present purposes there is space for only a brief account. Clark and his colleagues have shown that people who experience panic attacks make a greater number and more intensely negative interpretations of bodily sensations than do other people. There are meaningful links between cognitions and bodily sensations (Rachman and Levitt, 1988; Marks et al., 1991). Varying the instructions given to panic patients prior to undergoing the physiological lactate provocation test effects the probability that an episode of panic will occur, panics can be induced by cognitive or other psychological manipulations (Rachman, 1990), etc.

The theory has been criticized for being non-exclusive, unrelated to traditional cognitive psychology (e.g. Seligman, 1988), incomplete (Rachman, 1990), unable to account for important phenomena (Klein and Klein, 1988), and indistinguishable from conditioning theory and no advance on that theory (Wolpe and Rowan, 1988). These complex theoretical matters will be sorted out over the next few years, but to return to the therapeutic mechanisms of cognitive therapy, we need to ascertain whether or not the reduction/elimination of key cognitions is the critical element in this form of therapy.

We already know that the direct modification of cognitions can be a sufficient condition for treatment success, but we also know that direct modification is not a necessary condition for success (e.g. exposure alone can be as effective as cognitive therapy, imipramine and other medications produce therapeutic improvements, etc.).

COMPLEXITIES

These analytical tasks are easier to identify than to study because there are several obstacles to progress. As mentioned earlier, one is obliged to consider the probable existence of *key cognitions*: critical cognitions that are responsible for the panics and whose removal is necessary for elimination of the panics. During treatment, patients may express not one, but several, cognitions and endorse several cognitions from widely used standard lists, such as that constructed by Chambless (1988). Also, during the course of treatment, other and often idiosyncratic cognitions emerge. It is unlikely that all of these cognitions are equally critical, and we know that even after successful treatment some patients continue to endorse a diminished number of negative cognitions. Given that treatment is successful, these remaining cognitions cannot be regarded as critical. How then can we determine, in advance, as we need to do, which cognitions are critical and which are not?

The key cognitions may serve many functions. They may serve to drive fear and probably to stitch together different types of fearful cognitions. There are various ways in which one can define and measure key cognitions, none of them simple or straightforward. And as mentioned earlier, the detection of non-cognitive episodes is difficult. There is another layer of complexity because combinations or clusters of cognitions are more influential than single cognitions (Marks et al., 1991; Rachman, Levitt and Lopatka, 1987). The probability of panic is greater when the person has two or more threatening cognitions.

THE TIMING OF EVENTS

In analysing the treatment of anxiety, as in the treatment of depression, a serious obstacle to severe tests of the theory arises from the need for control over the timing of events. If the reductions in negative cognitions are no more than correlates of panic reduction, or if the cognitive changes follow rather than precede the reduction of panic, we need to study the sequence of events with care. Reductions in fear are easier to observe and record, but they can occur slowly, over weeks rather than minutes. In cases of panic, the measures typically range over days or weeks (e.g. the number of panics recorded per week or even per month). So if the patient records a decrease in panics, say from four per week to one per week, when exactly did this decline take place?

Cognitive changes can be even more difficult to track. It is true that in treatment, major changes can occur suddenly (e.g. Ost, 1989; Rachman and Whittal, 1989), and it is therefore possible to record the change in these instances. In many, perhaps most, occurrences, clinical or experimental, the cognitive shifts are slow to develop, changing over weeks rather than minutes [e.g. the cognitive therapy group in the Booth and Rachman (1992) study]. To make matters worse, the changes in fear and in fearful cognitions can and undoubtedly often do occur even when the affected person is separated from and out of contact with the fear-provoking stimulus (Rachman, 1990). It is not possible to determine precisely when the change occurred, assuming, of course, that there is a complete change in the first place. So we are left with the awkward task of timing the sequence of changes in the cognitions and in the episodes of panic, knowing that these changes may take place over an extended period and that the determination of the precise point of change will in many instances be impossible. We also have some evidence that cognitive shifts can initiate a process of change that becomes evident some time later. The existence of a so-called 'dual belief systems', in which the intensity and believability of fearful cognitions varies greatly from situation to situation (see Booth and Rachman, 1992), is one more complication. It confuses measurement and can mislead patient and therapist alike.

In the midst of these complexities and obstacles, it is worth drawing attention to the fact that useful progress has been made in developing methods to tackle these critical questions. For example, Salkovskis, Clark and Hackmann (1991) were able to show in a preliminary study that cognitive treatment that is focused on the (key?) cognitions produces larger and quicker changes than therapy that is more broadly aimed. In addition, we have early indications from the claustrophobia experiment that the *believability* of the cognitions plays a major part in therapy. A single strongly believed cognition may be more important than four or five cognitions with low believability (Shafran, Booth and Rachman, 1993). In 10 out of 13 claustrophobic subjects, an absence of believable cognitions at post-test was associated with a total loss of claustrophobia. Moreover, high belief in the cognition 'trapped' correlated with the return of fear.

PHOBIAS

Last (1987) concluded her comprehensive review of CBT for phobias with pessimism. There was little evidence to support the efficacy of CBT, but within the past few years some promising signs have appeared. Slight progress has been made in reducing snake/spider fears by CBT (Rachman and Whittal, 1989) and it was discovered that a sudden and complete elimination of fear occurs in some cases, reminding one of 'learning by insight'. In these instances the fearful person experiences a sudden transition and is certain the fear has been eliminated – e.g. 'I am no longer frightened of snakes; it has gone.'

Two interesting features of these so-called 'glass jar' experiences, of a sudden, complete elimination of fear, need to be taken into account in trying to identify the mechanisms of change. First, the elimination of fear is sometimes recognized and reported by the person to have taken place *between* CBT sessions with, say, a 45% fear reaction to the phobic stimulus remaining. On returning for the next session, perhaps a week later, they confidently announce that the fear has gone. At some point between sessions, the processes set in train during CBT reached a conclusion; in this sense, CBT sessions *initiate* emotional processing (Rachman, 1980, 1990) that reaches completion only after an interval in which the fearful person has no contact with the phobic stimulus and usually cannot recall having made deliberate attempts to facilitate the fear reduction between sessions. This apparent delay in the effects of CBT was also encountered in the experimental reduction of claustrophobia described by Booth and Rachman (1992). The comparison group received exposure-only treatment and made rapid progress; the CBT group made slow early progress but then caught up with the gains of the exposure-only group directly after the retest, in which the subjects were required to re-enter the closet, i.e. to be re-exposed. In seeking to explain the therapeutic action of CBT it is essential to look beyond the events that are known to occur during particular sessions of CBT. True, the sessions often are followed by an immediate reduction in fear, but in other instances a CBT session initiates a process that continues well past the duration of the session and the effects are not apparent until some period has passed.

A second feature of these rapid 'glass-jar' changes in fear carries a caution. The fearful person's confident report that the fear has been eliminated is not always followed by an equally rapid reduction in avoidance behaviour. Desynchronous changes sometimes take place, thereby complicating the task of explaining the mechanisms of change. Pending further progress, the simplest course to follow at present is to concentrate first on finding an explanation for the cognitively produced changes in self-reported fear.

In the comparative experimental analysis of the reduction of claustrophobia referred to above, a pure exposure condition proved as powerful in reducing claustrophobia as CBT (Booth and Rachman, 1992). Detailed analyses of the cognitive changes did, however, provide support for the cognitive theory as elaborated from Clark's theory (1986, 1988). High fear (and panic) was always accompanied by negative, fearful cognitions; moreover, zero fear was never reported in the presence of believable cognitions (Shafran, Booth and Rachman, 1993). Changes in the number and the believability of the cognitions were closely associated with reductions in fear. Continued belief in a central fearful cognition was, on the other hand, associated with maintenance of the fear. It was concluded that claustrophobia comprises a number of cognitions 'centred on key thoughts of trappedness, suffocation and loss of control' (Shafran, Booth and Rachman, 1993, p. 75). The removal of the belief in the pertinent cognition was followed by 'a dramatic reduction in claustrophobia' (p. 75).

Encouraging though these results are, one must remember that the non-cognitive comparison treatment, exposure-only, produced equally large reductions in claustrophobia. If the reduction of fearful cognitions is indeed the mechanism involved in successful treatment, it has to be conceded that the cognitions can be removed as effectively by indirect non-cognitive methods as by CBT.

OBSESSIONAL DISORDERS

In Salkovskis' (1985) refreshing cognitive analysis of obsessional compulsive disorders (OCD), the affected person's construal of the behaviour and urges was taken as the starting point and the conclusion of the problem. Salkovskis focused attention on the explanations which the affected person provides for his/her OC urges, behaviour and motives. In this way he succeeded in filling a previously empty stage. Previously, the nature and significance of the specific *content* of the obsessions and compulsions remained unexamined. This is, I believe, an important advance and one that will absorb a great deal of thought and effort in the next few years.

As a result of this analysis, therapists now devote serious attention to the cognitive contents of the OCD and attempt to modify the maladaptive ideas. Salkovskis also emphasized the importance of the person's sense of responsibility, claiming that in most cases the OCD is associated with an excessive and absurdly broad sense of responsibility (see Rachman, 1993). We now have some evidence to support this view, at least in respect of obsessions and of compulsive checking. For example, the urge to check declines steeply when the experimenter succeeds in persuading a compulsive subject to reduce his/her sense of responsibility for a specific outcome (Lopatka and Rachman, 1995); there is a need to translate this work from the laboratory to the clinic.

Additional trials of CBT are required, but the early results are promising. Arntz (1994), Emmelkamp and Beens (1991), van Oppen (1992, 1995) and

Salkovskis (1989) have all reported successful results with CBT, but in the comparisons with conventional behaviour therapy, CBT was not found to be superior. As in the therapeutic research on panic disorder, the dysfunctional cognitions of obsessional patients treated with 'pure exposure' have also been reported to decline. One more intriguing problem for investigation.

HYPOCHONDRIASIS

There are early signs that (non-cognitive) behavioural treatment of this disorder may tell the same story as that emerging from research on panic. Prompted by the novel reanalysis carried out by Warwick and Salkovskis (Salkovskis and Warwick, 1986; Warwick and Salkovskis, 1990), researchers in Holland compared CBT with pure behavioural treatment in a series of case-studies, only to find a slight superiority for the behavioural methods (Visser and Bouman, 1992). As in related research, dysfunctional beliefs declined after behavioural treatment, as they did after CBT.

Given their common ancestry (Salkovskis and Clark, 1993), is is no surprise that the cognitive analyses of hypochondriasis and of panic disorder are similar and that the results emerging from the CBT of panic disorder find an echo in the work of Visser and Bouman. The cognitive theory of hypochondriasis shares the boldness that characterizes the theory of panic disorder. It is argued that 'bodily signs and symptoms are perceived as more dangerous than they really are, and that a particular illness is believed to be more probable than it really is' (Warwick and Salkovskis, 1990, p. 110). In panic disorder, the affected person is assumed to make a catastrophic misinterpretation of bodily sensations and hence panic (Clark, 1986). Importantly, the panic theory pertains to expectations of *imminent* catastrophe (e.g. 'I am having a heart attack'). The hypochondriasis theory pertains to threats to one's health or wellbeing that can be equally catastrophic but are more remote (e.g. 'This bump on my skin will develop into a cancer'), but the underlying mechanisms are assumed to be common to both disorders. If follows therefore that the action of psychological treatment for hypochondriasis, as for panic disorder, should be directed at the identification of the dysfunctional misinterpretations of bodily sensations and signs, their modification, and replacement with a more benign (and accurate) interpretation of sensations and signs. In the treatment of hypochondriasis, greater emphasis is needed on the probability estimates made by patients, because of their postulated tendency to over-predict the likelihood of health disasters [see Rachman and Arntz (1991) on over-predictions of aversive events such as pain and fear]. Salkovskis and Warwick (1986) and Warwick and Salkovskis (1990) shaped their CBT of hypochondriasis on the basis of the new theory and the early results are promising, as are the findings from a completed but not yet fully analysed controlled trial (personal communication, Salkovskis, 1994).

The postulated mechanisms of change in treating hypochondriasis are similar to those for panic, but differ in detail, with greater emphasis placed on remote threats and on the correction of inflated probabilities of illness/injury. Confirmation of the postulated mechanisms of CBT in panic disorder would strengthen the likelihood of similar therapeutic actions in the CBT of hypochondriasis, just as a disconfirmation would reduce the plausibility of a cognitive explanation for the reduction of hypochondriasis. Anxious people are easily able to fear imminent and remote threats to their health and well-being simultaneously, and hence a high degree of co-morbidity is to be expected between hypochondriasis and panic disorder (Rachman, 1991).

In summary, the cognitive approaches to phobias, OCD and hypochondriasis have a common core that is derived mainly from the cognitive theory of panic. Intense anxiety arises when the person makes a catastrophic misinterpretation of internal or external events such that a serious threat is perceived. The idea is that if the misinterpretation can be identified, modified and then replaced by a more benign interpretation of the events, improvement will follow. The future of CBT in the treatment of panic disorder will have major ramifications for the cognitive approaches to all of the anxiety disorders.

To summarize, the advance of CBT, and especially the successes in treating panic, gave rise to the first and only major *psychological* alternative to the then widely accepted biological theory of panic (see Rachman and Maser, 1988). The debate will rumble along and also incorporate competing explanations for obsessional compulsive disorders. Importantly, the cognitive explanation for the results of cognitive therapy in treating panic is the best supported at present. Indeed, there is no plausible alternative explanation for the effects of cognitive therapy at present.

Therapeutic reductions in the frequency/intensity of panic are associated with reductions in negative cognitions. The magnitude of the therapeutic improvements is impressive. In addition, there is a growing amount of positive but indirect evidence, mainly in the form of support for the underlying theory of panic causation. Cognitive therapy is legitimately deduced from the theory, and the theory itself is gaining some support (Rapee, 1993). This cohesiveness of the theory and therapy is an added source of strength.

However, it remains to be shown that the reduction of panic is conditional on the reduction of critical negative cognitions. The temporal relations between cognitive change and panic reductions need close investigation, and a variety of other questions need to be answered. On a broader scale, we need to determine the extent to which the cognitive explanation can account for the therapeutic effects of exposure treatment and pharmacological treatment. As a first step we need to investigate the cognitive changes that accompany those other treatments. While aiming for a parsimonious explanation of the effects of therapy, we should leave open the possibility that a single explanation may prove unattainable. One possible candidate is the emotional processing model (Rachman, 1980, 1990).

The implications of the cognitive theory and the related research are manifold. Confirmation of the cognitive theory account of anxiety disorders, namely that dysfunctional cognitions play the major role in generating and sustaining abnormal anxiety and avoidance, will put us in a position to improve our current methods of treatment and, importantly, enable us to provide treatment for the full range of these disorders. However, if the cognitive theory is disconfirmed, we will be left with successful but embarrassingly puzzling therapy results.

During the next few years we can expect to see a forceful expansion of cognitive theory and therapy into a wide variety of non-psychiatric medical problems, in keeping with the fundamental expansion of clinical psychology itself. Before long a fully *cognitive clinical psychology* will be established.

REFERENCES

Arntz, A. (1994). Treatment of borderline personality disorder: A challenge for cognitive-behavioural therapy, *Behaviour Research and Therapy*, **32**, 419–430.

Barlow, D. (1988). *Anxiety and its Disorders*, Guilford Press, New York.

Barlow, D. (1993). Psychological and pharmacological treatment of panic disorder, paper presented at the Congress of Cognitive Behaviour Therapy, London.

Beck, A.T. (1967). *Depression: Clinical, Experimental and Theoretical Aspects*, Harper & Row, New York.

Beck, A.T. (1976). *Cognitive Therapy and the Emotional Disorders*, International Universities Press, New York.

Beck, A. (1988). Cognitive approaches to panic disorder, in *Panic: Psychological Perspectives*, Rachman, S.J. and Maser, J. (eds), Lawrence Erlbaum, Hillsdale, NJ.

Booth, R. and Rachman, S.J. (1992). The reduction of claustrophobia, *Behaviour Research and Therapy*, **30**, 207–222.

Chambless, D.L. (1988). Cognitive mechanisms in panic disorder, in Rachman, S. and Maser, J. (eds), *Panic: Psychological Perspectives*, Lawrence Erlbaum, Hillsdale, NJ.

Clark, D.M. (1986). A cognitive approach to panic, *Behaviour Research and Therapy*, **24**, 461–470.

Clark, D.M. (1988). A cognitive model of panic attacks, in Rachman, S.J. and Maser, J. (eds), *Panic: Psychological Perspectives*, Lawrence Erlbaum, Hillsdale, NJ.

Clark, D.M., Salkovskis, P., Hackmann, A. and Gelder, M. (1991). A comparison of cognitive therapy, applied relaxation and imiprimine in the treatment of panic disorder, paper presented at the AABT Meeting, New York, November.

Davison, G.C. (1968). Systematic desensitization as a counterconditioning technique, *Journal of Abnormal Psychology*, **73**, 91–99.

Ehlers, A. (1993). Somatic symptoms and panic attacks: A retrospective study of learning experiences, *Behaviour Research and Therapy*, **31**, 269–278.

Elkin, I., SHea, M.T., Watkins, J.T., Imber, S.D., Sotsky, S.M., Collins, J.F., Glass, D.R., Pilkonis, P.A., Leber, W.R., Docherty, J.P., Feister, S.J. and Parloff, M.B. (1989). National Institute of Mental Health treatment of depression collaborative research program: General effectiveness of treatments, *Archives of General Psychiatry*, **46**, 971–982.

Emmelkamp, P. and Beens, H. (1991). Cognitive therapy with obsessive-compulsive disorder: A comparative evaluation, *Behaviour Research and Therapy*, **29**, 293–300.

Evans, M.D. and Hollon, S.D. (1992). Differential relapse following cognitive therapy and pharmacotherapy for depression, *Archives of General Psychiatry*, **49**(10), 802–808.

Eysenck, H.J. (1994). The outcome problem in psychotherapy, *Behaviour Research and Therapy*, **32**, 477–496.

Frank, J.D. (1961). *Persuasion and Healing*, Johns Hopkins University Press, Baltimore, MD.

Giles, T.R. (ed.) (1993). *Handbook of Effective Psychotherapy*, Plenum Press, New York.

Jaspers, K. (1963). *General Psychopathology*, Chicago University Press, Chicago.

Jaycox, L.H., Reivich, K.J., Gillham, J. and Seligman, M.P. (1994). Prevention of depressive symptoms in school children, *Behaviour Research and Therapy*, **32**, 801–816.

Klein, D. and Klein, H. (1988). The nosology of anxiety disorders: A critical review of hypothesis testing about spontaneous panic, in Tyrer, P. (ed.), *Psychopharmacology of Anxiety*, Oxford University Press, Oxford.

Lambert, M., de Julio, S. and Stein, D. (1978). Therapist interpersonal skills, *Psychological Bulletin*, **83**, 467–489.

Lang, P.E. (1969). The mechanics of desentisization and the laboratory study of fear, in Franks, C.M. (ed.), *Behavior Therapy: Appraisal and Status*, McGraw-Hill, New York.

Lang, P.E., Melamed, B. and Hart, J. (1970). A psychophysiological analysis of fear modification, *Journal of Abnormal Psychology*, **72**, 220–234.

Last, C. (1987). Simple phobias, in Michelson, L. and Ascher, M. (eds), *Anxiety and Stress Disorders*, Guilford Press, New York.

Lewinsohn, P.M. (1974). A behavioral approach to depression, in Friedman, R.M. and Katz, M.M. (eds), *The Psychology of Depression: Contemporary Theory and Research*, John Wiley & Sons, New York.

Lewinsohn, P.M., Biglan, A. and Zeiss, A.M. (1976). Behavioral treatment of depression, in Davidson, P.O. (ed.), *The Behavioral Management of Anxiety Depression and Pain*, pp. 91–146, Brunner/Mazel, New York.

Lopatka, C. and Rachman, S.J. (1995). Perceived responsibility and compulsive checking: An experimental analysis, *Behaviour Research and Therapy*, **33**, 673–684.

Margraf, J., Barlow, D., Clark, D. and Telch, M. (1993). Psychological treatment of panic, *Behaviour Research and Therapy*, **31**, 1–8.

Margraf, J. and Schneider, S. (1991). Outcome and active ingredients of cognitive-behavioural treatments for panic disorder, paper presented at the AABT Meeting, New York, November.

Marks, M., Basoglu, M., Alkubaisy, T., Senguia, S. and Marks, I.M. (1991). Are anxiety symptoms and claustrophobic cognitions directly related? *Journal of Anxiety Disorders*, **5**, 247–254.

McNally, R. (1994). *Panic Disorder: A Critical Analysis*, Guildford Press, New York.
Mitchell, K., Bozarth, J. and Krauft, C. (1977). A reappraisal of the therapeutic effectiveness of accurate empathy, nonpossessive warmth and genuineness, in Gurman, A. and Razin, A. (eds), *Effective Psychotherapy*, Pergamon Press, Oxford.
Ost, L. (1989). One-session treatment for specific phobias, *Behaviour Research and Therapy*, **27**, 1–8.
Ost, L. and Westling, B. (1995). Applied relaxation vs. cognitive behavioural therapy in the treatment of panic disorder, *Behaviour Research and Therapy*, **33**, 145–158.
Rachman, S.J. (1965). Studies in desensitization, *Behaviour Research and Therapy*, **3**, 245–252.
Rachman, S.J. (1966). Studies in desensitization II. Flooding. *Behaviour Research and Therapy*, **4**, 1–6.
Rachman, S.J. (1967). Systematic desensitization, *Psychological Bulletin*, **67**, 93–103.
Rachman, S.J. (1980). Emotional processing, *Behaviour Research and Therapy*, **18**, 51–60.
Rachman, S.J. (1988). Panics and their consequences: A review and prospect, in Rachman S.J. and Maser, J.D. (eds), *Panic: Psychological Perspectives*, Lawrence Erlbaum, Hillsdale, NJ.
Rachman, S.J. (1990). *Fear and Courage*, 2nd edition, W.H. Freeman, New York.
Rachman, S.J. (1991). A psychological approach to co-morbidity, *Clinical Psychology Review*, **11**, 461–464.
Rachman, S.J. (1993) Obsessions, responsibility and guilt. *Behaviour Research and Therapy*, **31**, 149–153.
Rachman, S.J. and Arntz, A. (1991). The overprediction and underprediction of pain, *Clinical Psychology Review*, **11**, 339–355.
Rachman, S.J. and Levitt, K. (1988). Panic, fear reduction and habituation, *Behaviour Research and Therapy*, **26**, 199–206.
Rachman, S.J., Levitt, K. and Lopatka, C. (1987). Panic: The links between cognitions and bodily symptoms – 1, *Behaviour Research and Therapy*, **25**, 411–424.
Rachman, S.J. and Maser, J. (eds) (1988). *Panic: Psychological Perspectives*, Lawrence Erlbaum, Hillsdale, NJ.
Rachman, S.J. and Whittal, M. (1989). Fast, slow and sudden reductions in fear, *Behaviour Research and Therapy*, **27**, 613–620.
Rachman, S.J. and Wilson, G.T. (1980). *The Effects of Psychological Therapy*, Pergamon Press, Toronto.
Rapee, R. (1993). Psychological factors in panic disorder. *Advances in Behaviour Research and Therapy*, **15**, 85–102.
Rehm, L. (1977). A self-control model of depression, *Behavior Therapy*, **8**, 787–804.
Rehm, L.P. and Tyndall, C.I. (1993). Mood disorders: Unipolar and bipolar, in Sutker, P.B. and Adams, H.E. (eds), *Comprehensive Handbook of Psychopathology*, Plenum Press, New York.
Rodriguez, B. and Craske, M. (1993). The effects of distraction during exposure to phobic stimuli, *Behaviour Research and Therapy*, **31**, 549–558.
Rogers, C.R. (1957). The necessary and sufficient conditions of therapeutic personality change, *Journal of Consulting Psychology*, **21**, 95–103.
Russell, R.L., (ed.) (1994). *Reassessing Psychotherapy Research*, Guilford Press, New York.
Salkovskis, P. (1985). Obsessional compulsive problems: A cognitive behavioral analysis, *Behaviour Research and Therapy*, **5**, 571–583.
Salkovskis, P. (1989). Cognitive-behavioural factors and the persistence of intrusive thoughts in obsessional problems, *Behaviour Research and Therapy*, **27**, 677–682.
Salkovskis, P. and Clark, D. (1993). Panic disorder and hypocondriasis, *Advances in Behaviour Research and Therapy*, **15**, 23–48.

Salkovskis, P., Clark, D. and Hackmann, A. (1991). Treatment of panic attacks using cognitive therapy without exposure or breathing retraining, *Behaviour Research and Therapy*, **29**, 161–166.

Salkovskis, P. and Warwick, H. (1986). Morbid preoccupations, health anxiety and reassurance: a cognitive-behavioural approach to hypochondriasis, *Behaviour Research and Therapy*, **24**, 597–602.

Seligman, M.E.P. (1975). *Helplessness: On Depression, Development and Death*, W.H. Freeman, San Francisco.

Seligman, M.E.P. (1981). A learned helplessness point of view, in Rehm, L.P. (ed.), *Behavior Therapy for Depression: Present Status and Future Directions*, Academic Press, New York.

Seligman, M.E.P. (1988). Competing theories of panic, in Rachman, S.J. and Maser, J.D. (eds), *Panic: Psychological Perspectives*, Lawrence Erlbaum, Hillsdale, NJ.

Shafran, R., Booth, R. and Rachman, S.J. (1993). The reduction of claustrophobia – II. Cognitive analyses, *Behaviour Research and Therapy*, **30**, 75–85.

Shapiro, D.A., Harper, H., Startup, M., Reynolds, S., Bird, D. and Suokas, A. (1994). The high-water mark of the drug metaphor: A meta-analystic critique of process-outcome research, in Russell, R.L. (ed.), *Reassessing Psychotherapy Research*, Guilford Press, New York.

Shea, M.T. and Elkin, I. (1992). Course of depressive symptoms over follow-up: Findings from the National Institute of Mental Health treatment of depression collaborative research program, *Archives of General Psychiatry*, **49**(10), 782–787.

Sutker, P.B. and Adams, H.E. (eds) (1993). *Comprehensive Handbook of Psychopathology*, Plenum Press, New York.

Teasdale, J.D. (1988). Cognitive models and treatments for panic: a critical evaluation, in Rachman, S.J. and Maser, J.D. (eds), *Panic: Psychological Perspectives*, Lawrence Erlbaum, Hillsdale, NJ.

Teasdale, J.D. (1993). Emotion and two kinds of meaning: Cognitive therapy and applied cognitive science, *Behaviour Research and Therapy*, **31**, 339–354.

Teasdale, J.D. and Barnard, P. (1993). *Affect, Cognition and Change*, Lawrence Erlbaum, Hove.

Van Oppen, P., de Haan, E., van Balkan, M., Spinhoven, P., Hoogduin, K. and van Dyck, R. (1995). Cognitive therapy and exposure in the treatment of obsessive compulsive disorder. *Behaviour Research and Therapy*, **33**, 379–390.

Visser, S. and Bouman, T. (1992). Cognitive-behavioural approaches to hypocondriasis, *Behaviour Research and Therapy*, **30**, 301–306.

Warwick, H. and Salkovskis, P. (1990). Hypochondriasis of classical conditioning, *Behaviour Research and Therapy*, **28**, 105–118.

Wolfe, B. and Maser, J. (1994). *Treatment of Panic: NIMH Consensus Conference*, American Psychiatric Press, Washington, DC.

Wolpe, J. (1958). *Psychotherapy by Reciprocal Inhibition*. Stanford University Press, Stanford.

Wolpe, J. and Rowan, V. (1988). Panic disorder: A product of classical conditioning, Behaviour Research and Therapy, **27**, 583–585.

Chapter Two

PAUL M. SALKOVSKIS

Avoidance Behaviour is Motivated by Threat Beliefs: A Possible Resolution of the Cognitive–Behaviour Debate

COGNITIVE-BEHAVIOURAL THERAPY OR COGNITIVE AND BEHAVIOURAL THERAPIES?

Few now doubt the value of systematic assessment and modification of cognitive factors in the context of the broad approach previously known as behaviour therapy. As a result of this change in the clinical application of behaviour therapy and of the development of specifically cognitive approaches to treatment (Hawton et al., 1989), behaviour therapy has evolved into cognitive-behavioural therapy. Despite this (or perhaps because of this) theoretical arguments continue. A notable feature of this debate is the *post-hoc* process of redefining 'cognitive change' strategies as variants of 'exposure' and vice versa. Paradoxically, this type of exercise in redefinition probably arises because little detailed attention has been given to the predictions which flow from each approach. The theoretical issues involved are only going to be resolved by specific experimental studies which address specific predictions.

For most clinicians, the theoretical distinction between 'cognitive' and 'behavioural' procedures appears largely irrelevant, and few therapists have

Trends in Cognitive and Behavioural Therapies. Edited by P.M. Salkovskis.
© 1996 John Wiley & Sons Ltd.

much interest in studies which set 'pure behaviour therapy' against 'pure cognitive therapy'. It now seems clear that some believe change is necessary for people to undertake behavioural change; by the same token, it would be an unusual 'cognitive' therapist who did not believe that changes in behaviour are an especially powerful way of changing beliefs. No competent therapist ignores *either* behaviour *or* belief change in clinical treatment.

The failure to resolve the theoretical distinction between cognitive and behavioural views of therapeutic effects in the treatment of anxiety is unfortunate. In particular, it has a negative impact on treatment *development*. From the beginning, advances in both behavioural and cognitive treatments have emerged from the careful and systematic application of theory by committed and experienced clinicians (e.g. Beck, 1976; Wolpe, 1958). Refinements in theory and treatment follow based on further clinical experience, with a reciprocal influence between theory and practice being complemented by well-conducted empirical research. More recently, there has been a tendency to over-emphasize the *theoretical* importance of treatment outcome studies (especially controlled trials), based on a mistaken assumption that such studies are of crucial *theoretical* importance. Whilst such clinical studies are of undoubted importance in considering the relative merits of different treatment packages, they are seldom designed in a way which allows them to address theoretical issues.

THE POSSIBLE THEORETICAL CONTRIBUTION OF CLINICAL OUTCOME STUDIES

The effectiveness of treatment (or failure to differentiate the effectiveness of two contrasting treatments) is sometimes taken as evidence for or against theoretical formulations. However, the relative effectiveness of particular treatment packages, (whether cognitive, behavioural, psychoanalytic or pharmacological) has no direct bearing on the mechanism of change or the value of the underlying theory. As if this were not enough, treatment-based theorizing is littered with examples of a major logical fallacy which is seldom recognized. Commonly, new theories of psychopathology are generated by the demonstrated (or clinically assumed) effectiveness of a particular approach to therapy. The resulting theory is adapted to account for what are regarded as key aspects of the phenomenology of the problem. The main focus tends to be on the presumed (and preferred) mechanism of the treatment which triggered the development of the theory. Subsequently, those advocating this particular theory tend to regard the effectiveness of treatment as compelling evidence supporting that theory. The circularity of such theorizing is seldom recognized. Those advocating pharmacotherapy are prone to such argument, as testified by the serotonin hypothesis of obsessional problems (obsessional compulsive disorders – OCD). Clomipramine was serendipitously found to be effective in the treatment of OCD. Given that its primary mode of action is serotonergic, it was suggested that a deficit in serotonin causes OCD. Subsequent research indicates that the serotonin system of OCD patients is intact (see Salkovskis, 1996a, b). Those advocating the serotonin hypothesis now point to the effectiveness of selective serotonin reuptake inhibitors (particularly Clomipramine) as providing convincing evidence for the hypothesis!

Perhaps the most influential example of this type of unscientific reasoning is the unfortunate abandonment of theory which has accompanied the adoption so-called 'exposure principle'. The origin of exposure-based treatments can be directly traced to Wolpe (1958). Wolpe advocated treatment by systematic desensitization on the basis of a detailed theory derived from experimental work with animals, and from his clinical observations of the effectiveness of the treatment, documented in a remarkable case series. Subsequently, others (notably Paul, 1966) used experimental component analysis studies to identify that the key ingredient in systematic desensitization and related treatments was repeated/prolonged exposure to the feared stimulus or situation. A group of clinical researchers, notably Isaac Marks (e.g. Marks, 1987) has raised this important clinical observation to the status of a pseudo-theory, commonly described as 'the exposure principle'.

The Popperian approach to science suggests that two types of theory cannot be falsified: those which are true, and those which are so nebulous that they cannot be falsified. The 'exposure principle' is not only circular in the way it deals with the relationship between 'theory' and treatment (like the serotonin theory of OCD) but also has become so nebulous as to be untestable. There are no truly falsifiable predictions which arise from the present form of the theory. Those working from a pure exposure basis can, *post hoc*, come up with accounts of other techniques which assert that some exposure took place, thus accounting for the particular results obtained. To be valuable, such accounts must make specific predictions that are capable of experimental test and which go beyond the clinical findings which generated the theory in the first place.

There is a key issue which has been addressed; this is whether fear reduction is posible without exposure. A single convincing empirical demonstration of fear reduction in the absence of exposure will indicate whether exposure is *necessary*. Ost, Fellinius and Sterner (1989), found that applied tension (which involves exposure) and tension only (which does not) were both significantly better in the treatment of blood injury fear than a full exposure treatment.

There are two clear ways in which treatment outcome may inform theory directly. A convincing *disconfirmation* of a theory is achieved by the demonstration of the *ineffectiveness* of any intervention (if appropriate modification of a theoretically crucial ingredient has been achieved). Secondly, treatment outcome studies can evaluate *a priori* predictions concerning the key process or processes involved in change [see Clark et al. (1988) for an application of this type of prediction].

Regrettably, the more recent debate concerning the primacy of cognitive or behaviour change has focused almost exclusively on treatment *response*, to the exclusion of process variables, which tend to be accounted for *post hoc*. It has been argued that talking to the patient about their problem constitutes a type of exposure, and that the only way to show that exposure is not the key therapeutic variable is to use a treatment which does not involve discussion of the patient's problem. There is an uncomfortable similarity here with the earlier behavioural/psychoanalytic dispute (e.g. Breger and McGaugh, 1965), where it was argued that the therapeutic relationship was entirely responsible for the effectiveness of behavioural treatment. If the cognitive/behavioural debate is to be resolved, it is most likely to be by a two-stage process. Firstly, clear articulation of the competing theories and their predictions is needed, followed by experimental investigations in which mutually exclusive predictions are contrasted. Once theoretical issues are clarified, the data will decide. (Interestingly, psychoanalytic writers were quick to predict symptom substitution as a consequence of 'symptomatic' treatments such as behaviour therapy. Given that this prediction is based directly on psychodynamic theory, the clear absence of symptom substitution is a clear refutation of psychoanalytic theory.)

COGNITIVE-BEHAVIOURAL APPROACHES: TWO THEORIES OR ONE?

A major part of the continuing tension between cognitive-behavioural and unmodified behavioural approaches has been the tendency for cognitive-behaviour therapy to be an uneasy hybrid of cognitive theory (Beck, 1976; Beck, Emergy and Greenberg, 1985), two-process theory (Rachman, 1977) and the 'exposure principle' (Marks, 1987). Cognitive researchers and theoreticians have paid little direct attention to the role of behaviour in maintaining emotional problems. The cognitive therapist has been obliged to alternate between strategies directed towards belief change on the one hand and techniques intended to facilitate behaviourally based extinction of anxiety on the other. The parallel use of two such theories is associated with inconsistencies in clinical formulation and poorly integrated and inefficient interventions. In the rest of this chapter, behavioural perspectives on the importance of avoidance and escape will be reviewed, highlighting some specific problems. A related problem for the cognitive theory are described. A theoretical solution involving a properly integrated cognitive-behavioural account will then be outlined and its research and clinical implications considered.

FOUNDATIONS OF BEHAVIOUR THERAPY: TWO-PROCESS THEORY

According to the two-process model of the acquisition and maintenance of phobic anxiety (Rachman, 1977, 1990), phobias arise as a result of a formerly neutral stimulus (such as a dog) being associated with intrinsically aversive consequences or situations. The most obvious example of fear arising from such CS–UCS pairing would be dog phobia originating from the pain experienced when bitten by a dog; less obvious, but probably more important, would be instances where the UCS is observing an adult showing fear in the presence of the dog (adult fear being an intrinsically aversive stimulus to a child). The subsequent failure of phobias to extinguish is said to be due to both (i) the way in which avoidance behaviour prevents the occurrence of actual exposure to the feared stimuli and (ii) the way in which exposure to feared stimuli is terminated or shortened by escape behaviour (when exposure to the feared stimulus unavoidably occurs) (Rachman, 1977). In turn, the persistence of avoidance and escape behaviours is accounted for by the negative reinforcement associated with the omission or termination of anxiety ('anxiety relief'). This theory is of key clinical importance, because it dictates the way exposure to feared stimuli is conducted. The phobic is instructed to remain in the phobic situation *until their anxiety has begun to decline*. Leaving the situation when anxiety has not substantially decreased from the initial level is regarded as counter-productive (Mathews, Gelder and Johnston, 1981), having the effect of preventing fear reduction and reinforcing avoidance and escape on subsequent exposure to the stimulus. Based on this theory, graded exposure became the treatment of choice for phobic anxiety (Rachman, 1990). Problems with two-process theory (see Rachman, 1977) led to the atheoretical 'exposure principle' with an exclusive focus on the effectiveness of behavioural strategies. However, as outlined above, therapeutic success is an extremely misleading way of evaluating theories, especially when the effectiveness of therapy has itself played a part in the development of that theory.

Clinical treatment of anxiety using behavioural methods often highlights a problem upon which both two-process theory and the exposure 'principle' are entirely silent. Anxiety-prompted behaviours (such as distraction) are said to constitute avoidance and therefore play a crucial role in the maintenance of the problem, to be blocked in the course of effective exposure-based therapy (Borkovec, 1982). Apparently identical behaviours become an effective and valued component of a treatment such as anxiety management when presented to the patient in the course of therapy such as behaviourally based anxiety management. Behavioural theories are unable to specify the difference between anxiety management procedures, which are effective in producing significant reductions in severe clinical anxiety (Butler et al., 1987) and similar procedures which such patients are reported as constantly carrying out prior to treatment. Any theory which claims to account for the maintenance of anxiety must address the difference between *coping* behaviour and *avoidance* behaviour, particularly when they are often topographically identical.

This important point was highlighted in two studies by Rachman and colleagues (de Silva and Rachman, 1984; Rachman et al., 1986). These simple and elegant studies set out to test the central assertion of the two-process theory. The theory asserts that phobic anxiety persists because avoidance behaviour prevents exposure and escape behaviour rapidly terminates any exposure to the feared stimulus that unavoidably occurs. Rachman and colleagues reasoned that, if the two-process model is a valid account of the persistence of phobic behaviour and of the way in which exposure is effective as a treatment, then treatment by exposure should produce fear reduction whilst encouraging escape should not. Subjects were told to enter the feared situation and either (a) remain until their anxiety declined (as in exposure-based treatments) or (b) leave when their anxiety rose to 70 on a 100-point scale (as is hypothesized to normally occur in untreated agoraphobics). Unfortunately, the manipulation did not fully succeed, and escape was rare. Both groups showed anxiety reduction. There was, however, some evidence that the *second* (escape) group may show a tendency to experience greater anxiety reduction – an apparently paradoxical finding. Although methodological considerations limit the conclusiveness of these studies (the subjects allowed to 'escape' seldom did so), they are none the less difficult to account for in terms of purely behavioural accounts. Rachman suggests that perceived control over the possibility of panic may have been responsible for the effects observed (Rachman, 1990; Sanderson, Rapee and Barlow, 1989). However, this explanation does not deal with the issue of why the perception of control over escape in a clinical experiment should have produced an anxiety reducing effect compared with the usual situation experienced by these agoraphobic patients. Under normal circumstances, agoraphobics constantly remind themselves that they are able to escape, and much of their behaviour in phobic situations is designed to ensure that possibility remains open to them. They not only watch their escape route to ensure that it is clear, but also often choose to escape. In the experimental situation it might be expected that there was a certain amount of social pressure not to escape, which may have resulted in *lower* perception of control.

As part of a discussion on psychological theories of panic, Seligman (1988) attempted to discount both two-process and cognitive explanations, on the grounds of 'a central weakness in both the Cognitive and Pavlovian theories of the anxiety disorders: neither theory clearly distinguishes the rational from the irrational, the conscious from the unconscious'. Seligman suggests that the data are best accounted for by 'two distinguishable processes, obeying different laws'. He suggests that anxiety disorders are the result of 'prepared' learning, which is biologically relevant, irrational and not readily modified by cognitive means; it is presumably therefore pre-conscious. In support of this view, he describes the common clinical phenomenon of the patient who has experienced regular panic attacks for a decade or more. This person

> may have had about 1000 panic attacks. In each one, on the cognitive account, he misinterpreted his racing heart as meaning that he was about to have a heart attack, and this was disconfirmed. Under the laws of disconfirmation that I know, he received ample evidence that his belief was false, and he should have given it up. On the Pavlovian account, he has had 1000 extinction trials in which the CS was not followed by the US–UR . . . His panics should have extinguished long ago . . . but neither theory explains why the belief did not extinguish in the face of disconfirmation long ago. What is it about cognitive therapeutic procedures which makes them effective disconfirmations, and about the Pavlovian exposure procedures that make them effective extinction procedures? (Seligman, 1988, p. 326).

The value of the concept of 'irrationality' has been challenged by the cognitive theory (Beck, Emery and Greenberg, 1985); more recently, evidence has emerged that even simple phobias may be less 'irrational' than was previously supposed (Thorpe and Salkovskis, 1995). A reconsideration of how the cognitive hypothesis deals with the issues and problems raised above is required.

THE COGNITIVE HYPOTHESIS AND BEHAVIOUR: LOGICAL ASSOCIATIONS AND LEARNING INTERACT TO MAINTAIN NEGATIVE BELIEFS

Seligman's suggestion of biological preparedness resulting in the division of learning into two types, prepared and unprepared, rests on his analysis of anxiety problems such as panic as 'irrational'. In fact, the answer to this point is to be found in the same paper; he points out that ' "having" the cognition or "engaging" in the ideation is not all there is to ideation and cognitions. It is *believing* the cognition that is responsible for the cognitive disorders' . . . (Seligman, 1988, p. 328, original emphasis).

This point is, of course, the real basis for the cognitive hypothesis of anxiety; having the thought that palpitations means that one is about to have a heart attack is not necessarily anxiety provoking; *believing* this thought to be true is. If, as Seligman appears to assume, interpretations are inappropriately learned associations, it could be argued that the 'two types of learning' may, in human anxiety, represent associations which have a degree of internal consistency and logic and are thus strongly believed, as opposed to those which are internally inconsistent and are weakly believed. It therefore seems neither necessary nor parsimonious to propose that the cognitions involved in panic follow two different sets of *rules* according to whether or not the panic is prepared or not. Nor is it sensible to divide panic from other types of anxiety, including 'objectively rational' fear.

The cognitive hypothesis is based on the premise that anxiety (and panic) is a *rational* response to a given set of circumstances, and that there is fundamentally no difference between the type of anxiety and 'reasoning' involved in panic as opposed to other types of anxiety. The evidence upon which the misinterpretations made are based may be *inaccurate*, but as has already been described, the important point is that the patient experiencing panic has a logical basis for these misinterpretations. The rationality or irrationality of a person's beliefs to the outside observer is not the key issue. The degree of anxiety is proportional to the immediate appraisal of threat; in the case of panic attacks, the *catastrophic* nature of the misinterpretations generates spectacular levels of anxiety incomprehensible to the observer who does not share the patient's assumptions (and, in panic, the intense and apparently inexplicable bodily sensations which are the subject of misinterpretation). Consider the example of the victim of a practical joke who is held up by a masked friend carrying what turns out to be a fake gun; the informed observer who knows the true details of the situation might find the extreme fear and panic of the victim irrational (or even amusing).

There is another way in which anxiety is regarded as 'irrational', and this concerns fears which appear to be generally improbable or unlikely. It is extremely unlikely that a young woman will have a heart attack, or that a passenger plane will crash. On a probabilistic basis, such fears can be regarded as irrational. However, take the example of a particular flight, where some severe turbulence is encountered. For most people, the probability of plane crashes remains unchanged, but this is the plane that will crash, based on the evidence of the rough flight. In the same way, the young woman knows that it is very unusual for women of her age to have heart attacks, but the sensations she experiences during panic convince her that she is one of the unusual ones. Clearly, such a situation will not be helped by reminding her of how unlikely a heart attack is on the scale of things. Rather, it is important to help her re-evaluate the evidence upon which she bases her catastrophic conclusions. A particularly powerful way of doing this might be to help her *disconfirm* her fearful predictions. The cognitive theory must therefore account for the apparent failure of people experiencing frequent panic attacks to take advantage of naturally occurring disconfirmations.

The cognitive view suggests that the failure of what appears to be *objective* naturally occurring disconfirmation is in fact a key clue to the understanding of the maintenance of anxiety provoking beliefs, and therefore to more effective treatment. The cognitive theory proposes a functional and internally logical link between cognition and behaviour (Salkovskis, 1988b, 1989a, 1991). If the same rules of logic apply to anxiety and panic as to other areas of human behaviour, then the logical response to threat is to take action designed to prevent perceived negative outcomes which are perceived to be imminent. That is, a person panicking because he believes that a catastrophe is imminent will do anything he believes he can to prevent the *catastrophe*. The person afraid of fainting sits, the person afraid of having a heart attack refrains from exercising, and so on. By doing so, the patient not only experiences immediate relief because of the safety they believe they have achieved, but also inadvertently 'protects' his or her belief of the potential for disaster associated with particular sensations. Each panic attack, rather than being a disconfirmation, becomes another example of *nearly* being overtaken by a disaster: 'I have been close to fainting so many times: I have to be careful, or one of these times I won't be able to catch it in time.' This in effect means that the apparent failure of panic patients to take advantage of naturally occurring disconfirmations may be because the non-occurrence of feared catastrophes does not constitute an actual disconfirmation, and may often serve as an apparent confirmation of the imminence of disaster. The concept of 'safety seeking behaviour' accounts not only for escape behaviours and subtle avoidance, but also for general avoidance.

The difference between this account and previous behavioural explanations is that, in panic, it is not usually *anxiety* which is being avoided, but feared catastrophes. In most instances, if a person is convinced that the end point of exposure to a feared stimulus will be anxiety alone, then avoidance is relatively unlikely, other than the avoidance normally associated with mildly unpleasant emotional states. If, on the other hand, the person is anxious as a result of a perceived threatening or catastrophic event, then avoidance of that threat is both rational and advisable. An important extension of this view concerns the issue of anxiety sensitivity (i.e. the tendency to believe that anxiety *per se* is dangerous, which has been demonstrated to be a feature of panic, especially panic associated with agoraphobia (McNally and Lorenz, 1987; Reiss et al., 1986). Anxiety will be the focus of avoidance *if the subject strongly believes that anxiety can itself result in harm.* That is, the person who believes that anxiety itself can kill would reasonably avoid situations where they might become anxious. This phenomenon would be expected to be a major mechanism involved in the readiness of a particular individual to experience the transition from panic disorder to situational (agoraphobic) avoidance.

Previous research showing that there is a relationship between anxiety sensitivity and avoidence again provides additional but indirect support for the view described here (e.g. McNally and Lorenz, 1987). The problem with more direct investigation is that the proposed relationship between cognitions and behaviour is, by definition, highly idiosyncratic. Although there is a need for investigations using techniques which allow for the proposed idiosyncratic nature of the links between cognition and safety seeking behaviour, the relatively narrow range of misinterpretations involved in panic as opposed to other anxiety disorders means that a preliminary evaluation should be possible using more conventional assessments.

As a preliminary investigation of this view, data was collected from a questionnaire devised as an assessment of safety seeking behaviours in panic together with assessments of some of the more common panic-related cognitions in a sample of 147 panic patients. The pattern of associations was consistent with predictions from the safety seeking perspective. Holding on to an object was associated with fears of fainting and being paralysed with fear. Holding on to or leaning on another person was associated with fears of fainting. Sitting down was associated with fears of heart attack, acting foolishly and being paralysed with fear. As expected, keeping still was exclusively associated with fears of having a heart attack. Doing more exercise was only associated with being paralysed with fear. Focusing attention on one's body was associated with thoughts of having a tumour, choking to death and having a stroke. The specific asssociation of controlling one's behaviour were with thoughts of acting foolishly and not being able to control oneself. These cognitions were also associated with trying to move more slowly, reflecting the attempt to exercise control over one's behaviour. The beliefs associated with looking for an escape route are exclusively loss of control type concerns (acting foolishly, losing control and being paralysed with fear), and not thoughts concerning the more somatically focused catastrophes. This finding was expected; leaving a situation is a relatively ineffective remedy for internally located problems, where the catastrophe would be carried with the patient out of the situation. By contrast, the negative consequences of loss of control type events are almost exclusively social evaluative. Asking people around for help was associated with thoughts of having a heart attack and choking to death, both likely to be perceived as extremely serious and uncontrollable somatic catastrophes, likely to require immediate external aid.

The *pattern* of associations between specific behaviours and cognitions found in this study was therefore consistent with the hypothesis that cognitions may 'drive' the anxiety-related behaviours in a meaningful and idiosyncratic way. Particular avoidant behaviours may be occurring because they are *intended* by the patients as logical reactions designed to avert feared catastrophes. These findings are consistent with the cognitive hypothesis as a 'normalizing' account of panic and associated phenomena (particularly avoidance behaviours), highlighting the internal logic of the problem.

In another study, groups of panic, socially anxious and hypochondriacal patients and non-clinical subjects were compared with each other on measures of avoidance, escape and safety seeking behaviours. A number of behaviours (such as trying to control one's mind) were found to be common in both patients and non-patients and can be regarded as virtually universal coping strategies directed at the control of *anxiety* rather than the avoidance of feared catastrophes. This does not mean, of course, that such behaviours cannot, in some specific instances, become avoidant and catastrophe directed. A detailed experimental analysis of measures related to *specific* (identifiable) episodes of anxiety and/or panic is needed to evaluate the proposed relative impact of 'anxiety focused' as opposed to 'safety seeking' behaviours. Some behaviours (such as holding on to or leaning aginst an object or internal focus of attention) are more specific to the clinical groups, and fulfil the suggested criteria for the proposed category of safety seeking behaviour intended to prevent feared disasters. Taking the example of focus of attention on one's body; this strategy is not a helpful one for the control of anxiety, as it tends to call attention to the sensations which are associated with anxiety and is also likely to impair the subject's ability to continue with everyday activities. Similar considerations apply to the avoidance of being with other people; the interesting exception to this example is the group of hypochondriacal patients, who were also the only group to exhibit significantly higher levels of asking people around for help and the only clinical group which did not seek an escape route from anxious situations. This pattern of results is consistent with the exclusively somatic focus of such patients. The combined panic–hypochondriasis group showed an interesting admixture of somatically directed and situation-specific avoidance behaviours.

The data on the association between panic-related behaviours and beliefs demonstrate that the pattern of behaviour shown by the different patient groups (relative to each other and to non-clinical subjects) was consistent with the view that avoidance behaviour is purposeful in terms specified by the cognitive hypothesis. Such behaviours are generally present across anxiety disorders compared with non-clinical controls but the pattern also shows specificity consistent with the way the cognitive hypothesis differentiates each disorder. Within a larger group of panic patients, the *pattern* of associations between specific behaviours and cognitions was also consistent with the hypothesis that cognitions may 'drive' the anxiety-related behaviours in a meaningful and idiosyncratic way with a remarkable degree of internal consistency. Only detailed experimental studies can fully evaluate the extent to which behaviours and beliefs interact in the way proposed. These data provided a basis for the further investigation of the proposed role of safety seeking behaviours in the *maintenance* of panic-related cognitions. Failure to find any associations would have tended to argue against such a relationship.

SAFETY SEEKING VERSUS AVOIDANCE

The results of the studies described above are consistent with the hypothesis that there is a meaningful relationship between particular cognitions and safety seeking behaviours. These data do not, of course, bear *directly* on the hypothesis that safety seeking behaviours actually sustain negative interpretations by preventing disconfirmation. This requires more direct experimental evaluations, which are currently being undertaken by our group.

The analysis of the role of safety seeking behaviour in maintaining anxiety (Salkovskis, 1991) can be applied to all anxiety disorders and to severe health anxiety (often called hypochondriasis). There is emerging evidence that even avoidance in simple phobias may be strongly influenced by threat cognitions (Thorpe, 1994; Thorpe and Salkovskis, 1995). The cognitive model of obsessional problems (Salkovskis, 1985, 1989c, 1996a; Salkovskis, Richards and Forrester, 1995) suggests a similar concept can be invoked to account for the link between distressing thoughts and compulsive behaviour in obsessional problems. In some problems, particularly hypochondriasis and obsessions, the safety behaviours used by patients may serve to directly increase the symptoms which form the focus of misinterpretation and therefore anxiety. For example, obsessional patients try to exclude, suppress or neutralize intrusive thoughts with demonstrably counter-productive effects (Salkovskis and Campbell, 1994; Trinder and Salkovskis, 1994). Patients worried about their health may repeatedly prod areas of inflammation or pain, take inappropriate medication, excessively focus attention on particular bodily systems, and so on (Salkovskis, 1989b; Warwick and Salkovskis, 1990). More recently, our group has applied Salkovskis' (1991) safety seeking behaviour analysis to an experimental investigation of social phobics (Wells et al., 1995), where behaviours such as talking too much or too little, excessive self-directed focus, and so on, are hypothesized as involved in the maintenance of social anxiety. In that study, social phobic patients were exposed to a personally relevant anxiety provoking situation and either decreased or increased their safety seeking behaviours during an experimental session. Decreased safety be- haviour was associated with consistently greater drops in anxiety during a behaviour test conducted before and after the experimental session.

It is clear that the proposed link between specific avoidance behaviours and cognition depends on an analysis of the 'intention' of the behaviour. That is, the cognitive definition of avoidance behaviour (as opposed to adaptive 'cop- ing' behaviour, which has the effect of reducing anxiety in the longer term) depens on an understanding of *what is being avoided*, apparently representing a major departure from previous behavioural conceptualizations of avoid- ance, although perhaps consistent with the development of modern learning theory (e.g. Mackintosh, 1983; Rescorla, 1988).

CLINICAL IMPLICATIONS

Some of the most important implications of this proposed cognition– behaviour link concern treatment. In general, cognitive-behavioural treat- ment emphasizes the need to deal with idiosyncratic factors which are bolster- ing the continued misinterpretation of bodily sensations. For example, a patient who became confused during panic describes mentally 'holding on to my sanity'. In each successive panic he becomes *more* convinced that he would have gone mad were it not for this effort. After hundreds of very severe panic attacks, such patients still believe in each new attack that he or she is about to go crazy, pass out or die. Clinically, questioning of these patients reveals that no disconfirmation occurs because they believe that they have, in every instance, been able to take successful preventative action. Thus, each panic is a near miss and further confirmation of the risk. Once such be- havioural responses are identified, the patient can be helped to begin the process of reappraisal by withholding such protective responses and learning the true extent of risk. In many instances, this may involve suggesting to the patient that they challenge their worries by *actively trying* to bring about the feared disaster, for example, going into the supermarket and trying to faint, trying to go mad. This helps the patient to discover that their efforts to prevent these disasters have been misdirected; this can also help the patient to then reinterpret their past experiences as true disconfirmations instead of 'near misses'. The data described above suggest that this particular type of association might be a fruitful one for investigation, as controlling one's mind is a common response in panic patients as well as other groups, including non- clinical subjects. Given that observation and the readiness with which patients can reproduce this type of behaviour as either safety seeking or coping when requested in the laboratory, experiments concerning the use of the same degree of effort directed at different targets (i.e. reduction of anxiety versus preservation of sanity) could be used to assess the validity of the cognitive basis of such behaviour and its putative anxiety preserving effects when used as a safety seeking behaviour.

The present analysis also suggests ways of combining cognitive procedures and brief exposure in a way which should be particularly effective in bringing about belief change without *repeated* and *prolonged* exposure being necessary. Thus, exposure sessions are devised in the manner of behavioural experiments, intended as an information gathering exercise directed towards invalidation of catastrophic interpretations. Most previous studies in which cognitive and behavioural treatments have been combined [such as those reviewed by Marks (1987)] have used cognitive procedures as a way of dealing with general and 'background' life stresses, most of which tend not to be directly relevant to the specific experience of panic attacks. The particular strategy of using exposure as an exercise in testing alternative non-catastrophic interpretations of experience would be predicted to succeed better than brief exposure with 'supplementary' (panic-irrelevant) cognitive change procedures. That is, such a study should show that 'general' cognitive therapy combined with exposure has an additive effect, whilst 'panic-focused' cognitive therapy would be expected to multiply the effect of exposure, resulting in maximal cognitive change through behavioural experiments.

CONCLUSION

It is proposed here that there is a logical link between the cognitions which generate anxiety and the associated behaviours; these behaviours can be described as safety seeking behaviours which are intended by the patient to prevent danger from coming about. Apart from being a specific account of how particular patterns of behaviour become associated with anxiety, this explanation also explains how such behaviours can preserve the tendency to misinterpret in the face of apparent objectively convincing disconfirmation by repeated experience of episodes where threat does not materialize. Safety seeking behaviours have the subjective effect of 'saving' the person from the perceived danger, in the sense that the person comes to believe that their behaviour has been successful in averting disaster. Thus, disconfirmation is converted to *confirmation* by the subjective experience of 'a near miss'. This account also helps explain how *prolonged* graded exposure works, and provides a framework to understand the difficult and unresolved issue of the difference between a *coping* (adaptive) response and an *avoidance* (anxiety maintaining) response described above. The key to discriminating between avoidance and coping lies in evaluating *what the person is avoiding*. If the cognitive account is correct, then avoidance responses are those behaviours which are intended to avoid *disaster*, but thereby also having the secondary effect of preventing the disconfirmation that would otherwise take place. On the other hand, coping responses are those behaviours brought to bear by a person intending to deal with *anxiety alone*, with no further fears about the consequences of the anxiety, and so on. The second strategy is not catastrophe based, and therefore will not interfere with disconfirmation; in fact, it would be expected to enhance cognitive change because the strategy is based on an alternative, non-catastrophic account of symptoms and situations. The approach described here integrates cognitive and behavioural approaches, with cognitions (in the shape of threat beliefs) being the primary phenomena. Safety seeking behaviour is therefore one of several factors involved in maintaining anxiety disorders, along with selective attention, psychophysiological response and affect (Salkovskis, 1988a, 1996c).

REFERENCES

Beck, A.T. (1976). *Cognitive Therapy and the Emotional Disorders*, International University Press, New York.

Beck, A.T., Emery, G. and Greenberg, R. (1985). *Anxiety Disorders and Phobias*, Basic Books, New York.

Borkovec, T.D. (1982). Facilitation and inhibition of functional CS exposure in the treatment of phobias, in Boulougouris, J. (ed.) *Learning Theory Approaches to Psychiatry*, John Wiley & Sons, New York.

Breger, L. and McGaugh, J.L. (1965). Critique and reformulation of 'learning theory' approaches to psychotherapy and neurosis, *Psychological Bulletin*, **63**, 338–358.

Butler, G., Cullington, A., Hibbert, G., Klimes, I. and Gelder, M. (1987). Anxiety management for persistent generalized anxiety, *British Journal of Psychiatry*, **51**, 535–542.

Clark, D.M., Salkovskis, P.M., Gelder, M.G., Koehler, C., Martin, M., Anastasiades, P., Hackmann, A., Middleton, H. and Jeavons, A. (1988). Tests of a cognitive theory of panic, in Hand, I. and Wittchen, H.U. (eds), *Panic and Phobias II*, Springer Verlag, Berlin.

de Silva, P. and Rachman, S.J. (1984). Does escape behaviour strengthen agoraphobic avoidance? A preliminary study, *Behaviour Research and Therapy*, **22**, 87–91.

Hawton, K. Salkovskis, P.M., Kirk, J. and Clark, D.M. (eds) (1989). *Cognitive Behaviour Therapy for Psychiatric Problems: A Practical Guide*, Oxford University Press, Oxford.

Mackintosh, N.J. (1983). *Conditioning and Associative Learning*, Oxford University Press, New York.

McNally, R.J. and Lorenz, M. (1987). Anxiety sensitivity in agoraphobics, *Journal of Behaviour Therapy and Experimental Psychiatry*, **18**, 3–11.

Marks, I.M. (1987). *Fears, Phobias and Rituals*, Oxford University Press, New York.

Matthews, A.M., Gelder, M.G. and Johnston, D.W. (1981). *Agoraphobia: Nature and Treatment*, Guilford Press, New York.

Ost, L.G., Sterner, U. and Fellinius, J. (1989). Applied tension, applied relaxation, and the combination in the treatment of blood phobia, *Behaviour Research and Therapy*, **25**, 25–32.

Paul, G.L. (1966). *Insight Versus Desensitisation in Psychotherapy*, Stanford University Press, Stanford, CA.

Rachman, S. (1977). The conditioning theory of fear acquisition: a critical examination, *Behaviour Research and Therapy*, **15**, 375–387.

Rachman, S.J. (1990) *Fear and Courage* (2nd edn), W.H. Freeman, New York.

Rachman, S.J., Craske, M., Tallman, K. and Solyom, C. (1986). Does escape behaviour strengthen agoraphobic avoidance? A replication, *Behaviour Therapy*, **17**, 366–384.

Reiss, S., Peterson, R.A., Gursky, G.M. and McNally, R.J. (1986). Anxiety sensitivity, anxiety frequency and the prediction of fearfulness, *Behaviour Research and Therapy*, **24**, 1–8.

Rescorla, R.A. (1888). Pavlovian conditioning: it's not what you think it is, *American Psychologist*, **43**, 151–160.

Salkovskis, P.M. (1985). Obsessional-compulsive problems: a cognitive-behavioural analysis, *Behaviour Research and Therapy*, **25**, 571–583.

Salkovskis, P.M. (1988a). Hyperventilation and anxiety, *Current Opinion in Psychiatry*, **1**, 76–82.

Salkovskis, P.M. (1988b). Phenomenology, assessment and the cognitive model of panic, in Rachman, S.J. and Maser, J. (eds), *Panic: Psychological Perspectives*, Lawrence Erlbaum, Hillsdale, NJ.

Salkovskis, P.M. (1989a). Cognitive models and interventions in anxiety, *Current Opinion in Psychiatry*, **2**, 795–800.

Salkovskis, P.M. (1989b). Somatic problems, in Hawton, K., Salkovskis, P.M., Kirk, J. and Clark, D.M. (eds), *Cognitive Behaviour Therapy for Psychiatric Problems: A Practical Guide*, Oxford University Press, Oxford.

Salkovskis, P.M. (1989c). Cognitive-behavioural factors and the persistence of intrusive thoughts in obsessional problems, *Behaviour Research and Therapy*, **27**, 677–682.

Salkovskis, P.M. (1991). The importance of behaviour in the maintenance of anxiety and panic: a cognitive account, *Behavioural Psychotherapy*, **19**, 6–19.

Salkovskis, P.M. (1996a). Cognitive-behavioural approaches to the understanding of obsessional problems, in Rapee, R. (ed.), *Current Controversies in Anxiety Disorders*, Guilford Press, New York.

Salkovskis, P.M. (1996b). Obsessive compulsive disorder: redefinition does not necessarily increase understanding, in Rapee, R. (ed.), *Current Controversies in Anxiety Disorders*, Guilford Press, New York.

Salkovskis, P.M. (1996c). The cognitive approach to anxiety: threat beliefs, safety seeking behaviour and the special case of health anxiety and obsessions, in Salkovskis, P.M. (ed.), *Frontiers of Cognitive Therapy: The State of the Art and Beyond*, New York, Guilford Press.

Salkovskis, P.M. and Campbell, P. (1994). Thought suppression in naturally occurring negative intrusive thoughts, *Behaviour Research and Therapy*, **32**, 1–8.

Salkovskis, P.M., Richards, H.C. and Forrester, E. (1995). The relationship between obsessional problems and intrusive thoughts. *Behavioural and Cognitive Psychotherapy*, **23**, 281–299.

Salkovskis, P.M. and Warwick, H.M.C. (1986). Morbid preoccupations, health anxiety and reassurance: a cognitive behavioural approach to hypochondriasis, *Behaviour Research and Therapy*, **24**, 597–602.

Sanderson, W.C., Rapee, R.M. and Barlow, D.H. (1989). The influence of an illusion of control on panic attacks induced via inhalation of 5.5% carbon dioxide enriched air, *Archives of General Psychiatry*, **46**, 157–164.

Seligman, M.E.P. (1988). Competing theories of panic, in Rachman, S. and Maser, J.D. (eds), *Panic: Psychological Perspectives*, Lawrence Erlbaum, Hillsdale, NJ.

Thorpe, S.J. (1944). Unpublished D.Phil. thesis, Oxford University.

Thorpe, S.J. and Salkovskis, P.M. (1995). Phobic beliefs: Do cognitive factors play a role in specific phobias?, *Behaviour Research and Therapy*, **33**, 805–816.

Trinder, H. and Salkovskis, P.M. (1994). Personally relevant intrusions outside the laboratory: long-term suppression increases intrusion, *Behaviour Research and Therapy*, **32**, 833–842.

Warwick, H.M.C. and Salkovskis, P.M. (1990). Hypochondriasis, *Behaviour Research and Therapy*, **28**, 105–118.

Wells, A., Clark, D.M., Salkovskis, P.M., Ludgate, J., Hackmann, A. and Gelder, M.G. (1995). Social phobia: the role of in-situation safety behaviours in maintaining anxiety and negative beliefs, *Behaviour Therapy*, **26**, 153–162.

Wolpe, J. (1958). *Psychotherapy by Reciprocal Inhibition*, Stanford University Press, Stanford, CA.

Chapter Three

RICHARD G. HEIMBERG

Social Phobia, Avoidant Personality Disorder and the Multiaxial Conceptualization of Interpersonal Anxiety

Probably the most frequent question I have been asked since my first forays into research on social phobia in the early 1980s is 'What is the difference between social phobia and avoidant personality disorder?' The answer has changed over time as the definitions of these two disorders have evolved from DSM III (American Psychiatric Association, 1980) to DSM IIIR (American Psychiatric Association, 1987) and DSM IV (American Psychiatric Association, 1994). However, once we get beyond the particulars of the psychiatric nosology, the answer remains both complex and elusive.

The nature of the relationship between social phobia and avoidant personality disorder (APD) is an extremely important question because it asks us to go beyond the specific context and examine the relationships between Axis I and Axis II disorders and between acute and chronic anxiety and distress. Because of my own research interests, I approach this 'opinionated essay' from the social phobia side of the equation and ask the reader to consider whether the concept of APD serves a needed function, that is, whether it adds a useful increment to th diagnosis of generalized social phobia, a classification which I believe contains a greater amount of information than APD (see below). Furthermore, does the description of social anxiety and avoidance in terms of chronic and maladaptive personality traits increase our ability to identify,

Trends in Cognitive and Behavioural Therapies. Edited by P.M. Salkovskis.
© 1996 John Wiley & Sons Ltd.

understand and effectively treat affected individuals beyond conceptualization of these characteristics in terms of symptoms? From my opinionated position, the answer is no, and I will demonstrate why I believe this to be the case in the remainder of this chapter. I will address the question of the relationship between social phobia and APD by (a) examining the diagnostic criteria for social phobia and APD and the rate of overlap between these two diagnostic categories, (b) reviewing the research on similarities and differences in clinical presentation of patients with social phobia alone and social phobia with APD, and (c) reviewing the research on the outcomes of pharmacological and cognitive-behavioral treatments for social phobic patients with and without APD. In the final section of this chapter, I will examine the implications of the findings of the review for the definition and conceptualization of these two disorders.

DIAGNOSTIC CRITERIA

Both social phobia and APD were first recognized in the psychiatric nosology with the 1980 publication of DSM III. At that time, social phobia was conceptualized as something akin to a specific phobia of humiliation, embarrassment or scrutiny by others. Examples of social phobia in DSM III included fears of speaking or performing in public, using public lavatories, eating in public and writing in the presence of others. It was stated in DSM III that an individual generally has only one social phobia. Social phobia was not thought to be common or incapacitating unless it was very severe, although it was stated that considerable inconvenience might result from the need to avoid the phobic situation.

In DSM III (p. 323), APD was characterized by 'hypersensitivity to potential rejection, humiliation, or shame; an unwillingness to enter into relationships unless given unusually strong guarantees of uncritical acceptance; social withdrawal in spite of a desire for affection and acceptance, and low self-esteem.' Thus the focus of APD in DSM III was on fear of personal relationships rather than fear of humiliation or embarrassment in specific social situations. Five criteria were specified for the diagnosis of APD, and all five had to be met. In DSM III, the text of the social phobia section stated that social phobia was not to be diagnosed if the anxiety could be better explained by the presence of APD. However, in a seeming contradiction, the APD text stated that social phobia could be diagnosed *as a complication of APD* if fears of specific social situations were present in the context of more pervasive interpersonal anxiety.

Several revisions important to the current discussion were made to the diagnostic criteria in DSM IIIR. First, the exclusionary rule that social phobia could not be diagnosed in the presence of APD was removed. Second, the criteria for social phobia were expanded to include the notion of subtypes. Specifically, DSM IIIR (p. 243, italics in original) added the following language: '*Specify generalized type* if the phobic situation includes most social situations, and also consider the additional diagnosis of Avoidant Personality Disorder.' Third, the number of criteria listed for APD increased to seven, but the number of criteria necessary for the diagnosis decreased to four. Furthermore, as the criteria for social phobia broadened to include fears of social interaction, the criteria for APD were redirected away from personal relationships and low self-esteem and toward discomfort and fear of negative evaluation in social interaction.

The changes to the diagnostic criteria in DSM IIIR arose from a number of sources. Several investigators reported that social phobics reported fears of multiple situations rather than a single social fear as stated in DSM III (Liebowitz et al., 1985; Turner et al., 1986). Spitzer and Williams (1985) also noted that, despite directions to the contrary in DSM III, clinicians often classified persons with multiple social fears as social phobic. Liebowitz et al. (1985) further asserted that there was no empirical justification for DSM III's separation of social phobia and APD and expressed the concern that placement of interpersonal anxiety on Axis II would discourage research into the treatment of this disorder.

The changes in the DSM IIIR criteria did little to clarify the boundaries between social phobia and APD. In fact, they seemed to have done just the opposite. In DSM IIIR, persons with pervasive social fears (i.e. those who fear most social situations) could be classified as social phobic whereas DSM III criteria would place them in the APD category. More persons could be classified as having APD because only four of seven rather than five of five criteria were required for diagnosis. Additionally, several of the criteria for APD overlapped conceptually with the domain of social phobia (Turner, Beidel and Townsley, 1992), and DSM IIIR allowed the simultaneous assignment of both diagnoses. This confusing situation remains basically unchanged in DSM IV, although the criteria for APD have been refocused on discomfort in relationships rather than in social interaction *per se*.

DIAGNOSTIC OVERLAP

Several investigators have noted a high degree of overlap between social phobia and APD (Alnaes and Torgersen, 1988; Brooks, Baltazar and Munjack, 1989; Sanderson et al., 1994; Turner et al., 1991). However, this comparison seems most sensible when subtypes of social phobia are taken into account. Since the generalized type of social phobia is defined in DSM IIIR as the fear of most social situations and APD is described as 'a pervasive pattern of social discomfort, fear of negative evaluation, and timidity' (p. 352), it is reasonable that most of the overlap between social phobia and APD would involve the generalized type.

Six studies have examined the rate of diagnosis of APD in samples of generalized and non-generalized social phobics and support the prediction of a greater association between APD and the generalized type than between APD and the non-generalized type (i.e. social phobics who do not fear most social situations) (Brown, Heimberg and Juster, 1995; Herbert, Hope and Bellack, 1992; Holt, Heimberg and Hope, 1992; Schneier et al., 1991; Tran and Chambless, 1995; Turner, Beidel and Townsley, 1992). Despite differences in sample characteristics, assessment methods and definitions of social phobic subtypes (see Heimberg et al., 1993), all studies found a preponderance of APD among generalized, as compared to non-generalized, social phobics. The frequency of APD among generalized social phobics ranged from 25 to 89% (median = 57.6%) while the frequency of APD among non-generalized social phobics ranged from 0 to 44% (median = 17.5%).

A recent study by Jansen et al. (1994) also examined the frequency of APD and other personality disorders in social phobics. However, this study was unique in that it included another anxiety disorder group, patients with panic disorder, for purposes of comparison. Thirty-two social phobics (30 with the generalized type) were compared with 85 patients with panic disorder (with or without agoraphobia but without an additional diagnosis of social phobia). Thirty-one per cent of the social phobics received a diagnosis of APD compared with 23.5% of the patients with panic disorder, a nonsignificant difference. Social phobics did, however, receive higher scores on avoidant personality features than did panic disorder patients. This finding is difficult to interpret for two reasons. First, the percentage of social phobics with APD (31.3%) was well below the median figure for generalized social phobics reported above. Second, 84% of the social phobics were married or living with a partner, suggesting that this sample may have been less impaired than other samples of social phobics cited in the literature [e.g. Schneier et al. (1992) reported that only 34% of social phobics identified in the Epidemiological Catchment Area Study were married]. Nevertheless, it is important to recognize that APD was diagnosed with some frequency in anxious patients without social phobia, a phenomenon that has been reported by other investigators as well (Alnaes and Torgersen, 1988; Renneberg, Chambless and Gracely, 1992).

It is also of interest to examine the question of overlap at the level of individual diagnostic criteria rather than at the level of diagnosis *per se*, and four studies have attempted to do so. Schneier et al. (1991) reported that generalized social phobics endorsed four of the seven DSM IIIR criteria for APD significantly more frequently than non-generalized social phobics. However, the high rate of overlap between generalized social phobia and APD in this study (89%) makes this finding difficult to interpret. Holt, Heimberg and Hope (1992) and Brown, Heimberg and Juster (1995) examined the endorsement of these criteria during structured interviews in samples of non-generalized social phobics and generalized social phobics with and without APD. The findings of these two studies were highly similar, so only the data from the larger Brown, Heimberg and Juster (1995) study ($n = 102$) are reported here. Differences among groups were found on all criteria except for Criterion 2 (no close friends or confidants). Of the remaining six criteria, generalized social phobics with APD endorsed only three significantly more frequently than generalized social phobics without APD: Criterion 3 (unwilling to get involved with others unless certain of being liked), Criterion 4 (avoids social or occupational activities that involve significant interpersonal contact) and Criterion 6 (fears being embarrassed by blushing, crying or showing signs of anxiety in front of others). Generalized social phobics with APD endorsed Criterion 1 (easily hurt by criticism or disapproval), Criterion 5 (reticent in social situations) and Criterion 7 (exaggerates risks of activities outside usual routine) more frequently than non-generalized social phobics, but they did not differ from generalized social phobics without APD. Criterion 5 also distinguished between generalized social phobics without APD and non-generalized social phobics. Criteria 5 and 6 also differentiated social phobics from panic disorder patients in the study by Jansen et al. (1994).

Further examination of these data reveals that Criteria 1, 2 and 7 were endorsed by no more than 11 of the 102 subjects (10.8%), suggesting that they have limited utility in the diagnosis of APD. Criterion 5 was the most frequently endorsed but did not separate generalized social phobics with APD from those without. The remaining criteria (3, 4, 6), while they did distinguish between these groups, were endorsed with decreasing frequency by generalized social phobics with APD, generalized social phobics without APD, and non-generalized social phobics. This pattern leaves open the possibility that differences in endorsement frequency are related to the severity of social phobia, with more severe social phobics being more likely to endorse these criteria for APD.

APD AND CLINICAL PRESENTATION AMONG SOCIAL PHOBICS

In this section, differences between generalized social phobics with and without APD are reviewed. In most cases, both groups of generalized social phobics differed from non-generalized social phobics [see Heimberg et al. (1993) for a review of subtype differences].

DEMOGRAPHIC CHARACTERISTICS

Tran and Chambless (1995) reported that generalized social phobics with APD (13.3%) were significantly less likely to be married than generalized social phobics without APD (57.1%). Brown, Heimberg and Juster (1995) reported a similar finding (17.9% and 55.6% for generalized social phobics with and without APD, respectively). In the latter study, generalized social phobics with APD also reported lower annual earnings than generalized social phobics without APD.

Feske et al. (in press) reported that generalized social phobics with APD had experienced their social anxieties for a longer period of time than generalized social phobics without APD. While Holt, Heimberg and Hope (1992) and Brown, Heimberg and Juster (1995) found generalized social phobics with and without APD to report a younger age at onset than non-generalized social phobics, Tran and Chambless (1995) did not replicate this finding. No other demographic differences have been noted in the literature.

DIAGNOSTIC COMORBIDITY

Generalized social phobics with APD appear to be more likely than other social phobics to receive additional DSM IIIR diagnoses. Herbert, Hope and Bellack (1992) and Feske et al. (in press) reported that patients with generalized social phobia and APD met criteria for another Axis I or II diagnosis more often than patients with generalized social phobia but without APD. Holt, Heimberg and Hope (1992) and Brown, Heimberg and Juster (1995) reported that patients with both generalized social phobia and APD were more likely than generalized social phobics without APD or non-generalized social phobics to have a comorbid mood disorder.

CLINICAL ASSESSOR MEASURES

Several measures completed by clinical assessors have suggested greater severity of symptoms and impairment among generalized social phobics with APD. These include: lower scores on the Global Assessment of Functioning Scale (Herbert, Hope and Bellack, 1992) and higher scores on the Global Impairment of Social Domains Scale (Tran and Chambless, 1995), the Clinical

Global Impressions (Guy, 1976) Severity Scale (Turner, Beidel and Townsley, 1992), the Clinician's Severity Rating of the Anxiety Disorders Interview Schedule – Revised (DiNardo and Barlow, 1988) (Brown, Heimberg and Juster, 1995; Holt, Heimberg and Hope, 1992), and the anxiety subscale of the Liebowitz (1987) Social Anxiety Scale (LSAS) (Brown, Heimberg and Juster, 1995; Holt, Heimberg and Hope, 1992). Brown, Heimberg and Juster (1995) also reported higher scores among generalized social phobics with APD on the avoidance subscale of the LSAS, but Holt, Heimberg and Hope (1992) did not. Neither Turner, Beidel and Townsley (1992) nor Brown, Heimberg and Juster (1995) reported differences between generalized social phobics with and without APD on the Hamilton (1959) Anxiety Scale. While a number of differences occurred between generalized social phobics with and without APD, these findings must be interpreted with caution because the clinical assessor also determined the diagnosis of APD in several of these studies.

SELF-REPORT OF SOCIAL ANXIETY, DEPRESSION AND PSYCHOPATHOLOGY

Several investigators have administered large questionnaire batteries to samples of social phobics. However, the differences between generalized social phobics with and without APD have been considerably less notable than the similarities, and inconsistent findings across studies have been the rule. Herbert, Hope and Bellack (1992) reported differences between these groups on the Beck Depression Inventory (BDI; Beck et al., 1961), Social Avoidance and Distress Scale (SADS; Watson and Friend, 1969), Social Phobia and Anxiety Inventory (SPAI; Turner et al., 1989) and the trait subscale of the State–Trait Anxiety Inventory (STAI-T; Spielberger, 1983). However, the difference on the BDI has been replicated in only two of five studies, the difference on the SADS has been replicated in only one of three studies and the differences between generalized social phobics with and without APD on the SPAI and STAI-T were no longer significant when depression was statistically controlled (Feske et al., in press). Both Turner, Beidel and Townsley (1992) and Feske et al. (in press) reported lower scores on the Social Adjustment Scale – Self-Report (Weissman and Bothwell, 1976) among generalized social phobics with APD. Herbert, Hope and Bellack (1992) reported higher scores on the Global Symptom Index of the Symptom Checklist-90 – Revised (SCL-90R; Derogatis, 1977), Turner, Beidel and Townsley (1992) reported higher scores on the interpersonal sensitivity subscale of the SCL-90R, and Feske et al. (in press) reported lower scores on the Gambrill–Richey Assertion Inventory (Gambrill and Richey, 1975) and the Personal Self Scale of the Tennessee Self-Concept Scale (Roid and Fitts, 1988) among generalized social phobics with APD, but these measures have not been included in any other study. Brown, Heimberg and Juster (1995) and Tran and Chambless (1995) reported no differences between generalized social phobics with and without APD on questionnaire measures of anxiety, depression or other psychopathology.

BEHAVIORAL MEASURES

Several studies (Brown, Heimberg and Juster, 1995; Herbert, Hope and Bellack, 1992; Holt, Heimberg and Hope, 1992; Tran and Chambless, 1995; Turner, Beidel and Townsley, 1992) examined the anxiety and performance of subjects during behavioral tests. While Herbert, Hope and Bellack (1992) reported that generalized social phobics with APD demonstrated greater anxiety during their behavioral test situations than generalized social phobics without APD, this finding was not replicated in the other studies. No study employing DSM IIIR criteria reported differences in the quality of behavior test performance. An early study by Turner et al. (1986) found that social phobics exhibited more appropriate gaze and voice tone and were rated as more socially skilled than patients with APD. However, it is important to remember that this study utilized DSM III diagnostic criteria. Most patients described in other studies as having generalized social phobia (with or without APD) per DSM IIIR criteria would probably meet criteria for DSM III APD but not DSM III social phobia, making the results of this study very difficult to interpret in the current context.

COGNITIVE MEASURES

Cognitive assessment measures administered after behavioral tests have failed to distinguish between generalized social phobics with and without APD (Herbert, Hope and Bellack, 1992; Trans and Chambless, 1995; Turner, Beidel and Townsley, 1992). In another recent study, McNeil et al. (1995) found no differences between these groups in response to a modified Stroop task in which subjects were asked to name the colors in which various anxiety evoking social word stimuli were presented.

APD AND RESPONSE TO TREATMENT AMONG SOCIAL PHOBICS

Is there any difference in the response to treatment of generalized social phobics with and without APD? Does treatment for social phobia have an impact on APD? Several studies of pharmacological and cognitive-behavioral treatments have addressed this question.

In the realm of pharmacological treatment, Reich, Noyes and Yates (1989) treated 14 DSM IIIR social phobics with alprazolam in an open trial. Alprazolam led to reduced ratings on several criteria for APD, but only one of these ratings remained improved following treatment discontinuation. Leibowitz et al. (1992) and Versiani et al. (1992) reported similar findings in controlled studies of the monoamine oxidase inhibitors (MAOIs) phenelzine and moclobemide. Versiani et al. (1992) also reported that 24 of 27 patients with APD were no longer diagnosed with APD after 8 weeks of MAOI treatment, whereas this was the case for only two of sixteen patients receiving placebo.

Turner (1987) conducted a preliminary study of the effects of a diagnosis of personality disorder (PD) on the cognitive-behavioral treatment of social phobia. PD diagnosis was determined on the basis of DSM III criteria and response to the Minnesota Multiphasic Personality Inventory. Seven of the thirteen social phobic patients meet criteria for a PD, and three of these met criteria for APD. Patients without a PD improved significantly more than patients with a PD on a variety of measures, and this pattern remained evident one year after treatment. However, the results of this study are difficult to interpret because of the unusual method of diagnosis of PDs, the broad range of PDs present in the small sample and the failure to follow DSM III diagnostic conventions (the combination of primary social phobia and APD is technically not possible under DSM III).

Hope, Herbert and White (1995), Brown, Heimberg and Juster (1995), Lucas and Telch (1993) and Feske et al. (in press) have also examined the impact of APD on the outcome of cognitive-behavioral treatment of social phobia. With the exception of Feske et al. (in press), these studies examined Heimberg's protocol for Cognitive Behavioral Group Therapy (CBGT) for Social Phobia (see Heimberg et al., 1995; Hope and Heimberg, 1993).

While Lucas and Telch (1993) reported that APD was significantly and negatively associated with outcome in their study of CBGT, a similar but individually administered cognitive-behavioral treatment and an educational supportive control treatment, these authors did not include subtype of social phobia in their prediction equation. Since generalized social phobics are more likely to have APD than non-generalized social phobics, subtype differences in response to treatment may have accounted, at least in part, for their results. Similarly, although Hope, Herbert and White (1995) found no effect for APD on CBGT outcome, they did not simultaneously classify patients into subtype and APD groups. In a separate set of analyses which did not consider APD, non-generalized social phobics began treatment less impaired than generalized social phobics, and, despite overall sample improvement, remained less impaired after treatment.

Brown, Heimberg and Juster (1995) administered CBGT to 23 non-generalized social phobics, 20 generalized social phobics with APD and 20 generalized social phobics without APD. This design allowed the simultaneous examination of the impact of subtype of social phobia and APD on treatment outcome. Assessments before and after treatment consisted of a battery of self-report questionnaires, measures derived from an individualized behavioral test and measures derived from an interview with an independent assessor. Similar to the findings of Hope, Herbert and White (1995), non-generalized social phobics were less impaired than generalized social phobics (with or without APD) on most measures before treatment, and despite improvement among all groups they remained less impaired after treatment on all 10 measures of social phobia which revealed significant group differences. In 8 of these 10 analyses, there was no post-treatment difference between generalized social phobics with and without APD. In the other two analyses, generalized social phobics with APD remained more symptomatic after treatment than generalized social phobics without APD. When patients were classified as responders or non-responders to treatment by the independent assessor, a higher percentage of non-generalized social phobics (79%) were classified as responders than was the case for generalized social phobics with APD (41%) or without APD (47%).

Brown, Heimberg and Juster (1995) also examined the effect of CBGT on the diagnosis of APD. Notably, 8 of 17 generalized social phobics who met criteria for APD before treatment no longer did so after completing treatment.

Feske et al. (in press) examined the effect of APD on the treatment response of 48 patients with generalized social phobia. Treatment in this study consisted of 32–42 hours of group exposure, relaxation training, systematic desensitization and social skills training, and there was improvement for the sample as a whole. Generalized social phobics with APD began treatment more impaired than generalized social phobics without APD and remained that way, despite significant improvement, at post-test and 3-month follow-up assessments. Several analyses suggest that greater depression among generalized social phobics with APD may have accounted for at least a portion of these differences.

COMMENTS

With the review of the literature behind us, we return to the question, 'What is the difference between (generalized) social phobia and avoidant personality disorder?' We know the following:

1. The diagnostic criteria for generalized social phobia and APD address several common areas, and generalized social phobics with and without APD differ in the frequency with which they endorse only three of the seven criteria.

2. Approximately 60% of generalized social phobics also receive a diagnostic of APD compared with about 20% of non-generalized social phobics.

3. Despite its greater frequency among generalized social phobics, APD does not necessarily occur more frequently in social phobia than in other anxiety disorders. However, few studies have directly addressed this issue.

4. Generalized social phobics with APD are less likely to be married than generalized social phobics without APD and may differ in earned income and duration of social fears.

5. Generalized social phobics with APD are more likely than generalized social phobics without APD to receive additional Axis I or Axis II disorders, and it is quite likely that these additional diagnoses will be mood disorders.

6. Generalized social phobics with APD receive more extreme scores on measures of severity and impairment when administered by clinical assessors, although this conclusion is made cautiously because the same clinical assessors also made the diagnosis of APD in some of the studies reviewed. As noted by Brown, Heimberg and Juster (1995), this aspect of design may increase the appearance of differences between generalized social phobics with and without APD.

7. Generalized social phobics with APD sometimes achieve more extreme scores on self-report measures of anxiety, depression and other psychopathology than generalized social phobics without APD. However, the specific pattern of these differences varies widely from study to study, and many of these differences have not withstood replication.

8. Generalized social phobics with and without APD do not appear to differ on measures of social performance when diagnosed according to DSM IIIR criteria, although such differences have been noted between social phobics and patients with APD as defined in DSM III.

9. Generalized social phobics with and without APD do not appear to differ on measures of cognitive content or process, although this is an area of research that has received very little attention.

10. The presence of APD does not appear to influence the outcome of pharmacological treatment for social phobia as far as this has been investigated, although pharmacological treatment for social phobia does appear to affect APD.

11. The presence of APD has been negatively associated with the outcome of cognitive-behavioral treatment in two studies and not associated with outcome in two others. Some of these studies have not simultaneously accounted for subtype of social phobia and APD. Thus, it is difficult to draw conclusions. However, cognitive-behavioral treatment does appear to affect APD.

Widiger (1992) provided a commentary on three of the studies of DSM IIIR social phobia and APD (Herbert, Hope and Bellack, 1992; Holt, Heimberg and Hope, 1992; Turner, Beidel and Townsley, 1992), which were published together as a mini-series in the *Journal of Abnormal Psychology*, and concluded (p. 340) that generalized social phobia and APD are 'overlapping constructs that have only minor differences with respect to severity of dysfunction.' While more studies have now been conducted, this conclusion remains quite tenable. However, a number of competing hypotheses, discussed by Widiger (1992), Heimberg et al. (1993) and others, may explain this pattern of results. Generalized social phobia with APD may simply be a more severe instantiation of generalized social phobia alone (i.e. a quantitative difference). Generalized social phobia and APD may be two different disorders that both affect interpersonal interaction and anxiety, and may or may not occur together in the same person (i.e. a qualitative difference). The criteria for generalized social phobia and APD may simply be too similar, leading us to an artificial debate. Generalized social phobia and APD may represent the same disorder described in different fashion by researchers with backgrounds in anxiety versus personality or by different workgroups within the DSM revision process.

Certainly, it will be difficult to determine the actual nature of these differences. Before addressing them, we must acknowledge the limitations of the data on which this discussion is based. Most of the studies reviewed herein involve the comparison of generalized social phobia alone with generalized social phobia with the additional diagnosis of APD. However, APD also occurs in the context of non-generalized social phobia, albeit less frequently than with generalized social phobia. Although this combination is less common, its existence may be critical to our understanding of the relationship between social phobia and APD. APD has also been found to co-occur with Axis I disorders other than social phobia (Jansen et al., 1994; Renneberg et al., 1992), and personality disorders other than APD (e.g. dependent or obsessive-compulsive PD) occur in social phobia, at times together with APD (Alnaes and Torgersen, 1988; Jansen et al., 1994; Turner et al., 1991). The current data base does not include persons with a primary diagnosis of APD, nor does it address the question of the co-occurrence of multiple (simultaneous) personality disorders with generalized social phobia.

The above notwithstanding, cases of APD without generalized social phobia will be rather infrequent. While approximately 60% of generalized social phobics have APD, 71–100% (median = 87%) of patients with APD have been classified as generalized social phobics. Of course, in most of these studies, all patients have some form of social phobia since they have been almost universally conducted in social phobia research centers. It seems important to thoroughly examine the frequency of generalized social phobia in patients with a primary diagnosis of APD, but these studies have not been conducted, and it has not been determined whether or not these patients exist.

Although studies of APD and panic disorder (e.g. Jansen et al., 1994) typically exclude patients with additional diagnoses of social phobia, they still report a percentage of patients who meet criteria for APD. While APD is not the primary diagnosis in these patients, the existence of APD independent of social phobia is an enigma. I have always found it difficult to conceptualize the patient with panic disorder who meets criteria for APD but not social phobia. How can the APD criteria be satisfied without the presence of interpersonal anxiety of magnitude sufficient to meet the criteria for social phobia, generalized or non-generalized? As noted earlier in this chapter, the two criteria sets are sufficiently similar that overlap should be substantial on that basis alone. It is tempting to call for much more thorough assessment of social phobia in these studies.

Despite the complications and confusions, generalized social phobia and APD do not appear to be the same thing. However, they refer to the same general domain of symptoms. As noted, almost all patients with APD in the studies reviewed also have the generalized type of social phobia. Herbert, Hope and Bellack (1992, p. 337) assert that 'Such a high degree of overlap, particularly when one disorder is wholly subsumed within another, raises serious questions about the validity of the two disorders as separate diagnostic entities.' They argue further that it is important for different diagnostic categories to be 'conceptually distinct, discriminable from one another, and as mutually exclusive as possible and that they must demonstrate relations with theoretically meaningful variables apart from those initially used to define them' (p. 337). It appears that generalized social phobia and APD do not pass this test as defined in the DSM IIIR. Widiger (1992) asserts that generalized social phobia and APD may represent boundary conditions of the anxiety and personality disorders that involve essentially the same psychopathology. If so, it is misleading to provide both diagnoses to the same patient since this practice suggests that the patient suffers from two distinct and co-morbid mental disorders. However, the patient who currently receives diagnoses of generalized social phobia and APD does not suffer from two distinct and comorbid mental disorders, but instead exhibits a set of symptoms that meets the criteria for two diagnoses.

The responsiveness of generalized social phobia and APD to treatment also bears on the current discussion. If APD (at least in the context of social phobia) is a 'true' personality disorder, then it is reasonable to think that generalized social phobia with APD should be harder to treat than generalized social phobia without APD. It is also reasonable to expect that the time-limited treatments for social phobia that are common in the literature would do little to affect APD. However, neither of these assertions appears to be supported by the available data. Pharmacological treatment, at least with alprozolam and the MAOIs, appears to reduce avoidant traits during the time that medication is administered, and one study (Versiani et al., 1992) reported that patients treated with MAOIs were less likely to meet criteria for APD after 8 weeks of treatment than patients receiving placebo treatment. While studies of the effect of APD on the outcome of cognitive-behavioral treatment are somewhat divided, Brown, Heimberg and Juster (1995) report that generalized social phobics with and without APD showed similar degrees of treatment response. Like Versiani et al.'s experience with MAOI treatment, several patients with generalized social phobia and APD no longer met the criteria for APD after 12 weeks of treatment.

These data suggest to me that there is a quantitative difference between generalized social phobia alone and generalized social phobia with APD, and that they are not, as suggested by Widiger (1992), two boundary conditions. They also suggest to me that it is time for us to consider the conceptual implications of how we currently talk about these disorders and of placing them simultaneously on Axis I and Axis II. First, although it is appropriately placed on Axis I, generalized social phobia with APD is not really a phobia as usually conceptualized. It is experienced in response to too many stimuli to comfortably fit that classification, even if these stimuli are functionally related to fears of scrutiny and negative evaluation. For the patient with broadly generalized social phobia, the experience seems more akin to a social version of generalized anxiety disorder, in which worry and anxiety apprehension are ever-present. DSM IV has quietly acknowledged this position by including *social anxiety disorder* as an alternative name for social phobia. Second, the severe impairment and pervasive avoidance that sometimes accompanies generalized social phobia may arguably *not* constitute a personality disorder. On the one hand, this may be a semantic argument, focusing on the definition of a 'symptom' versus the definition of a 'personality trait'. On the other hand, common conceptualizations of personality disorders not only suggest pervasiveness and chronicity but also imply poor response to therapeutic intervention. However, since APD does not uniformly detract from the outcome of treatment for social phobia, and is itself reduced by social phobia, this does not appear to be the case. It may be better to conceptualize generalized social phobia as a disorder of interpersonal anxiety that often begins early in life, that may be associated with substantial active and passive avoidance behavior, and that may systematically and negatively influence the development of personality traits and self-esteem over the life span.

As has been described in the context of panic disorder with agoraphobia (Barlow, 1988), some patients with generalized social phobia may develop an avoidant pattern and others may not. Instead, as described in DSM IIIR, they may endure social situations with dread. While there may be some genetic predisposition to social avoidance, its development may also be as much a response to the contingencies applied to the expression of anxiety during the early stages of the disorder as the presence of predisposing personality traits, and these contingencies may shape those very traits. In that case, avoidance and personality styles may be viewed as associated features of generalized social phobia rather than an independent personality disorder. In another paper, we (Heimberg et al., 1993) suggested that avoidance in the context of social phobia might be indexed as mild, moderate or severe, as was the case for panic disorder with agoraphobia in DSM IIIR. This approach removes us from the conceptual confusion of looking at the same symptomatology from two very different points of view.

A couple of other issues about the nature of generalized social phobia and APD should be discussed. First, it is often stated that one of the differences between social phobia and APD is that patients with APD are deficient in social skills (see, for instance, Marks, 1985). Although DSM III social phobics exhibited more appropriate gaze and voice tone and were rated as more socially skilled than patients with DSM III APD (Turner et al., 1986), this has not been the case in any study comparing patients with DSM IIIR generalized social phobia with patients with DSM IIIR generalized social phobia and APD. With DSM IIIR criteria, the quality of social behavior does not appear to discriminate between the two groups (see earlier discussion of the differences between DSM III and DSM IIIR criteria for social phobia and APD). However, it is important to keep in mind that some patients in each group may have social skills deficits while others will not. Furthermore, *deficits in performance on behavioral roleplay tests do not directly imply deficits in social skills*. Poor performance may occur for any number of reasons, including but not limited to poor social skills. Other reasons may include inhibition due to anxiety, maladaptive attentional focus, etc. See Heimberg and Juster (1995) for further discussion of this issue.

One of the more robust findings in this review is the potential association between generalized social phobia with APD and depression. Three of six studies found higher scores among generalized social phobics with APD on the Beck Depression Inventory, and multiple studies found an association between generalized social phobia with APD and additional mood disorder diagnoses. Furthermore, Feske et al. (in press) attribute a portion of the poorer response of generalized social phobics with APD to cognitive-behavioral treatment in their study to the fact that several of them were depressed. This is an area worthy of much further examination. Does pervasive social anxiety and avoidance (that is, in current parlance, the combination of generalized social phobia and APD) produce sufficient suffering that hopelessness and depression may result? Does the functional impairment (e.g. less likelihood of marriage, reduced earning capacity) associated with the combination mediate this connection? Does the development of avoidance follow the development of depression which follows repeated (real or perceived) social failure that is part of the generalized social phobia? These are questions that may most profitably occupy our time and help us help persons suffering from this difficult syndrome.

NOTES

Thanks to Harlan R. Juster and Elissa J. Brown for their comments on an earlier draft of this paper. Preparation of this paper was supported in part by grant 44119 from the National Institute of Mental Health to Richard G. Heimberg. Address correspondence or requests for reprints to Richard G. Heimberg, Social Phobia Program, Center for Stress and Anxiety Disorders, Pine West Plaza, Building 4, Washington Avenue Extension, Albany, NY 12205, USA.

REFERENCES

Alnaes, R., and Torgersen, S. (1988). The relationship between DSM III symptom disorders (Axis I) and personality disorders (Axis II) in an outpatient population, *Acta Psychiatrica Scandinavica*, **78**, 485–492.
American Psychiatric Association (1980). *Diagnostic and Statistical Manual of Mental Disorders* (3rd edn), APA, Washington, DC.
American Psychiatric Association (1987). *Diagnostic and Statistical Manual of Mental Disorders* (3rd edn – revised), APA, Washington, DC.

American Psychiatric Association (1994). *Diagnostic and Statistical Manual of Mental Disorders* (4th edn), APA, Washington, DC.

Barlow, D.H. (1988). *Anxiety and its Disorders*, Guilford Press, New York.

Beck, A.T., Ward, C.H., Mendelson, M., Mock, J. and Erbaugh, J. (1961). An inventory for measuring depression, *Archives of General Psychiatry*, **4**, 561–571.

Brooks, R.B., Baltazar, P.L. and Munjack, D.J. (1989). Co-occurrence of personality disorders with panic disorder, social phobia, and generalized anxiety disorder: a review of the literature, *Journal of Anxiety Disorders*, **3**, 259–285.

Brown, E.J., Heimberg, R.G., & Juster, H.R. (1995). Social phobia subtype and avoidant personality disorder: effect on severity of social phobia, impairment, and outcome of cognitive-behavioral treatment, *Behavior Therapy*, **26**, 467–486.

Derogatis, L.R. (1977). *SCL 90R: Administration, Scoring and Procedures Manual*, Clinical Psychometrics Research, Baltimore.

DiNardo, P.A. and Barlow, D.H. (1988). *The Anxiety Disorders Interview Schedule – Revised (ADIS-R)*, Graywind Publications, Albany, NY.

Feske, U., Perry, K.J., Chambless, D.L., Renneberg, B. and Goldstein, A.J. (in press). Avoidant personality disorder as a predictor for severity and treatment outcome among generalized social phobics, *Journal of Personality Disorders*.

Gambrill, E.D. and Richey, C.A. (1975). An assertion inventory for use in assessment and research, *Behavior Therapy*, **6**, 550–561.

Guy, W. (ed.) (1976). *ECDEU Assessment Manual for Psychopharmacology*, (DHEW Publication No. ADM, pp. 218–222), US Government Printing Office, Washington, DC.

Hamilton, M. (1959). The assessment of anxiety states by rating, *British Journal of Psychiatry*, **32**, 50–55.

Heimberg, R.G., Holt, C.S., Schneier, F.R., Spitzer, R.L. and Liebowitz, M.R. (1993). The issue of subtypes in the diagnosis of social phobia, *Journal of Anxiety Disorders*, **7**, 249–269.

Heimberg, R.G. and Juster, H.R. (1995). Cognitive-behavioral treatments: literature review, in Heimberg, R.G., Liebowitz, M.R., Hope, D.A. and Schneier, F.R. (eds), *Social Phobia: Diagnosis, Assessment, and Treatment* (pp. 261–309), Guilford Press, New York.

Heimberg, R.G., Juster, H.R., Hope, D.A. and Mattia, J.I. (1995). Cognitive behavioral group treatment for social phobia: description, case presentation, and empirical support, in Stein, M. (ed.), *Social Phobia: Clinical and Research Perspectives* (pp. 293–321), American Psychiatric Press, Washington, DC.

Herbert, J.D., Hope, D.A. and Bellack, A.S. (1992). Validity of the distinction between generalized social phobia and avoidant personality disorder, *Journal of Abnormal Psychology*, **101**, 332–339.

Holt, C.S., Heimberg, R.G. and Hope, D.A. (1992). Avoidant personality disorder and the generalized subtype in social phobia, *Journal of Abnormal Psychology*, **101**, 318–325.

Hope, D.A. and Heimberg, R.G. (1993). Social phobia and social anxiety, in Barlow, D.H. (ed.), *Clinical Handbook of Psychological Disorders: A Step-by-Step Treatment Manual* (2nd edn), pp. 99–136, Guilford Press, New York.

Hope, D.A., Herbert, J.D. and White, C. (1995). Diagnostic subtype, avoidant personality disorder, and efficacy of cognitive behavioral group therapy for social phobia. *Cognitive Therapy and Research*, **19**, 399–417.

Jansen, M.A., Arntz, A., Merckelbach, H. and Mersch, P.P.A. (1994). Personality disorders and features in social phobia and panic disorder, *Journal of Abnormal Psychology*, **103**, 391–395.

Liebowitz, M.R. (1987). Social phobia, *Modern Problems of Pharmacopsychiatry*, **22**, 141–173.

Liebowitz, M.R., Gorman, J.M., Fyer, A.J. and Klein, D.F. (1985). Social phobia: review of a neglected anxiety disorder, *Archives of General Psychiatry*, **42**, 729–736.

Liebowitz, M.R., Schneier, F., Campeas, R., Hollander, E., Hatterer, J., Fyer, A., Gorman, J., Papp, L., Davies, S., Gully, R. and Klein, D.F. (1992). Phenelzine vs. atenolol in social phobia: a placebo-controlled comparison, *Archives of General Psychiatry*, **49**, 290–300.

Lucas, R.A. and Telch, M.J. (1993). Group versus individual treatment of social phobia, paper presented at the annual meeting of the Association for Advancement of Behavior Therapy, Atlanta, GA, November.

Marks, I.M. (1985). Behavioral treatment of social phobia, *Psychopharmacology Bulletin*, **21**, 615-618.

McNeil, D.W., Reis, B.J., Taylor, L.J., Boone, M.L., Carter, L.E., Turk, C.L. and Lewin, M.R. (1995). Comparison of social phobia subtypes using Stroop tests, *Journal of Anxiety Disorders*, **9**, 47–57.

Reich, J., Noyes, R. and Yates, W. (1989). Alprazolam treatment of avoidant personality traits in social phobic patients, *Journal of Clinical Psychiatry*, **50**, 91–95.

Renneberg, B., Chambless, D.L. and Gracely, E.J. (1992). Prevalence of SCID-diagnosed personality disorders in agoraphobic outpatients, *Journal of Anxiety Disorders*, **6**, 111–118.

Roid, G.H. and Fitts, W.H. (1988). *Tennessee Self-Concept Scale: Revised Manual*, Western Psychological Services, Los Angeles, CA.

Sanderson, W.C., Wetzler, S., Beck, A.T. and Betz, F. (1994). Prevalence of personality disorders among patients with anxiety disorders. *Psychiatry Research*, **51**, 167–174.

Schneier, F.R., Johnson, J., Hornig, C.D., Liebowitz, M.R. and Weissman, M.M. (1992). Social phobia: comorbidity and morbidity in an epidemiologic sample. *Archives of General Psychiatry*, **49**, 282–288.

Schneier, F.R., Spitzer, R.L., Gibbon, M., Fyer, A.J. and Liebowitz, M.R. (1991). The relationship of social phobia subtypes and avoidant personality disorder. *Comprehensive Psychiatry*, **32**, 1–5.

Spielberger, C.D. (1983). *Manual for the State–Trait Anxiety Inventory* (revised edn), Consulting Psychologists Press, Palo Alto, CA.

Spitzer, R.L. and Williams, J.B.W. (1985). Proposed revisions in the DSM III classification of anxiety disorders based on research and clinical experience. In Tuma, A.H. and Maser, J. (eds), *Anxiety and the Anxiety Disorders*, pp. 759–773, Lawrence Erlbaum, Hillsdale, NJ.

Tran, G.Q. and Chambless, D.L. (1995). Subtypes of social phobia and avoidant personality disorder, *Journal of Anxiety Disorders*, **9**, 489–501.

Turner, R.M. (1987). The effects of personality disorder diagnosis on the outcome of social anxiety symptom reduction, *Journal of Personality Disorders*, **1**, 136–143.

Turner, S.M., Beidel, D.C., Borden, J.W., Stanley, M.A. and Jacob, R.G. (1991). Social phobia: Axis I and II correlates, *Journal of Abnormal Psychology*, **100**, 102–106.

Turner, S.M., Beidel, D.C., Dancu, C.V. and Keys, D.J. (1986). Psychopathology of social phobia and comparison to avoidant personality disorder, *Journal of Abnormal Psychology*, **95**, 389–394.

Turner, S.M., Beidel, D.C., Dancu, C.V. and Stanley, M.A. (1989). An empirically derived inventory to measure social fears and anxiety: the Social Phobia and Anxiety Inventory, *Psychological Assessment: A Journal of Consulting and Clinical Psychology*, **1**, 35–40.

Turner, S.M., Beidel, D.C. and Townsley, R.M. (1992). Social phobia: a comparison of specific and generalized subtype and avoidant personality disorder, *Journal of Abnormal Psychology*, **101**, 326–331.

Versiani, M., Nardi, A.E., Mundim, F.D., Alves, A.B., Liebowitz, M.R. and Amrein, R. (1992). Pharmacotherapy of social phobia: a controlled study with moclobemide and phenelzine, *British Journal of Psychiatry*, **161**, 353–360.

Watson, D. and Friend, R. (1969). Measurement of social-evaluative anxiety, *Journal of Consulting and Clinical Psychology*, **33**, 448–457.

Weissman, M.M. and Bothwell, S. (1976). Assessment of social adjustment by patient self-report, *Archives of General Psychiatry*, **33**, 1111–1115.

Widiger, T.A. (1992). Generalized social phobia versus avoidant personality disorder: a commentary on three studies, *Journal of Abnormal Psychology*, **101**, 340–343.

Chapter Four

J.M.G. WILLIAMS

Personality Disorder and the Will: A Cognitive Neuropsychological Approach to Schizotypal Personality

INTRODUCTION

The spirit of this volume is to encourage cognitive researchers and therapists to speculate. In this chapter, I have accepted the challenge by speculating about the origins of schizotypal personality disorder. Schizotypal traits rarely occur in isolation. I first became aware of their importance in the course of researching suicidal behaviour. Many parasuicide patients show 'borderline' symptoms (such as affective and interpersonal instability). However, when we assessed schizotypal traits, we found they were surprisingly high, and their occurrence highly correlated with borderline traits (Marker et al., 1991). This association has rarely been commented upon in the literature on suicidal behaviour, but it needs to be taken seriously.

The premise of my argument is that theorizing about personality needs to take seriously the constraints of neuropsychology. I therefore ask the question: what neuropsychological mechanism might come closest to helping an understanding of schizotypal disturbance?

Trends in Cognitive and Behavioural Therapies. Edited by P.M. Salkovskis.
© 1996 John Wiley & Sons Ltd.

THE NATURE OF SCHIZOTYPAL AND BORDERLINE PERSONALITY DISORDER

The understanding and treatment of people who have 'personality disorders' has always been difficult (Beck and Padesky, 1989; Gunderson, 1984; Kroll, 1988; Linehan, 1988, 1993; Young, 1989). This is particularly true of a group of patients who suffer from affective instability, self-harming acts, dissociative symptoms, identity disturbance, paranoia and ideas of reference. Because of the range and nature of the symptoms, it used to be thought that such patients were 'on the borderline' between neuroses and psychoses (see Kroll, 1988, for review). They were thus referred to as 'borderline' patients.

Historically, the concept of borderline personality disorder emerged from psychodynamic theory. In this theory, both the disturbances in cognition and the affective instability result from underlying dynamic disturbances. For example, Kernberg et al. (1981) separated 'psychotic' 'neurotic' and 'borderline intra-psychic organisations'. In this system, 'borderline' was defined by: (a) absence of stable sense of identity (b) use of primitive defence mechanisms (splitting and projective identification) and (c) partial retention of reality testing (unlike full-blown psychotic states). In these accounts, the schizophrenic-like disturbances are seen as reactions and attempts to cope with extremes of affective disturbance. They are all part of the same 'borderline' personality structure.

However, recent diagnostic systems have separated the schizophrenic-like 'schizotypal' symptoms from 'borderline' symptoms. The category 'schizotypal personality disorder' now refers to people with such symptoms as magical thinking, ideas of reference, social isolation, recurrent illusions, odd speech, inadequate rapport in face-to-face interaction, suspiciousness or paranoid ideation and undue social anxiety or hypersensitivity to criticism. The 'borderline' category now refers to those who show impulsivity in self-damaging behaviour, unstable and intense interpersonal relationships, inappropriate and intense anger, problems with the experience of self, affective instability, intolerance of being alone, physically self-damaging acts, occasional dissociative states and chronic feelings of emptiness or boredom. The value in separating borderline from schizotypal personality disorder is that it helps avoid the danger that schizophrenic-like symptoms are seen as merely the result of intense and prolonged affective disturbance. Nevertheless, one must avoid the opposite danger of separating the two types of symptom clusters too widely. There is general agreement that personality disordered clients very commonly have both borderline and schizotypal symptoms, especially the symptom of dissociation (Kroll, 1988; Tarnopolsky and Berelowitz, 1987). This co-occurrence of schizotypal and borderline symptoms exists whether such symptoms are rated by the patients themselves or independently by a clinician (Marker et al., 1991). They co-exist sufficiently frequently to prompt questions about what the relations between them might be. Whereas the separation into separate diagnostic entities has more clearly revealed the absence of a coherent theory that explains schizotypal phenomena, the co-occurrence of such traits and symptoms with borderline-type affective disturbance reminds us that any theory of schizotypy must explain the close relation between them.

This chapter will therefore be concerned primarily with understanding symptoms that have most commonly been associated with schizotypal disturbance, the increases in perceptual aberration, magical thinking and dissociative experience to which I give the generic term 'self-coherence dysfunction'. What is it that requires explanation about disturbance in self-coherence? A central feature of these phenomena appears to be the failure to draw appropriate boundaries between self and non-self. Such boundaries are important for smooth communication, for attributing motives appropriately, for distinguishing events in the environment from events in the mind, for attributing *causes* of events in the environment appropriately to self or other people or other things. But what processes underlie our abilities to make such distinctions? I will suggest that neuropsychology offers us a way of understanding self-coherence and its dysfunction, using a model attributable to Frith (1987, 1993). This explains such phenomena in terms of a breakdown in the mechanisms that normally monitor willed intentions. It can help us understand how self-coherence dysfunction can lead to, and in turn be caused by, the affective dysregulation of borderline personality disorder. I will conclude that schizotypal and borderline personality traits and symptoms, although mediated by different systems, co-occur for a number of reasons, including the exposure to similar stressors in early life, the weakening of goal-directed behaviour by fragmentation of intention monitoring, and a vicious circle in which the affective consequences of the helplessness induced by lack of control over mental events puts further pressure on the processes which monitor intentions. As background to Frith's model, previous work on the neuropsychology of the limbic frontal lobes will be briefly reviewed.

THE RELEVANCE OF NEUROPSYCHOLOGY: DYSFUNCTION OF THE LIMBIC FRONTAL LOBES

Limbic system dysfunction has often been implicated in discussions of the neuropsychological basis of motivation and emotion since the early suggestion (Papez, 1937) that it was an important central mechanism subserving emotional feeling and expression. Both experimental observations in animals and observation of limbic dysfunction in humans have shown that stimulation or lesion in various parts of the limbic system can produce rage-like states or emotional passivity. One of the difficulties in interpreting these data is that the limbic system projects to a large number of different parts of the brain, and it is difficult to know whether any effects that are produced by stimulation or by oblation are the direct effect on that part of the brain or more indirect effects through the complex network of connections. However, interest has particularly focused on connections between the limbic system and the frontal lobes.

These findings have suggested that the frontal lobes are responsible for the most high-level supramodal executive functions: planning, actions based on anticipation, monitoring and adjusting actions according to feedback. This programming of sequences of willed movements which require co-ordination over time is due to the frontal lobe's ability to maintain information in meaningful chunks that can be serially related (Alexander, Benson and Stuss, 1989). Thus the frontal lobes represent the supramodal regulation of external and internal milieu. Damasio (1979) compares it with the hypothalamus, which, at a lower level, adjusts behaviour according to motivational state on a 'thermostat' principle. The frontal lobes act as a comparator, but provide mechanisms that mediate between stimuli and responses and regulate behaviour on the basis of a greater range of information, long-term goals, anticipation of a likely outcome of a range of possibilities, and time sequences.

Some personality disorders may directly result from frontal damage: pseudo-depression (especially caused by damage to the dorsal–lateral convexity) or pseudo-psychopathy [especially caused by damage to the orbital aspect (Eslinger and Damasio, 1985; Stuss and Benson, 1984)]. None of these phenomena quite capture the particular range of symptoms found in schizotypal personality disorder, however. To understand these, we need to refer to one particular frontal pathway, and one particular aspect of phenomenal experience, that of knowing that an action has been willed by oneself.

THE SUPPLEMENTARY MOTOR AREA AND WILLED ACTION

There is one limbic frontal pathway (the cingulate–supplementary motor area (SMA) frontal pathway) which is particularly relevant to understanding schizotypal phenomena, since it appears to regulate a fundamental aspect of cognition – the sense of being in control of one's actions. The SMA is important in programming and execution of willed action, including speech and thoughts. Further, it helps record and co-ordinate willed action, speech and thoughts via a *central monitor* (Frith, 1987, 1993). To understand how this occurs, it is relevant to consider the underlying neuropsychology of action control.

In a review of the structure and function of the SMA, Goldberg (1985) suggests a dualism in the routes to action, re-emphasizing earlier conclusions by other investigators (e.g. Mackay, 1978; Sanides, 1964). The two systems, which compliment each other (and which interact with each other in the prefrontal orbital region), consist of:

1. A lateral system corresponding to the arcuate pre-motor area (APA) in primates (Schell and Strick, 1984). This is a 'data driven', responsive system dependent on a feedback control mechanism.

2. A second, medial system, involving the supplementary motor area (SMA) which derives from the hippocampal formation, and is involved in the context-sensitive, goal-setting functions of the pre-frontal cortex.

Of particular note are the clinical phenomena associated with damage to the SMA. Under some circumstances this is confined to impaired initiation of action. But in other cases, there occur movements of the arm and hand (contralateral to the damage) which are 'extra volitional'. This 'alien hand movement' is in conflict with the verbalized intentions of the patient. They say they do not mean to move their hands. One function the SMA may therefore have is the regulation of actions to be consistent with a current goal (Goldberg, 1985).

THE IMPLICATIONS OF SMA DISRUPTION

The evidence strongly suggests that the SMA damage disrupts the balance between environmentally contingent automatic actions, which are responsive in nature, and willed, internally generated actions, which are anticipatory in nature due to a disconnection between the limbic system and the SMA. 'Just as it may appear from the dissociative sensory phenomena seen with temporal lobe seizures that a neocortically elaborated percept requires limbic association to assume experiential immediacy, so actions may require limbic participation to assume its volitional or self-referenced origin' (Goldberg, 1985, p. 579).

There are two major consequences of this. The first concerns the interruption of output to the pre-frontal cortex. Since this area may be responsible for formulating goal-oriented action and integrating information from both the lateral and the medial system (Fuster, 1980) such a breakdown would allow actions to occur which were based solely on immediate response to external objects with motivational significance (based solely on their past reinforcement history), rather than on integration with an anticipatory model of the external world. We suggest that dysfunction in the SMA-mediated system would render a person vulnerable to act in ways that take no account of long-term goals. The second major consequence concerns the occurrence of 'alien phenomena'. If speech, thought and action is intended, but does not have limbic participation, it will not be experienced as being 'willed' or 'self-referenced'. Rather, they will appear to be alien, giving rise to the self-coherence disturbances which are a core feature of schizotypal patients.

This feature of SMA function and breakdown has been suggested to be a crucial factor in the experiential positive symptoms of Type I schizophrenia (Frith, 1987, 1993). Such patients may experience thoughts being inserted or withdrawn from their head. They hear voices apparently from outside. They believe events and conversations refer to themselves. They experience a disintegration of identity and delusions that external forces are controlling their actions. Frith proposes that such phenomena arise from a breakdown in the 'central monitor', the mechanism which normally monitors willed intentions to act, think or speak. The result is that the patients are unable to distinguish actions which arise in response to current environmental inputs (which Frith calls 'stimulus intentions' – SIs) from actions arising in anticipation of predicted states of affairs ('willed intentions' – WIs).

DISRUPTION OF WILL AND SCHIZOTYPAL SYMPTOMS

I noted earlier that there were several key features of schizotypal personality disorder which represent a failure to draw boundaries between self and non-self. If Frith is correct that the feeling that actions are 'willed by me' (be they thoughts, speech or limb movements) is dependent on the function of a central monitor, then dysfunction of this system will result in the occurrence of thoughts, speech and movements which appear to the person to have occurred without their having willed them to happen. Furthermore, the ability of the monitor to distinguish between actions which are willed and those which are responsive to external stimuli will be impaired. The monitor will be subject to errors of commission and errors of omission. In the extreme, if something occurs in the environment at the same moment at which the central monitor is activated, the result may be an erroneous attribution of the external event to the person's will. For example, if a picture falls off the wall and at that moment my (faulty) willed intention system is active, it will seem to me that I have willed the picture to fall.

A second consequence of failing to distinguish willed from responsive action is that the patient will find it difficult to clamp attention on to a single goal

(Duncan, 1990). Any salient stimulus in the environment will compete for attention on equal terms since the assignment of priority between different tasks, channels or messages depends on being able to decide which 'candidate' intentions are consistent with my goals and which are consistent only with moment-to-moment environmental stimulation. Speech and thought patterns underlying them will be odd because of this failure to discriminate dominant, willed, from non-dominant rival and respondent speech and thoughts [see Hoffman (1986) for an account of auditory hallucinations in closely related terms of verbal images which are unintended and extraneous to current goals of discourse].

Third, depersonalization, dissociative experiences and illusions of sensing 'presences' in the room are explained by the fact that patients feel and think things, but these do not feel as if *they* feel and think them. A person who has repeated alien experiences may attempt to give a coherent account of the experience in terms of the reality of 'presences', in terms of his or her own telephathic abilities, and in terms of magical control. It is not difficult to see how, in negative mood, they become paranoid, suspicious that others are attempting to control them, or that events and people's conversations are constantly referring to them.

Finally, although the disruption of the limbic–SMA–pre-frontal–limbic loop is partial compared with that which occurs in schizophrenia, we suggest that similar systems are involved and that it is vulnerability in this system which underlies the findings of schizophrenic spectrum disorders in the relatives of schizophrenic patients. There is evidence that the relatives of schizophrenic patients also have some schizophrenic characteristics (Claridge, 1987). More recently Shenton et al. (1989) have found evidence of thought disorder in the relatives of psychotic patients. Furthermore, Lenzenweger and Loranger (1989) have found that high scores on a scale assessing schizotypal traits in non-psychotic psychiatric patients, the Perceptual Aberration Scale, predicted the extent to which these patient's relatives were likely to have had schizophrenia.

VULNERABILITY TO AND PRECIPITATION OF SELF-COHERENCE DYSFUNCTION

Recently it has become clear that schizotypal traits, especially prominent in relatives of schizophrenics, are actually normally distributed in the population (Claridge, 1987; Bentall, Claridge and Slade, 1989). It appears that the extent to which one experiences a range of aberrant or alien thoughts, feelings and sensations arises from individual differences in temperament, which is under genetic control. I suggest that individual differences in the functioning of the monitoring of stimulus and willed intention underlie this distribution. Yet the fact that one may have these experiences, yet not show personality distur-bance, shows that the deficient functioning of intention monitoring cannot by itself be sufficient to produce the chaotic mental life of a personality-disturbed patient.

For the schizotypal patient, fragmentation of the central monitor (which may already be vulnerable as a matter of inherited temperament) takes place in response to stress. Often the first remembered occurrences of dissociative phenomena were at times of severe stress. Many of these patients have suffered extreme trauma in their past lives (Herman, Perry and van der Kolk, 1989). Physical and sexual abuse is common, as is actual and threatened abandonment (Kroll, 1988). Reports of post-traumatic stress disorder in Vietnam veterans show how similar personality disturbances may result from prolonged stress (Kolb, 1989). Early experience of trauma of this type is an element common to both schizotypal and borderline personalities. It is to the explanation of this co-occurrence of the two types of personality traits that I now turn.

CO-OCCURRENCE OF 'BORDERLINE' SYMPTOMS

Fragmentation of the 'intention monitoring processes' may explain schizoty-pal phenomena, but how is the common co-occurrence with borderline symp-toms to be explained? These include impulsivity, instability both in affect (especially anger) and in interpersonal relationships (which are experienced as very intense), problems with self-identity linked to chronic feelings of emptiness and boredom and intolerance of being alone. There are also fre-quently physically self-damaging acts including multiple overdoses and the inflicting of cuts or burns on the body. I have already alluded to one reason why borderline and schizotypal traits co-occur: that is, the similar stressors which patients have undergone (especially physical and sexual abuse). Note that these commonly occur during unpleasant dissociative states brought about by the rapid uncontrolled escalation of negative affect.

The co-occurrence of schizotypal and borderline traits may also be partly due to the repeated experience of having no control over mental events. In order to reduce such feelings of helplessness, individuals may attribute their lack of control over mental events to control from other people or outside forces. Although such attribution has benefits, it also has costs. The benefit is that it reduces an immediate sense of helplessness and lack of control. If others are controlling your thoughts, then there is still some chance that one may dis-cover how they are doing it and stop them. The cost is an increased hypervigilance for external sources of hostility, making the person perceptually sensitive (Bentall and Kaney, 1989) analogous to the sensitivity shown by highly anxious patients (Williams et al. 1988, and in press). In the longer term it produces a chronic helplessness due to the eventual realization that these external factors cannot be controlled either.

Finally, schizotypal and borderline symptoms co-occur because these affective consequences feed back to the processes underlying intention monitoring to complete a vicious circle. As discussed earlier, the first episodes of schizotypal experiences often occur during a time of stress, such as sexual abuse. Even if such stress were not to occur again, subsequent affective disturbance later in life may reinstate the context due to mood-dependent memory effects. Such extremes of stress may once again cause the monitor to fragment. Any situation which produces large conflict between goals – particularly between stimulus intention and willed intention – may be particularly likely to cause fragmentation of the monitor. Consider the situation in which a person has been punished for the expression of emotion, for example in the case of sexual abuse where a child has been threatened with punishment if he or she becomes upset (Linehan, 1993). In this case there is conflict between the expression of emotion (stimulus intention) and the suppression of emotion to avoid future punishment (willed intention). The result is a rapid escalation of negative emotion due to such a positive feedback loop: the expression of emotion itself violates a goal ('do not feel or show emotion'), but the consequence of violating any goal is increased emotion (Oatley and Johnson-Laird, 1987). This leads to the invalidation strategies (patients feeling upset but telling themselves they should not), treatment for which is at the heart of recent therapy strategies for borderlines (Linehan, 1993). The central monitor becomes dysfunctional when there is no behavioural repertoire by which the stimulus or willed intention system can resolve such conflicts.

Even for people who are relatively low in schizotypal traits, extremes of stress resulting in such conflicts will cause fragmentation of the monitor so that actions are not seen as being under the control of the will. In the most extreme cases, all sense of self (of being a voluntary agent, having personal memories and body schema) disintegrates. The phenomenal experience is that of being 'out of body', of seeing the scene from another angle as observer rather than as participant. Experiences of alien control and of hallucinations may also occur following extreme or long-lasting stress associated with such affective dysregulation and escalation. These experiences occur spontaneously for the first time under extreme stress, but the threshold for the appearance of such phenomena is then lowered so that they can be activated under conditions of future (and often lesser) stress. Affective instability can thus play a moderating role in the dysfunctional organization of the self.

People with high schizotypal traits require lower amounts of stress for such dissociation to occur, for weakening of the central monitor is a chronic feature of such people. As we have seen, it explains the high occurrence of beliefs in telepathy and clairvoyance among such people. They will chronically experience actions, thoughts and words which do not feel as if they belong to them. They will be more likely to believe that they have received messages telepathically, and that things or events that occur in their environment either refer to them (ideas of reference) or were caused by them (magical ideation). They are always therefore more likely to become suspicious that others are attempting to control them (as a plausible account of their phenomenal experience) or talking about them.

The fragmentation of the monitor will have major consequences for the pursuit of interpersonal goals. Schizotypal individuals are often unusual in their interpersonal behaviour. This arises partly from the paranoia and suspiciousness which can result from the experience of alien control, but also because interpersonal interaction involves the co-ordination of goals and intentions between people. Not only does one need to be aware of one's own intentions, one needs a model of the other person's goals and intentions in order to construct and execute mutual plans. Schizotypal individuals find considerable difficulty in entering into shared intentions, because their own self-model is inherently unstable. The complex balance of approach and avoidance in social interaction makes heavy demands on a system for detecting whether one's behaviour represents an appropriate response to another person's 'messages'. Particularly important will be the ability to have 'insight' about situations where there is no longer positive reinforcement to be had from a certain course of action (a social analogue of the reversal learning paradigm). As Frith (1987), 1993) indicates, such insight depends on the integrity of a monitor which can give reliable information about whether an action taken is appropriate to the stimulus and to one's intentions. Without such a monitor, 'switching off' inappropriate behaviour will be difficult because they are unsure what the source of the social error is.

Finally, are there implications for treatment? In the model, the processes underlying borderline and schizotypal personality disorder are separate, but interact due to schizotypal symptoms sometimes arising from extreme stress, which gives rise to conflict which cannot be resolved within the current repertoire of the SI or WI system. The model predicts that treatment studies will find a dissociation between improvement in affect and in improvement in behaviour and that any such dissociation will be especially marked in those borderline patients who also show schizotypal traits.

Detailed descriptions of structured psychotherapies such as those of Young (1989), Beck and Freeman (1990) and Linehan (1993) are beyond the scope of this paper, but it it interesting that the most extensively explored structured psychotherapy for personality-disordered patients, Dialectical Behaviour Therapy (DBT) (Linehan, 1993), does reveal a dissociation between action and affect. In her studies of the effectiveness of DBT, Linehan shows that it can be successful in reducing impulsive self-harm behaviour. However, this occurs in the absence of any marked reduction of depression, hopelessness and suicidal ideation. It is difficult to explain if impulsive behaviour is seen only as the outcome of affective dysregulation. Such a dissociation is, however, consistent with the theory proposed here that a neuropsychological sub-system, independent of those subserving affect and concerned with the control of willed acts, is responsible for much of the disturbance these patients suffer.

CONCLUDING REMARKS

Many clinicians and researchers who have worked with personality disordered clients have identified affective intensity/instability as well as behavioural impulsivity and brief psychotic episodes as common or even core features to be explained. I have suggested that symptoms of schizotypal personality disorder arise from dysfunction in those mechanisms that underlie the activity of will, action, thought and speech, particularly the monitoring of intentions and discriminating stimulus from willed intentions. I have suggested that activation in the SMA normally underlies these functions. The projection of this area to the pre-frontal cortex allows information about willed intentions (based on predicted states of the world) to be integrated with information about the current environmental situation. I have suggested that borderline symptoms often co-occur with schizotypal symptoms not only because of commonalities in early experience, but also because weakening of intention monitoring disrupts the smooth pursuit of goals (especially interpersonal goals which depend on perceiving mutual intentions). Such fragmentation of intention monitoring is also itself a source of affective disturbance as the person tries in vain to gain control of his or her own mental states. This affective disturbance, especially that relating to conflict between stimulus and willed intentions, produces a vicious circle effect in which further fragmentation of intention monitoring (further dissociative experiences etc.) result.

One needs to assume dysfunction in both affective and conative (intentional) mechanisms to explain these personality disorders. Explanations confined to discussions of early maladaptive schemas, (e.g. Beck and Freeman, 1990; Young, 1989) have been very valuable in codifying the contents of the pathology, but by themselves they do not explain why such hypersensitivity should have just these effects. Similarly, emphasizing the aberrant perception and schizophrenia-like symptoms in personality disorder is insufficient to explain personality disorder itself. Many people in the normal population have a range of schizotypal experiences, yet do not show personality disturbance [and indeed may find such experiences increase their well-being (Jackson, 1991)]. It is possible that the extreme stress experienced by some patients would itself be sufficient to account for personality disorder in later life. However, in most cases it is a combination of stress and vulnerable temperament which contribute to the final clinical picture. Thus both drug therapy and psychotherapy will need to take account of these multiple dysfunctions, and allow for the fact that, although they undoubtedly interact, improvement in one aspect (e.g. behaviour, affect or alien experiences) may not entail improvement in the others.

ACKNOWLEDGEMENTS

I am grateful to Andrew MacLeod, Alan Wing, Susan Goodrich, Marsha Linehan, Gordon Brown, David Fowler, David Healy and Chris Frith for helpful discussions of earlier drafts of this paper; and to Caroline Muncey, Moira Stephenson and Sharon Fraser for typing the manuscript.

REFERENCES

Alexander, N.P., Benson, D.F. and Stuss, D.T. (1989). Frontal lobes and language, *Brain and Language*, **37**, 656–691.

Beck, A.T. and Freeman, A. (1990). *Cognitive Therapy of Personality Disorders*, Guilford Press, New York.

Beck, A.T. and Padesky, C. (1989). Cognitive approaches to personality disorder, Workshop presented at the World Congress of Cognitive Therapy, Oxford.

Bentall, R.P., Claridge, G.S. and Slade, P.D. (1989). The multi-dimensional nature of schizotypal traits: a factor-analytic study with normal subjects, *British Journal of Clinical Psychology*, **28**, 363–375.

Bentall, R.P. and Kaney, S. (1989). Content specific information processing and persecutory delusions: an investigation using the emotional Stroop test, *British Journal of Medical Psychology*, **62**, 355–364.

Claridge, G.S. (1987). 'The schizophrenias as nervous types' revisited, *British Journal of Psychiatry*, **151**, 735–743.

Damasio, A.R. (1979). The frontal lobes, in Heilman, K.L. and Valenstein, E. (eds), *Clinical Neuropsychology*, pp. 360–412, Oxford University Press, Oxford.

Duncan, J. (1990). Goal weighting and the choice of behaviour in a complex world. *Ergonomics*, **33**, 1265–1279.

Eslinger, P.J. and Damasio, A.R. (1985). Severe disturbance of higher cognition after bilateral frontal lobe ablation: Patient EVR, *Neurology*, **35**, 1731–1741.

Frith, C.D. (1987). The positive and negative symptoms of schizophrenia reflect impairments in the perception and initiation of action, *Psychological Medicine*, **17**, 631–648.

Frith, C.D. (1993). *The Cognitive Neuropsychology of Schizophrenia*, Lawrence Erlbaum, Hove.

Fuster, J.M. (1980). *The Prefrontal Cortex: Anatomy, Physiology and Neuropsychology of the Frontal Lobe*, Raven Press, New York.

Goldberg, G. (1985). Supplementary motor area structure and function: review and hypothesis, *Behavioural and Brain Sciences*, **8**, 567–616.

Gunderson, J.G. (1984). *Borderline Personality Disorder*. American Psychiatric Press, Washington, DC.

Herman, J.L., Perry, J.C. and van der Kolk, B.A. (1989). Childhood trauma in borderline personality disorder, *American Journal of Psychiatry*, **146**, 490–495.

Hoffman, R.E. (1986). Verbal hallucinations and language production processes in schizophrenia. *Brain and Behavioural Sciences*, **9**, 503–548.

Jackson, M.C. (1991). The relationship between psychotic and religious experience, unpublished D.Phil Thesis, University of Oxford.

Kernberg, O.F., Goldstein, E.G., Car, A.C., Hunt, H.F., Bauer, S.F. and Blumenthal, R. (1981). Diagnosing borderline personality: a pilot study using multiple diagnostic methods, *Journal of Nervous and Mental Disease*, **169**, 225–231.

Kolb, L.C. (1989). Chronic post-traumatic stress disorder: implications of recent epidemiological and neurospsychological studies. *Psychological Medicine*, **19**, 821–824.

Kroll, J. (1988). *The Challenge of the Borderline Patient, Competency in Diagnosis and Treatment*, W.W. Norton, New York.

Lenzenweger, M.F. and Loranger, A.W. (1989). Detection of familial schizophrenia using a psychometric measure of schizotypy, *Archives of General Psychiatry*, **46**, 902–907.

Linehan, M. (1988). Behavioural treatment of chronically parasuicidal patients, paper presented at the Behaviour Therapy World Congress, Edinburgh, September.

Linehan, M. (1993). *Cognitive Behavioural Treatment of Borderline Personality Disorder*, Guilford Press, New York.

Mackay, C. (1978). The dynamics of perception, in Buser, P.A. and Rougeul-Buser, A. (eds), North Holland, Amsterdam.

Marker, H.R., Williams, J.M.G., Wells, J. and Gordon, L. (1991). Occurrence of schizotypal and borderline symptoms in parasuicide patients: comparison between subjective and objective indices, *Psychological Medicine*, **21**, 385–392.

Oatley, K. and Johnson-Laird, P.N. (1987). Towards a cognitive theory of emotions, *Cognition and Emotion*, **1**, 29–50.

Papez, J.W. (1937). A proposed mechanism of emotion, *Archives of Neurology and Psychiatry*, **38**, 725–744.

Sanides, F. (1964). The cyto-myeloarchitecture of the human frontal lobe and its relation to phylogenetic differentiation of the cerebral cortex, *Journal Fur Hirnforschung*, **6**, 269–282.

Schell, G.R. and Strick, P.L. (1984). The origin of thalamic input to the arcuate premotor and supplementary motor areas, *Journal of Neuroscience*, **4**, 539–560.

Shenton, M.E., Solovay, M.R., Holzman, P.S., Coleman, M. and Gale, H.J. (1989). Thought disorder in the relatives of psychotic patients. *Archives of General Psychiatry*, **46**, 897–901.

Stuss, D.T. and Benson, D.F. (1984). Neuropsychological studies of the frontal lobes, *Psychological Bulletin*, **95**, 3–28.

Tarnopolsky, A. and Berelowitz, M. (1987). Borderline personality: a review of recent research, *British Journal of Psychiatry*, **151**, 724–734.

Williams, J.M.G., Watts, F.W., MacLeod, C. and Mathews, A. (1988). *Cognitive Psychology and Emotional Disorders*, John Wiley & Sons, Chichester.

Williams, J.M.G., Watts, F.W., MacLeod, C. and Mathews, A. (in press). *Cognitive Psychology and Emotional Disorders (2nd edn)*, John Wiley & Sons, Chichester.

Young, J. (1989). Schema focused cognitive therapy for difficult patients and characterological disorders, Workshop presented at the World Congress of Cognitive Therapy, Oxford.

Chapter Five

MARK B. SOBELL AND LINDA C. SOBELL

Control as a Pathway to Recovery from Alcohol Problems

Although the best evaluated treatments for alcohol problems are cognitive-behavioral (Miller, 1992), such interventions are little used in community treatment programs. In fact, the interventions that currently dominate treatment for alcohol problems have not been rigorously evaluated (Miller and Hester, 1986). Why have front line service providers failed to use empirically validated techniques to treat alcohol abusers? One reason is because cognitive-behavioral methods are identified with studies showing that some alcohol abusers can control their alcohol consumption. At the outset, it is important to distinguish between the academic question of whether or not individuals *can* regulate their alcohol consumption and the pragmatic issue of whether they *should* seek a recovery that involves limited alcohol consumption.

This chapter explores the pivotal role that the concept of 'control' plays in the two major approaches to alcohol problems. Although traditional and cognitive-behavioral approaches differ in several ways, the most important difference is in how they view alcohol abusers' ability to regulate their drinking. According to the traditional view, alcohol abusers intrinsically lack the ability to exert volitional control over their drinking. In a cognitive-behavioral view, alcohol abusers' excessive drinking is considered a learned response, subject to the same rules of behavior that govern other learning. From this perspective, therefore, alcohol abusers are viewed as able to control their drinking (even abstinence is conceptualized as a demonstration of control).

Trends in Cognitive and Behavioural Therapies. Edited by P.M. Salkovskis.
© 1996 John Wiley & Sons Ltd.

The fervor with which the traditional view of alcohol problems is held has led to extensive and vehement controversy in the alcohol field. The resulting conflicts have hampered the establishment of needed services for persons whose alcohol problems are not severe. However, self-control approaches have recently gained ground. Although the growing availability of such treatments reflects an important trend in cognitive-behavioral therapies, the increasing use of self-control approaches has not resulted from debate between traditionalists and cognitive-behaviorists. Rather, it stems from the growing acceptance of the importance of taking a public health approach to alcohol problems. As will be discussed, the increasing acceptance of a public health approach offers opportunities for cognitive-behavioral therapies to make significant contributions to public health.

VIEWS OF CONTROL

Two questions have perplexed the alcohol field for decades: (1) Why do some people develop alcohol problems while others do not? and (2) Why do alcohol abusers repeatedly engage in a behavior that brings turmoil and tragedy to their lives? Over the past quarter century there have been two major ways of explaining these phenomena.

THE TRADITIONAL VIEW OF CONTROL

The traditional view of control had its origins in the ideas of Alcoholics Anonymous (AA) and in a small group of interested professionals who were working in the alcohol field when AA became established. These views attributed alcohol problems to putative physical and personal failings. The AA view was formulated in the 1930s at a time when scientists were beginning to understand allergies. The book *Alcoholics Anonymous* states 'We believe, and so suggested a few years ago, that the action of alcohol on these chronic alcoholics is a manifestation of an allergy; that the phenomenon of craving is limited to this class and never occurs in the average temperate drinkers. These allergic types can never safely use alcohol in any form at all' (Anonymous, 1939, p. 4). The nature of the allergy was explained as 'once he [the alcoholic] takes any alcohol whatever into his system, something happens, both in the bodily and mental sense, which makes it virtually impossible for him to stop' (p. 33).

Even if the allergy hypothesis were true, it would not explain why people who experience drinking problems choose to drink again. Whether the allergy is to dairy products, animal fur or pollen, allergic individuals typically do not repeatedly expose themselves to the allergen. Instead, they usually avoid behaving in ways that have previously resulted in negative consequences. The phenomenon of repeatedly returning to drinking was explained by AA as 'the *obsession of the mind* that compels us to drink' (Anonymous, 1939, p. 13), and the obsession was further defined as 'the idea that somehow, someday he will control and enjoy his liquor drinking is the great obsession of every abnormal drinker' (p. 41). Consistent with this, the AA position on control states 'most alcoholics, for reasons yet obscure, have lost the power of choice in drink. Our so-called will power becomes practically nonexistent. We are unable at certain times to bring into our consciousness with sufficient force the memory of the suffering and humiliation of even a week or a month ago' (p. 34). Others echoing this philosophy have addressed the issue of control directly 'With alcoholics, choice is no longer possible, whether to drink or not to drink, or of the amount consumed, or the effects of that amount upon them, or the occasions upon which drunkenness occurs' (Mann, 1968, p. 9).

Shortly after the establishment of Alcoholics Anonymous, the disease concept of alcoholism began to gain favor. Although a disease approach was advocated during the 1800s, its advocacy during the mid twentieth century was largely for social reasons – to change public perceptions of people with drinking problems from moral transgressors to victims of a biological abberation who should not be held responsible for their problem. This approach was put forward without empirical support for the primary purposes of reducing the stigma felt by persons with an alcohol problem and encouraging the provision of health care for these individuals as an alternative to criminal justice interventions (i.e. get them out of jails and into hospitals). Although the advance of the disease concept was greatly facilitated by the American Medical Association's (AMA) pronouncement in the 1950s that alcoholism was a disease, there was little consensus for this position among physicians. Seldon Bacon has described the development of the AMA position as follows: 'Perhaps one-tenth of one percent of the medical profession fought for medical adoption of the medical definition. Thank God for their dedication. But this adoption was foisted upon the medical profession by the others' (Bacon, 1973, p. 23). This approach has been referred to as the traditional approach (Pattison, Sobell and Sobell, 1977) because it has long been championed by members of Alcoholics Anonymous, by the media and by treatment programs that are not research based. Those familiar with the alcohol literature will note that the traditional approach described here differs in a critical way from the disease concept as formulated by Jellinek (1960). Jellinek did hypothesize that for a chronic alcoholic, physical dependence would be initiated by consumption of just a small amount of alcohol, and that further drinking was then necessary in order to forestall withdrawal symptoms, but he clearly distinguished between '(a) the mechanism that leads from the completion of one bout to the beginning of another, and (b) the continuation of drinking within a single bout' (Jellinek, 1960). The former, he offered, was a learned behavior used 'as a means of "problem solution" ' (p. 66). This aspect of Jellinek's disease concept is surprisingly consistent with a cognitive-behavioral approach but has not typically been part of common understandings of the disease approach.

A central defining characteristic of the traditional approach is the assertion that individuals considered to be 'alcoholics' cannot control their drinking. Yet these individuals are repeatedly driven to test themselves, thus accounting for the high relapse rate that characterizes attempted recovery from alcohol problems. The importance of the control issue is nowhere more apparent than in the first of the 12 steps of the AA program – to admit we were powerless over alcohol. The 12 steps of AA form the basis for the treatment approach that is still dominant in North America. Recently, Hickey (1994) described the traditional approach as basically religious in nature:

> It is difficult to formulate a definition of a religion that AA wouldn't meet. The organization has a body of dogma which stresses man's inherent weakness and this need for a personal relationship with a forgiving God; it has its own sacred literature and rituals; and it holds regular meetings for the purpose of prayer and fellowship. (Hickey, 1994, p. 83)

The foregoing illustrates several points. First, a central tenet of the traditional approach is that the drinking behavior of alcoholics is not amenable to normal decision making and action processes, and cannot be regulated in the way that other behaviors are regulated (e.g. choosing to go to a restaurant or where to go on holiday). Second, according to the traditional approach the main way that recovery is achieved is by the individual accepting that control is not possible and incorporating this into his or her lifestyle by forever avoiding alcohol. This process has sometimes been viewed as 'surrender.' Third, this view has not been put forth as an academic theory or even as a common-sense explanation, but as a dogma akin to religious philosophy (Cook, 1985). This final point is important because it probably best accounts for why traditional treatment has shunned research advances.

THE COGNITIVE-BEHAVIORAL VIEW OF CONTROL

Behavioral and later cognitive-behavioral concepts of alcohol problems emerged in work done at research facilities as extensions of behavior therapy and in relative isolation from traditional thinking about alcohol problems. Starting in the mid-1960s, early behavioral research involved simple scientific explorations of the nature of intoxication, especially with chronic alcoholics. These experimental intoxication studies had considerable impact on broader conceptualizations that subsequently developed. Two research groups had a particularly significant impact on the field.

The first group consisted of Jack Mendelson and his colleagues. They conducted pioneering studies of alcohol consumption and intoxication in alcoholics (Mello, 1972; Mello and Mendelson, 1965, 1970; Mendelson, LaDou and Solomon, 1964; Mendelson and Mello, 1966). An important influence on cognitive social learning accounts of excessive drinking was this group's finding that chronic alcoholics given easy access to alcohol in an experimental setting did not drink themselves into oblivion. Rather, they maintained relatively high blood alcohol levels (around 25 mg %, well above legal levels for intoxication, but not a particularly high level for highly tolerant alcoholics) over several days by titrating their consumption (e.g. their levels might vary between 21 mg % and 30 mg %). Although these subjects were continuously intoxicated, they also clearly regulated their intake.

The second research group consisted of George Bigelow and his colleagues (Bigelow et al., 1972; Bigelow, Griffith and Liebson, 1975; Bigelow and Liebson, 1972; Bigelow, Liebson and Griffiths, 1974; Cohen et al., 1971a, b; Cohen, Liebson and Faillace, 1971a, b, 1972, 1973; Faillace et al., 1972). This group used operant learning theory to demonstrate that the drinking of even severely dependent alcoholics could be controlled by the application of contingencies, and especially by reward contingencies. One study, for example, demonstrated that in a hospital environment, chronic alcoholics could be induced to consume specified limited amounts (e.g. 5 oz) of 95-proof spirits per day to earn a daily payment ranging from $7 to $20 (Cohen, Liebson and Faillace, 1972). Considerable behavioral research leading to similar conclusions has been reported by other investigators [for reviews, see Adesso (1980), Fingarette (1988), Marlatt (1978), Marlatt and Rohsenow (1980), Pattison, Sobell and Sobell (1977), Sobell and Sobell (1975)].

At about the same time that these experimental studies were being conducted, Bandura's (1969) highly influential text on *Principles of Behavior Modification* became popular and advanced the notion that excessive drinking was a learned and functional behavior. Our own early work, in fact, was greatly influenced by Bandura's formulation (Sobell and Sobell, 1973, 1994). Implicit in a behavioral approach, whether from a social learning theory perspective (Wilson, 1988) or from theories of appetitive behavior (Orford, 1985), is the thesis that excessive drinking is a learned behavior that is a function of particular situations and learning histories and can be extinguished. In the early 1980s, cognitive factors (self-efficacy, perception of control) were added to this formation, largely from Marlatt's model of relapse

(Cummings, Gordon and Marlatt, 1980). Based on this conception, most cognitive-behavioral treatment approaches help individuals regain control over their drinking, whether the goal is abstinence or reduced drinking. For example, Guided Self-Change treatment, a motivationally based treatment that we have developed for problem drinkers (i.e. persons whose alcohol problems are not severe), emphasizes individuals selecting their own goal (based on an informed choice) performing a functional analysis of their drinking, and developing and implementing their own treatment plans (Sobell and Sobell, 1993a). Although the therapist serves as a source of information and advice, the purpose of the treatment is to 'help people help themselves.'

IMPLICATIONS FOR UNDERSTANDING THE BEHAVIOR CHANGE PROCESS

An interesting aspect of the traditional approach to treating alcohol problems is that while its philosophic underpinnings point to people's inability to control their behavior, the procedures advocated for achieving change emphasize that people are responsible for their behavior. For example, individuals are urged to exercise alternative behaviors such as calling their Alcoholics Anonymous sponsor when they feel tempted to drink. Other self-control procedures advocated in the traditional approach include frequent attendance at AA meetings (an activity inconsistent with spending time in a drinking environment), and changing social relationships to be with others who do not facilitate alcohol consumption (McCrady, 1986; Nowinski, Baker and Carroll, 1992).

Thus, at a very general level both traditional and cognitive-behavioral approaches place responsibility for change with the client, and the key to success is thought to be clients *choosing* to use alternative, non-drinking strategies to deal with high-risk situations. What then is the difference between the approaches? The difference is not so much in the strategies used to enact change, but rather in the underlying explanation imparted to the client as the rationale for the procedures. In the traditional approach, the rationale for using alternatives to drinking is that the individual is not capable of regulating his or her alcohol consumption. This leads directly to a strategy of never drinking at all. Not drinking is achieved by exercising self-control (i.e. purposefully engaging in alternative behaviors). In the cognitive-behavioral approach, clients are given an explanation of their behavior in terms of learning theory. Excessive drinking is viewed as a functional behavior that has become a problem because of the consequences or risks it has incurred. The individual, however, is *not* viewed as inherently incapable of exercising control over drinking. Thus, a major difference between the approaches is that a cognitive-behavioral approach is consistent with the use of flexible goals while the traditional approach requires a commitment to abstinence.

Although it is not our purpose to review the literature on alcohol treatment outcome evaluation, there is considerable evidence for the effectiveness of cognitive-behavioral treatment (Miller and Hester, 1986) and some evidence for the effectiveness of traditional treatment (Timko et al., 1994). If we accept that some people recover through either pathway – traditional or cognitive-behavioral – this raises the question of how approaches that differ so fundamentally can both facilitate recovery? A related question is for what reasons might one approach be preferred over the other?

RECOVERY AND COGNITIVE SCHEMAS

Functionally, treatments for alcohol problems have two main objectives: motivating individuals to recover, and assisting individuals in identifying and exercising alternatives to drinking. Both the traditional and cognitive-behavioral approaches accomplish these purposes for some individuals. Since the approaches converge in recommending that individuals exercise alternatives to drinking, this suggests that the main difference is in how they motivate persons to become committed to behavior change.

In this regard, implicit in a learning theory explanation of drinking is that drinking is largely a function of external stimuli that serve either as classically conditioned cues or as events signalling reinforcement contingencies. Excessive drinkers, therefore, are viewed as largely controlled by environmental factors. In contrast, in the traditional view excessive intake of alcohol is thought to be driven mainly by a biologically abnormal reaction to alcohol. However, both approaches stress that it is only the individual's actions that can bring about recovery and prevent relapse. According to the traditional approach, this is because the individual, aware of his or her vulnerabilities, exercises self-control by avoiding consumption of a first drink. Latent in this schema, however, is the self-fulfilling prophecy that should any alcohol be consumed, the individual will then lack control over further drinking. As noted in Marlatt's work on relapse prevention (Marlatt and George, 1984; Marlatt and Gordon, 1985), this is a very important difference between the approaches, and one that can have potentially serious consequences should the individual begin to drink.

Nevertheless, the fact that such widely disparate approaches can be effective suggests that it is not simply the specific philosophy of treatment that serves to increase motivation, but rather the *consistency* between the explanation and how the individual views the forces that influence his or her drinking. It would be predicted that difficulties should arise for individual who cannot accommodate an orientation to which they are exposed. Therefore, although both approaches appear to constitute viable pathways to recovery, they would be expected to differ in terms of the individuals for which they are most applicable. Using a quasi-experimental design, information on whether this prediction is correct should eventually be provided by a multicenter project presently underway in the United States (Project MATCH Research Group, 1993).

APPEAL OF THE DIFFERING APPROACHES

The acceptability of the approaches for individuals with alcohol problems is where the differences between the traditional and cognitive-behavioral approaches are most evident. To appreciate these differences, it is necessary to understand an issue that has long plagued the alcohol field. As described earlier, traditional concepts in the alcohol field arose concurrent with efforts to gain health care for alcohol abusers. Because the most obvious cases involved persons whose problems were severe, the conception was directed at explaining these highly visible cases. Over the past 25 years, however, accumulated epidemiological evidence has made clear that the spectrum of individuals with alcohol problems is much broader than suggested by traditional concepts. In fact, the population of individuals who have identifiable but not severe alcohol problems is far larger than that of individuals whose problems are severe (Institute of Medicine, 1990; Sobell and Sobell, 1993b). Most of this evidence has been ignored by the alcohol treatment field, and thus the field has not responded to the needs of persons whose problems are not severe (i.e. problem drinkers). The most obvious explanation of this lack of response relates to the underlying assumptions of the traditional approach, and the fact that that approach can only explain severe drinking problems. Moreover, because many problem drinkers are able to control their drinking on some or even most occasions (Sobell and Sobell, 1993a), their drinking is not amenable to approaches that require a belief that control is not attainable. The traditional view, therefore, is unable to explain the full range of alcohol problems. Likewise, because many service providers in the alcohol field are individuals who have recovered through traditional programs, those providers are likely to have serious problems working with clients who seek to regain control over their drinking.

As pressures mount for cost containment and for efficacy and efficiency in health care, there have been corresponding calls to establish services for problem drinkers (e.g. Babor et al., 1994; Institute of Medicine, 1990). Nearly all current treatment models developed for problem drinkers are cognitive-behavioral in orientation. More importantly, traditional programs have not produced good results with problem drinkers. Pomerleau et al. (1978), for example, found problem drinkers showed a significantly greater rate of attrition from treatment when treated using group confrontation methods derived from the traditional orientation than when treated using behavioral procedures. More recently, Miller, Benefield and Tonigan (1993) compared problem drinkers treated using either a confrontive therapist interviewing style (based on the traditional approach) or a motivational enhancement therapist style (based on motivational interviewing and other cognitive-behavioral procedures for increasing commitment to change). They found that the confrontive style elicited more resistance from clients during treatment and was associated with poorer outcomes at one year follow-up. In particular, the amount of confrontation by the therapist during treatment was directly and positively associated with the amount the client drank during follow-up. Such findings suggest that cognitive-behavioral treatments are more appropriate than traditional treatment for problem drinkers.

CONCLUSIONS

The cognitive-behavioral approach, which emphasizes individuals learning to reassert control over their drinking (either to not drink at all or to drink in moderation) has considerable appeal to a large and under-served population of persons with low-severity alcohol problems (problem drinkers). In contrast, the traditional approach, based on the assumption that alcohol abusers are inherently incapable of controlling their drinking, has little application or appeal for problem drinkers. This is the main difference between the cognitive-behavioral and traditional approaches, and for this reason the application of cognitive-behavioral procedures can be expected to increase. Nevertheless, the fact that both approaches have been associated with successful outcomes suggests that it is not so much the underlying philosophy of the approaches, but rather the extent to which the philosophy is consistent with the individuals's own view of his or her condition that is the more important determinant of success.

REFERENCES

Adesso, V.J. (1980). Experimental studies of human drinking behavior, in Rigter, H. and Crabbe, J. (eds), *Alcohol Tolerance and Dependence*, pp. 123–153, Elsevier/North-Holland Biomedical Press, New York.

Anonymous (1939) *Alcoholics Anonymous*, Works Publishing, Inc., New York.

Babor, T.F., Grant, M., Acuda, W., Burns, F.H., Campillo, C., Delboca, F.K., Hodgson, R., Ivanets, N.N., Lukomskya, M., Machona, M., Rollnick, S., Resnick, R.,

Saunders, J.B., Skutle, A., Connor, K., Ernberg, G., Kranzler, H., Lauerman, R. and Mcree, B. (1994). A randomized clinical trial of brief interventions in primary health care: Summary of a WHO project, *Addiction*, **89**, 657–660.

Bacon, S.D. (1973). The process of addiction to alcohol: Social aspects, *Quarterly Journal of Studies on Alcohol*, **34**, 1–27.

Bandura, A. (1969). *Principles of Behavior Modification*, Holt, Rinehart & Winston, New York.

Bigelow, G., Cohen, M., Liebson, I. and Faillace, L.A. (1972). Abstinence or moderation? Choice by alcoholics, *Behaviour Research and Therapy*, **10**, 209–214.

Bigelow, G., Griffith, R. and Liebson, I. (1975). Experimental models for modification of human drug self-administration-methodological developments in study of ethanol self-administration by alcoholics, *Federal Proceedings*, **34**, 1785–1792.

Bigelow, G. and Liebson, I. (1972). Cost factors controlling alcoholic drinking, *Psychological Record*, **22**, 305–314.

Bigelow, G., Liebson, I. and Griffiths, R. (1974). Alcoholic drinking: Suppression by a behavioral time-out procedure, *Behaviour Research and Therapy*, **12**, 107–115.

Cohen, M., Liebson, I.A. and Faillace, L.A. (1971a). Case histories and shorter communications – the role of reinforcement contingencies in chronic alcoholism: An experimental analysis of one case, *Behaviour Research and Therapy*, **9**, 375–379.

Cohen, M., Liebson, I.A. and Faillace, L.A. (1971b). The modification of drinking in chronic alcoholics, in Mello, N.K. and Mendelson, J.H. (eds), *Recent Advances in Studies of Alcoholism*, pp. 745–766, US Goverment Printing Office, Washington, DC.

Cohen, M., Liebson, I.A. and Faillace, L.A. (1972). A technique for establishing controlled drinking in chronic alcoholics, *Diseases of the Nervous System*, **33**, 46–49.

Cohen, M., Liebson, I.A. and Faillace, L.A. (1973). Controlled drinking by chronic alcoholics over extended periods of free access, *Psychological Reports*, **32**, 1107–1110.

Cohen, M., Liebson, I.A., Faillace, L.A. and Allen, R.P. (1971a). Moderate drinking by chronic alcoholics: A schedule-dependent phenomenon, *Journal of Nervous and Mental Disease*, **153**, 434–444.

Cohen, M., Liebson, I.A., Faillace, L.A. and Speers, W. (1971b). Alcoholism: Controlled drinking and incentives for abstinence, *Psychological Reports*, **28**, 575–580.

Cook, D.R. (1985). Craftsman versus professional: Analysis of the controlled drinking controversy, *Journal of Studies on Alcohol*, **46**, 433–442.

Cummings, C., Gordon, J.R. and Marlatt, G.A. (1980). Relapse: Prevention and prediction, in Miller, W.R. (ed.), *Addictive Behaviors*, pp. 291–321, Pergamon Press, New York.

Faillace, L.A., Flamer, R.N., Imber, S.D. and Ward, R.F. (1972). Giving alcohol to alcoholics: An evaluation, *Quarterly Journal of Studies on Alcohol*, **33**, 85–90.

Fingarette, H. (1988). *Heavy Drinking: The Myth of Alcoholism as a Disease*, University of California Press, Berkeley, CA.

Hickey, P. (1994). Behaviour therapy and traditional chemical dependency treatment, *the behaviour therapist*, **17**, 79–83.

Institute of Medicine (1990). *Broadening the Base of Treatment for Alcohol Problems*, National Academy Press, Washington, DC.

Jellinek, E.M. (1960). *The Disease Concept of Alcoholism*, Hillhouse Press, New Brunswick, NJ.

Mann, M. (1968). *New Primer on Alcoholism*, Holt, Rinehart & Winston, New York.

Marlatt, G.A. (1978). Craving for alcohol, loss of control, and relapse, in Nathan, P.E., Marlatt, G.A. and Løberg, T. (eds), *Alcoholism: New Directions in Behavioral Research and Treatment*, pp. 271–314, Plenum Press, New York.

Marlatt, G.A. and George, W.H. (1984). Relapse prevention: Introduction and overview of the model, *British Journal of Addiction*, **79**, 261–273.

Marlatt, G.A. and Gordon, J.R. (eds) (1985). *Relapse Prevention*, Guilford Press, New York.

Marlatt, G.A. and Rohsenow, D.J. (1980). Cognitive processes in alcohol use: Expectancy and the balanced placebo design, *Advances in Substance Abuse*, **1**, 159–199.

McCrady, B.S. (1986). Implications for behavior therapy of the changing alcoholism health care delivery system, *The Behavior Therapist*, **9**, 171–174.

Mello, N. (1972). Behavioral studies of alcoholism, in Kissin, B. and Begleiter, H. (eds), *The Biology of Alcoholism. Vol. 2, Physiology and Behavior*, pp. 219–291, Plenum Press, New York.

Mello, N.K. and Mendelson, J.H. (1965). Operant analysis of drinking patterns of chronic alcoholics, *Nature*, **206**, 43–46.

Mello, N.K. and Mendelson, J.H. (1970). Experimentally induced intoxication in alcoholics: A comparison between programmed and spontaneous drinking, *Journal of Pharmacology and Experimental Therapeutics*, **173**, 101–116.

Mendelson, J.H., LaDou, J. and Solomon, P. (1964). Experimentally induced chronic intoxication and withdrawal in alcoholics, Part 3. Psychiatric findings, *Quarterly Journal of Studies on Alcohol*, **25**, (Suppl. No. 2), 40–52.

Mendelson, J.H. and Mello, N.K. (1966). Experimental analysis of drinking behavior of chronic alcoholics, *Annals of the New York Academy of Sciences*, **133**, 828–845.

Miller, W.R. (1992). The effectiveness of treatment for substance abuse: Reasons for optimism, *Journal of Substance Abuse Treatment*, **9**, 93–102.

Miller, W.R., Benefield, R.G. and Tonigan, J.S. (1993). Enhancing motivation for change in problem drinking: A controlled comparison of two therapist styles, *Journal of Consulting and Clinical Psychology*, **61**, 455–461.

Miller, W.R. and Hester, R.K. (1986). The effectiveness of alcoholism treatment: What research reveals, in Miller, W.R. and Heather, N. (eds), *Treating Addictive Behaviors: Processes of Change*, pp. 121–174, Plenum Press, New York.

Nowinski, J., Baker, S. and Carroll, K. (1992). *Twelve Step Facilitation Therapy Manual*, National Institute on Alcohol Abuse and Alcoholism, Project MATCH Monograph Series, Vol. 1. Rockville, Maryland: National Institute on Alcohol Abuse and Alcoholism, DHHS Publication No. (ADM) 92–1893.

Orford, J. (1985). *Excessive Appetites: A Psychological View of Addictions*, John Wiley & Sons, New York.

Pattison, E.M., Sobell, M.B. and Sobell, L.C. (eds) (1977). *Emerging Concepts of Alcohol Dependence*, Springer, New York.

Pomerleau, O., Pertschuk, M., Adkins, D. and Brady, J.P. (1978). A comparison of behavioral and traditional treatment for middle income problem drinkers, *Journal of Behavioral Medicine*, **1**, 187–200.

Project MATCH Research Group (1993). Project MATCH: Rationale and methods for a multisite clinical trial matching patients to alcoholism treatments, *Alcoholism: Clinical and Experimental Research*, **17**, 1130–1145.

Sobell, M.B. and Sobell, L.C. (1973). Individualized behavior therapy for alcoholics, *Behavior Therapy*, **4**, 49–72.

Sobell, M.B. and Sobell, L.C. (1975). The need for realism, relevance and operational assumptions in the study of substance dependence, in Cappell, H.D. and LeBlanc A.E. (eds), *Biological and Behavioral Approaches to Drug Dependence*, pp. 133–167, Addiction Research Foundation, Toronto.

Sobell, M.B. and Sobell, L.C. (1993a). *Problem Drinkers: Guided Self-change Treatment*, Guilford Press, New York.

Sobell, M.B. and Sobell, L.C. (1993b). Treatment for problem drinkers: A public health priority, in Baer, J.S., Marlatt, G.A. and McMahon, R.J. (eds), *Addictive*

Behaviors Across the Lifespan: Prevention, Treatment, and Policy Issues, pp. 138–157, Sage, Beverly Hills, CA.

Sobell, M.B. and Sobell, L.C. (1994). Controlled drinking research, *Addiction*, **89**, 483–484.

Timko, C., Moos, R.H., Finney, J.W. and Moos, B.S. (1994). Outcome of treatment for alcohol abuse and involvement in Alcoholics Anonymous among previously untreated problem drinkers, *Journal of Mental Health Administration*, **21**, 145–160.

Wilson, G.T. (1988). Alcohol use and abuse: A social learning analysis, in Chaudron, C.D. and Wilkinson, D.A. (eds), *Theories on Alcoholism*, pp. 239–287, Addiction Research Foundation, Toronto.

Chapter Six

ROBERT LADOUCEUR AND MICHAEL WALKER

A Cognitive Perspective on Gambling

Two myths about gambling must be dispelled. The first is the belief that gambling is an activity of a minority: of rich playboys, social misfits and sections of the poor who know no better. The second is the belief that gambling is a harmless activity, or, as was blandly stated at a conference in 1984, 'there is no such thing as compulsive gambling.'

With regard to the first claim, gambling is a common activity among most people in most countries in the world. Throughout America, Australia, Canada and most parts of Western Europe, the majority of the population approve of gambling. Comparisons across countries suggest that the highest levels of involvement in gambling (Haig, 1985), and the highest levels of problems generated by gambling (Dickerson, 1993), are to be found in Australia. In Canada, Ladouceur (1991) reported that 88% of the adults in the province of Quebec played the lotteries. In Germany, more than 60% of adults have played a form of lotto (Hand, 1992) and 10% of adults actively play slot machines (Buhringer and Konstanty, 1992). Similarly, slot machines have become very popular in Spain (Becona, 1994). Furthermore, rates of gambling and the sum invested have increased over the years. In 1974, 61% of Americans gambled a total of $17.4 billion in the USA, but by 1992, the amount had reached $329.9 billion, an increase of 1900% in 18 years (Christiansen, 1993). A similar trend was found in Quebec where, from 1974 to 1992, money wagered on lotteries grew from $51 million to $1.2 billion per year, an

Trends in Cognitive and Behavioural Therapies. Edited by P.M. Salkovskis.

increase of 2000%! At this time, 48 American states have legalized at least one form of gambling, and there is a trend towards an increasing diversity of types of gambling (Lesieur, 1992). In Australia, a wide range of gambling activities including casino games, slot machines, racing, lotteries and bingo are available in every state (Walker, 1992b). This liberal attitude concerning the legalization of gambling activities is typical of most western countries and rarely seems to be questioned.

Concerning the claim that gambling is essentially harmless, the available data demonstrates unequivocally that heavy involvement in gambling is associated with both large debts and a range of personal, and societal problems that flow from debt. Since 1980, with the introduction of the Diagnostic and Statistical Manual of the American Psychiatric Association (DSM III), severe gambling problems have been accepted as symptomatic of 'pathological gambling'. Although the causes and nature of pathological gambling are not agreed (Walker, 1992b), the existence of a set of criteria for categorization of a gambler as pathological has enabled some comparison of gambling problems across countries. Despite a range of criticisms of both the survey methods used and the South Oaks Gambling Screen (SOGS) questionnaire given to respondents, it is clear that large numbers of people do not have severe personal problems associated with their gambling involvement. Table 6.1 shows the prevalence of 'probable pathological gambling' among adults in a range of different countries.

The evidence that gambling is causing severe personal hardship among 1% or more of the adult populations across a wide range of countries suggests that we are confronted with a major social problem. At this time, the explanation

Table 6.1   Estimates of the prevalence of pathological gambling

Author(s)	Country	State	Sample size	Problem gamblers (%)	Pathological gamblers (%)
Volberg and Steadman (1988)	USA	New York	1000	3.9	1.4
Volberg and Steadman (1989)	USA	Maryland	1000	4.1	1.4
	USA	New Jersey	1000	4.4	1.7
Ladouceur (1991)	Canada	Quebec	1002	2.6	1.2
Cayuela (1990)	Spain		1230	2.5	n/a*
Abbott and Volberg (1992)	New Zealand		4053	4.2	2.7
Dickerson et al. (1994)	Australia		2744	n/a	7.1

*Cayuela provides only one estimate for 'potential gambling pathology'.

of why gamblers persist with the activity at such personal cost is not understood. However, one thing is clear: gambling frequently begins before adulthood. A recent study in Quebec showed that 90% of the 1471 adolescents surveyed had gambled, and that 22% of them engaged in this behavior once a week or more often (Ladouceur, Dubé and Bujold, 1994b). In order to identify more precisely when individuals have their first contact with gambling, 1320 children from the 4th, 5th and 6th grade school were surveyed. Unexpectedly, the majority of the children had already bet money: from the three grade levels, 81%, 84% and 92% respectively had gambled. These results suggest that gambling is not confined to adults, but is widespread among grade school children (Ladouceur, Dubé and Bujold, 1994a). Similar results have been obtained in the United Kingdom (Fisher, 1993; Griffiths, 1994) and in the United States (Jacobs, 1989).

From a clinical perspective, the fundamental question concerns why some people persist with gambling until the gambling causes serious hardship. A satisfactory explanation for pathological gambling must be found if clinicians are to cope effectively with this problem in the years ahead and social scientists are to evaluate the social impacts of gambling on society (Ladouceur et al., 1994). Among the competing explanations for heavy involvement in gambling, the cognitive perspective is gaining increasing credence (Walker, 1992b). The following section will discuss the different biases and cognitive errors found in gamblers, and will illustrate how they must be included in all therapeutic interventions.

THE HETEROGENEITY OF GAMBLING

Many papers on gambling implicitly assume that gambling is an unitary activity. For example, it is commonly assumed that gamblers chase their losses: that after losing money the gambler continues to gamble in order to get it back. Such claims and assumptions are at risk of being too general. First of all, gambling occurs in many forms and contexts. The social, structural and computative differences between betting at the racecourse, playing poker in a casino and driving a slot machine are so great that more than the usual care must be taken in making statements about the general nature of gambling. Secondly, the intensity of gambling in terms of time spent and money staked varies from as little as an occasional raffle ticket to as much as the commitment of all available time and resources. It is immediately clear that the explanation of occasional raffle ticket buying may have little in common with the explanation of so-called compulsive or pathological gambling. Finally, given that the discussion is limited to heavy involvement in one particular form of gambling, it may be important to draw a distinction between the explanation of why a gambling session starts and, once started, why it continues. Given this heterogeneity of gambling, it is important to be clear about the aspect of gambling with which this discussion is concerned. From both the applied and theoretical viewpoints, the focus of gambling explanations is the gambler whose involvement is so great that the problems caused require a treatment agency. Such a gambler may attend Gamblers Anonymous, a specialized clinic, a financial counselling centre or some other agency. Frequently, such gamblers are heavily in debt, have lost their families and employment, and may be facing criminal charges. Thus, the central question for psychology concerns why a person will persist with gambling until all aspects of value in his or her life are lost. Such self-defeating behavior is an enigma which challenges the validity of current psychological theories. Why does the habitual gambler continue with behavior which is clearly not in his or her best interests? At the clinical level, an answer to this question is fundamental to the design of treatment strategies.

A COGNITIVE PERSPECTIVE ON GAMBLING

Gambling involves staking money on an uncertain event in the hope of winning more money at the expense of the risk of losing the money staked. Although gambling, as so defined, includes a wide range of activities, discussions of gambling are usually limited to institutionalized gaming and wagering such as betting on the outcome of horse-races or playing casino games and slot machines. The core feature of all gambling within this limited context is that the expected outcome of each gamble is less than the money staked: the economic utility of gambling is negative. In objective terms, gambling should never take place for expected winnings since no gamble is economically profitable. Thus, explaining why people gamble is not a matter of rational economics, but must involve the psychology of the individual in relation to gambling.

Basically, there are two possible explanations of why people gamble, and they are not mutually exclusive. The first explanation is that the utility of gambling is not purely economic. That is, gambling provides something of value beyond the expected return. For example, the excitement of gambling may be suficiently positive for many people that it more than compensates in utility terms for the expected economic loss. A person may treat the losses incurred by gambling as payment for the privilege of gambling and the excitement that that entails. The second explanation is that the utility of gambling is misperceived. That is, contrary to the objective expectation of overall loss, many people may have a subjective expectation of monetary gain. For example, if certain numbers are believed to be lucky, then taking a ticket in a lottery with

Figure 6.1   Research has shown that gambling is frequently associated with irrational thinking. Reproduced by permission from *Psychology*, 2nd edn, Jacaranda Wiley, Brisbane

those numbers may have a positive expected utility. Of course, how the utility of a gamble could be misunderstood must be explained. The cognitive perspective on gambling assumes that the utility of gambles is sometimes misperceived and sets out to clarify the processes that are involved.

Although cognitions are believed to play a role in all aspects of gambling, reference to the cognitive perspective usually applies to the factors involved in maintaining habitual gambling. Social, cultural and situational factors may well be central to any explanation of the origins of gambling in a person and to any continuation of gambling at infrequent intervals and for low stakes. However, the cognitive perspective on gambling focuses on the frequent or regular gambler and the explanation of his or her persistence with gambling despite losses. What is common across different types of gambling is that the habitual gambler is repeatedly confronted with a gambling decision where the overall expectation in monetary terms is negative. The horse-race punter must choose whether to bet on the next race, and, if so, which horse to back. The roulette player is confronted by the choice of 37 numbers on the next spin of the wheel; the blackjack player by the choice of whether or not to take another card; the poker player by whether to stay in the pot; the slot machine player by whether to play again; and so on. In each case, the gambling situation is set up so that, in the long run, the gambler should expect to lose. Despite this negative expectation, the habitual gambler chooses to continue. The cognitive perspective refers to a set of beliefs held by the gambler which, if true, would constitute sufficient reason to continue with the gambling. Most importantly, some or most of these beliefs are false. These false beliefs have been labelled in various ways: irrational thinking, erroneous cognitions, misperceptions and superstitutions. Some have also been identified as more general processes applying to a wide range of social cognitions: illusion of control, biased evaluation, entrapment and illusory correlation.

The cognitive perspective assumes that the motivation to gamble is the desire to win money or at least to beat the game. It is understood that these acquired motivations might be subjected to further analysis. However, the cognitive perspective is not concerned with this analysis. Rather, it is assumed that this motivation combined with false beliefs such as will be discussed next are sufficient to explain why the habitual gambler persists with the gambling. For example, if the roulette player believes that 10 is his or her lucky number, and that 10 will therefore occur more frequently than other numbers, then the overall expectation of a fixed stake on 10 will be positive, thus it is reasonable for the player to continue to bet on 10. In practice, the beliefs of roulette players are generally more complex, but the outcome is the same: the gambler continues to play. In the sections that follow, some of the common false beliefs held by gamblers are described and the relevant experimental evidence is examined.

COGNITIVE BIASES AMONG GAMBLERS

Gambling takes place where money is staked on the outcome of an event which is in some degree unpredictable. It is common to speak loosely of random events or events governed by chance. However, these terms refer simply to the fact that the gambler does not know some or all of the events which determine an outcome. For example, it may be said that the outcome of spinning the roulette wheel is random or governed by chance. In fact the roulette wheel is a finely designed machine in which the outcome is quite predictable once the starting parameters (speed of ball, speed of wheel, and so on) are known (Thorp, 1984). It is simply that the gamblers do not have the information or skill to make an accurate prediction. From the gambler's perspective the outcome is simply unpredictable, not random or governed by chance.

The gambler's task is to predict an outcome which is essentially unpredictable. In attempting this difficult task, gamblers typically display two kinds of bias. First of all they behave as if they can influence the outcome of the unpredictable event. Secondly, they behave as if the event is more predictable than in fact it is. Clearly, these two sources of bias may occur together. These biases are identified in the experimental literature by a variety of names: illusion of control, superstitious beliefs, biased evaluations, erroneous perception and irrational thinking.

ILLUSION OF CONTROL

The illusion of control refers to the fact that the gambler behaves as if gambling involves some element of skill, and that exercise of that skill determines the outcome to some extent. In fact many forms of gambling do allow the exercise of skill: horse-racing and blackjack, for example. However, in these cases, illusion of control refers to the belief that one's skill is excessively influential. Langer (1975) suggested that in situations of chance (unpredictable outcomes), individuals tend to behave as they would in a situation requiring skill; they perceive themselves as the principal agent responsible for the outcome. They do not correctly perceive that there is no relationship between their behavior and the outcome of the event; they do not perceive correctly that they have no control over the outcome. Anecdotal evidence for the illusion of control is plentiful. Craps players roll the dice slowly for low numbers and faster for higher numbers (Henslin, 1967). Blackjack players rap the table to obtain an ace (Walker, 1994) and slot machine players avoid hungry machines (Caldwell, 1974). The use of lucky charms, the selection of lucky seats, wearing lucky clothes, choosing lucky numbers and finding lucky dealers are all examples of the belief that the outcomes of essentially unpredictable events can be controlled to some extent. Anecdotal evidence is never strong evidence, since the events observed may be a biased selection of the whole realm of events available. However, the illusion of control in gambling has been demonstrated in many studies. Langer (1975) demonstrated the pervasive nature of the phenomenon in an amusing and informative study. Lottery tickets were offered to office workers employed by two firms. Individuals (subjects) were approached and offered the chance to purchase a ticket. Subjects were randomly assigned to one of the two conditions. In the first condition, subjects were given a box of tickets and told to select the ticket that they wanted. In the second condition, the individuals were handed a ticket by the experimenter (no-choice condition). Each subject paid $1 for a ticket and all subjects were treated similarly, apart from whether or not they chose their own tickets. Prior to drawing the winning ticket, all subjects were approached and were told: 'Someone in the other office wanted to get into the lottery, but since I am not selling tickets anymore, he asked me if I'd find out how much you would sell your ticket for?' (Langer, 1975). The choice/no-choice manipulation had a tremendous effect on the value placed on the ticket. The mean amount requested was $1.96 in the no-choice condition, but was $8.67 in the choice condition! The subjects behave as if they can increase their chance of winning by choosing their own ticket.

If it is the case that gamblers frequently exhibit illusion of control, we can ask what factors are likely to increase or decrease the strength of the illusion of control. Several can be suggested on the basis that any situation which increases the apparent similarity of the gambling game to a game of skill, should increase the illusion of control. Thus competition should increase the illusion of control since competition is based upon the exercise of skill. Active participation and involvement should increase the illusion of control, since participation provides examples of actions that are rewarded by favourable outcomes. Again, any opportunity to use devices or introduce mechanisms, increases the similarity to games of skill where devices and mechanisms are common. Finally, familiarity with the task would be expected to be a positive factor. Practice increases skill where skill is possible. Any belief in control within the task would thus be heightened by practice and familiarity.

As previously postulated by Langer, active participation in a situation would be expected to increase the illusion of control. Ladouceur and Mayrand (1987) experimentally manipulated the active/passive role in the following manner. Subjects were invited to play a game of roulette in a laboratory, which resembled a small casino with a roulette table, Blackjack table, a video poker machine and a slot machine. Subjects received $10 for their participation in the study. In order to create ecological validity subjects were instructed: 'Before the game starts, if you decide to participate you may exchange your money for tokens. For each dollar you will receive 20 tokens. At the end of the game, you will receive in dollars 5% of the total number of tokens you have.' The game was over when the subject had no more money, voluntarily quit the game or had played 40 times. Subjects were randomly placed in the active or passive condition. In the active condition, subjects threw the ball themselves whereas in the passive condition the experimenter threw the ball, as in casinos. The amount of money bet each turn served as dependent variable. Results showed that active subjects wagered significantly more money than subjects in the passive conditions. Apparently, active participation induces the belief that the outcome of spinning the wheel can be controlled to some extent. Any such belief would constitute an illusion of control.

Familiarity is another variable hypothesized as increasing perceived control: the more an individual becomes familiar with a task involving an unpredictable outcome, the more he or she has the impression of controlling the situation and of developing a skill-oriented attitude. It was hypothesized that the amount of direct exposure to a situation increases the degree of perceived control. During prolonged involvement in gambling, individuals may develop strategies in which the subjective probability is much greater than the objective probability of winning. In order to empirically test this hypothesis, 38 subjects were invited to play roulette, either alone or with two or three other individuals (Ladouceur, Tourigny and Mayrand, 1986). Subjects received similar instructions to those described above. They played three sessions of 25 spins of the roulette wheel, with a break between each session. As expected, monetary risk taking behavior increased with direct exposure to gambling, whether subjects played individually or in group. Level of risk increased not only between sessions, but also within a session. Also, on subjective measures, their levels of confidence increased as the game went on: the feeling of mastering the game significantly increased after direct exposure. In order to evaluate if this increase in monetary risk behavior is transient or stable, this study was replicated with a 24-hour interval between sessions (Ladouceur, Mayrand and Tourigny, 1987). Again, the monetary risk taking behavior was significantly higher at the beginning of the second and third session than at the start of the initial session, even after a 24-hour break. Since the outcomes in roulette are unpredictable, it is amazing to find that subjects report a feeling of mastering the game. These results are consistent with Bandura's self-efficacy theory: task familiarity or exposure enhances personal efficacy in the sense that the players have more confidence in themselves as the game progresses.

To the extent that the player can exercise choice in some aspect of the game, so the opportunity for the illusion of control is increased. For example, if the choice of number on which to bet is made before the roulette wheel is spun, then all manner of strategies might be used to forecast the result. By contrast, if the wheel has already spun, any chance to influence the outcome is lost. Thus, a greater illusion of control would be expected before the wheel is spun and a greater bet size corresponding to that control would be expected. Subjects were randomly assigned to one of the following conditions: (1) the regular condition in which the player placed his or her bet before the throw of the ball; (2) the artificial condition in which the individual bet after the ball had been thrown and had fallen in the slot, but the outcome was hidden by a large piece of cardboard. From an objective or probabilistic standpoint, both conditions are equally unpredictable. But from a cognitive perspective, betting before the throw allows more possibilities for prediction and influence, and stimulates the construction of various strategies. The results supported the hypothesis: bets placed before the throw were significantly higher than bets placed after the throw of the ball. The player behaves as if he or she believes that, 'As long as the ball is not in the slot, I still have to 'decide' which number is hot!' (Ladouceur and Mayrand, 1987). This experimental manipulation is instructive and rich in attempting to identify beliefs held by gamblers.

SUPERSTITIONS

The illusion of control has much in common with superstition. Whenever a player carries out some behavior unconnected with the gambling event, in the belief that the behavior will influence the gambling event, it is perhaps correct to speak of superstition even if the behavior implies illusion of control as well. Gamblers frequently have special clothes, jewellery and lucky talismen, which they believe will bring luck, and without which they would feel unlucky. A rabbit's foot is, perhaps, the most famous talisman, but the pockets and purses of gamblers may contain a wide range of goodluck charms. Croupiers at one Las Vegas casino tell the story of a gambler who lost his sight in an accident. The defective eye was removed by surgery, and the gambler had it mounted on a chain around his neck. For good luck he would strike his 'lucky eye'. With respect to gambling, we can define as superstitious any behavior which is repeated by the gambler while gambling, but which is not required for the purpose of gambling. Thus, if the gambler always holds a gold coin in the left hand while gambling with the right, holding the gold coin would be regarded as superstitious. If the gambler believes that the behavior can influence the chance of winning, then the behavior is superstitious.

According to the cognitive perspective, superstitious behavior in relation to gambling is an example of the illusion of control. Superstitious behavior is carried out because the gambler believes that the behavior can influence long-term success in gambling, if not short-term success. However, behavioral theories of gambling also predict superstitious behavior. Any behavior which is rewarded from time to time may continue even though it has no connection to the process by which the reward is achieved. Rats in Skinner boxes, for example, develop superstitious behaviors. If the cognitive perspective is correct, then preventing the superstitious behavior should lead to a decrease in gambling.

In order to test this hypothesis, slot machine players were recruited from slot machine clubs in Sydney, Australia (Walker, 1994). A slot machine player was included if some observable repetitive behavior unrelated to the actions of playing the machine was present, and if the player reported playing the game one or two times each week for at least an hour on each occasion. Since these players play the machines each week they can be regarded as regular players though not as heavy players, who might play the machine three or more times each week. In terms of the experiment, the subjects were required to play the machine of their choice with thier own money, and for as long as they wished. Each subject played the machines on two separate occasions, one week apart. They played under two sets of conditions: either with their repetitive behavior permitted and required, or with their repetitive behavior forbidden. Half of the subjects played with their repetitive behavior in the first session, whereas the other half played without their repetitive behavior in the first session. An observer recorded the following aspects of the play: (1) the length of the session in minutes; (2) the number of coins entered into the machine; (3) the number of games played; (4) the number of coins won; (5) the total of money won or lost. As expected by the cognitive perspective, subjects in the permitted repetitive behavior condition, compared with the forbidden repetitive behavior condition, played for longer (60 minutes versus 30 minutes), entered more coins (200 coins versus 100 coins), won more coins (100 coins versus 50 coins), and played more games (100 games versus 50 games). Interestingly, there was no significant difference in the amount of money lost ($10 versus $10).

ERRONEOUS BELIEFS ABOUT GAMBLING

The experiments described above were concerned with differences in the behavior of players that implied erroneous beliefs about gambling. To set a value on the ticket one chooses oneself that is higher than the value set on the ticket one is given without choice, implies the belief that the player's choice has more merit. The erroneous belief that one's own choice has more merit is inferred from the behavior. Since cognitions are not observable, they must always be inferred. However, the inferences may be indirect, as in the case where choice behavior is interpreted as implying cognitive beliefs, or direct, as in the case where the beliefs are stated. Thus, the direct measurement of erroneous beliefs is an important validation for experiments in which observed behavior is interpreted in terms of erroneous beliefs.

The first attempts to measure cognitive activity of players used paper and pencil questionnaires. The evidence from questionnaires was inconclusive (Ladouceur et al., 1984; Ladouceur and Mayrand, 1984). In some cases, players described the outcomes as purely chance (Caldwell, 1974). Although the questionnaire did not elicit descriptions of erroneous beliefs, informal observation of gamblers suggested that they frequently make comments during the game which reflect the presence of such beliefs. One possible explanation for the failure of questionnaires to elicit these statements was the timing of the data collection: subjects answered questionnaires after rather than during play. It was clear that the spontaneous verbalizations of some players were precisely the kind of erroneous beliefs that would validate the research on behavioral strategems such as the illusion of control. In order to conduct research on these verbalizations, a procedure was required that: (1) would elicit the cognitions of all players while the action was under way: (2) would not interrupt the game; (3) was as unobtrusive as possible. The procedure chosen has been called 'the thinking aloud method' (Gaboury and Ladouceur, 1989).

In the thinking aloud method, subjects are invited to provide a commentary on their play as the game is proceding. They are to say everything that goes through their minds. They are urged not to censor intentions, ideas or images. They are instructed not to judge whether what they are saying is interesting or not. The players are encouraged to speak continuously or as much as they are able, and they are given practice in doing so. The players are told that the clarity or completeness of thoughts are not at issue, and that there is no need to try to justify what is said. Thus, the thinking aloud method attempts to record the 'stream of consciousness' of the player while gambling. Across studies there are minor differences in the exact instructions given, but the task for the player is essentially the same.

In the original study using the thinking aloud method, 10 subjects were first invited to play a slot machine under laboratory conditions (Gaboury and Ladouceur, 1989). After training, the subjects received 200 tokens worth 5 cents each and were instructed to play for 30 minutes, while verbalizing all thoughts, images, perceptions or cognitions. The subjects were paid their winnings in cash at the end of play. All verbalizations were tape-recorded and then rated as accurate or erroneous (see Gaboury and Ladouceur, 1989). Essentially, accurate perceptions reflected the idea that the outcome of the game is determined by change, whereas erroneous perceptions implied some control, predictability or agency of the machine that is, in fact, not present. Examples of accurate and erroneous verbalizations include:

Accurate

'The odds aren't any better if I bet on three rows instead of one, it doesn't change anything.'

'It's a machine, we have no control over it, it's all luck.'

'There's more chance of losing than winning at this game.'

Erroneous

'I played many times on one row. In about five trials, I'll play on three rows, it should be a better bet then.'

'I knew it. I told you so. It wasn't this turn that I was supposed to win.'

'I'm getting good at this game. I think I've mastered it.'

Inter-judge reliability in categorizing the verbalizations as erroneous or accurate was over 85%. The results clearly showed that the erroneous perceptions outnumbered accurate perceptions (70% versus 30%) despite the fact that a questionnaire administered before and after the game elicited the view that the slot machine was a game of chance! Before playing, the game was rated 98% chance, whereas after the game, it was rated 91% chance. The slot machine, a game based entirely on chance, triggered many distorted perceptions, thus suggesting that most perceptions associated with this form of gambling are erroneous. Although subjects correctly perceived the game as being based on chance before and after play, verbalizations revealing erroneous perceptions outweighed accurate verbalizations during play.

The first result was quite striking, if one considers the simplicity of the game (slot machine). However, generalization from one gambling game to all gambling games should be avoided, given the heterogeneity issue discussed earlier. In order to extend the base of results for generalization, it was decided that a second experiment should be designed using the more complex game of roulette. Roulette allows the player a greater range of choice than does the slot machine, and would for this reason be expected to heighten the illusion of control. In fact, data from preliminary questionnaires given to the subjects suggested that many of them believe that strategies used at roulette can enhance the probability of winning (an erroneous belief). In the experiment conducted, half of the subjects endorsed the view that winning at roulette is purely chance, whereas the other half of the subjects endorsed the view that winning was influenced by the strategy used. The general procedure, using the thinking aloud method, was similar to the one described above for slot machines, except that the subjects played 50 games of roulette. The results were quite clear cut: the number of erroneous perceptions was significantly greater than the number of accurate perceptions, regardless of the group. Seventy-five per cent of the verbalizations were erroneous, and erroneous beliefs were as frequent among subjects who believed that winning is a matter of chance as among subjects who believed that some skill was involved (Gaboury and Ladouceur, 1989).

Given that players on slot machines and roulette players can be induced to express a large number of erroneous beliefs during play, the important question remains whether or not these beliefs have a causal role in maintaining the play. Two hypotheses have an important bearing on this issue. First of all, if erroneous cognitions are important in maintaining gambling involvement, then one would expect that the higher the involvement, the more erroneous beliefs that players would hold. Secondly, the more skill that a game requires from the player, the greater the number of accurate statements that can be made about influence and control in the game. Thus, we should expect that the percentage of erroneous verbalizations would be highest for games involving no strategic skill at all, such as slot machines, and lowest for games demanding very high levels of skill, such as bridge or chess.

The first of these hypotheses has been tested in experiments published by Griffiths (1993) and Walker (1992a) and in both cases the thinking aloud method was used. Griffiths recruited 60 university students, half of whom were regular fruit machine players (play once a week or more often), whereas the remainder were non-regular players (play less than once per month). Griffiths used the thinking aloud method while the players were playing fruit machines on site, but with an innovative design that had equal groups of both regulars and non-regulars either thinking aloud or not thinking aloud. In this way the impact and intrusiveness of the thinking aloud method on actual play could be assessed. In fact, the thinking aloud group on average played for longer in a session than the non-thinking aloud group (10.7 versus 8.5 minutes), but the rate of play was not significantly different. Analysis of the verbalizations of the players in the thinking aloud condition showed that greater involvement in playing fruit machines is associated with a higher frequency of erroneous statements. Fourteen per cent of the verbalizations of regular players were erroneous compared with only 2.5% for non-regular players.

Walker (1992a) recruited nine avid slot machine players, eight avid video card machine players and nine avid amusement arcade video machine players from among introductory psychology students at the University of Sydney, Australia. In order to take part, the players must have been playing their preferred game at least two times per week. Each player was requested to play for 30 minutes on his or her preferred game and for 20 minutes on each of the non-preferred games. Thus a given subject might be an avid slot machine player, and would be required to play for 30 minutes on the machine of their choice in the club of their choice. They would also play for 20 minutes on a video card machine and for a further 20 minutes on a video amusement machine. Thus the extent to which different kinds of games are associated with different rates of erroneous statements could be investigated. As expected, the video amusement machines elicited the smallest proportion of erroneous statements (12%), the video card machines a moderate proportion (59%) and the slot machines the highest proportion (69%). Furthermore, avid slot machine players produced more erroneous statements than other players across the three types of machine. Finally, the rate of erroneous statements made by avid slot machine players when playing their chosen machines was 80%, which is of the same order as the 70% reported by Ladouceur with Canadian subjects. The lower rate obtained by Griffiths (14%) can be explained by differences in the categorization process and the calculation of the rate of erroneous statements. The rate of erroneous statements can be calculated with reference to all statements concerned with strategies for playing the machine, or with reference to all statements regardless of their content. The high rates obtained by Walker and Ladouceur reflect the limited population of strategic verbalizations, whereas Griffiths included all verbalizations. When Walker's data is analyzed based on all verbalizations, the percentage of erroneous verbalizations is 11.8% for video card machine players and 37.9% for slot machine players.

Thus, the results from these experiments can be summarized as follows: (1) regular slot machine players make a high percentage of erroneous statements when thinking aloud while playing the machine; (2) the higher the involvement of the player, the higher the rate of erroneous statements; (3) there is reason to believe that these rates are higher in games where the skill factor is lower. However, the discrepancy between the perception of the slot machine game before and after playing and the statements made while playing the game is puzzling. Before and after the game, subjects report that it is a game of chance: nothing they can do will influence the outcome. During the game, subjects say many things about the game which suggest that the outcome is predictable and can be influenced. It is as if there are two modes of thinking about the game: spontaneous, uncensored reactions to the events in the game while the game is in progress, and rational consideration of the realities of the game when not involved. The following empirical study provided indirect support for this view. After completing one of the above studies, 10 subjects were invited to return on another day to help the experimenter interpret the 'conflicting' results obtained. Each subject was shown three figures illustrating the following ratios of accurate to erroneous verbalizations: 80:20% (mostly accurate), 20:80% (mostly erroneous) and 50:50% (moderately erroneous). The subject was told:

> A few days ago, you participated in one of our gambling studies. Here are three figures illustrating the perception of the game reported by three subjects, including yourself, who participated in the study. Would you first identify the figures which represent your perception of the game. Also, could you describe the personality of the other two individuals.

Surprisingly, 6 out of 10 subjects identified the 'accurate' graph as best illustrating their own performance. More interestingly, without knowing that they were describing themselves based on their own figures, they described the personality of the individual who produced the data as a person with serious gambling problems, with poor insight, and in some case with low intelligence level. The person who produced the 50:50 data was generally described as an individual at risk of becoming a pathological gambler. When we debriefed them, they had difficulty believing that they had acted so 'stupidly' during the game, and two did not believe the experimenter when told that they had produced the set of 80% erroneous statements. The only way that they could be convinced of the truth was by playing back their own tape recorded during the study! Only then did they become aware of their erroneous statements and false perceptions.

BIASED EVALUATION OF OUTCOMES

Biased evaluation of outcomes refers to the tendency of gamblers to believe that successful outcomes are the result of successful prediction or effective influence of the gambling event. By contrast, unsuccessful outcomes are discounted or explained away. Thus, playing roulette, the player may note that low numbers are coming up frequently, but that the number 7 has not occurred for a long time. So when 7 is chosen successfully for the next bet, the player believes that he or she has successfully predicted the sequence of roulette numbers. In fact, the successful 7 is a coincidence of the calculations of the player yielding the expectation that 7 will win, and the unpredictable roulette outcome of 7. If the player continues to make calculations on every spin of the roulette wheel, these coincidences will continue to occur at a rate of approximately 1 in 37, and the player will believe on each occasion that they have shown insight into the roulette process. In fact, we can expect a distribution of these coincidences such that in some roulette sessions the coincidences will be more frequent, and in other sessions less frequent, than 1 in 37. The poor sessions may be explained away as associated with the croupier on duty, poor concentration or any factor that the gambler can bring to mind. By contrast, the session rich in coincidences will convince the gambler that his or her calculations are successful. Thus, whether winning or losing, the gambler continues to believe in his or her methods by means of this biased evaluation.

The role of biased evaluation of outcomes has been demonstrated in sports betting (Gilovich, 1983) and was subsequently investigated in more detail by Gilovich and Douglas (1986). In the sports betting study, Gilovich used as his subjects bettors who had bet on a very close game of basketball between UCLA and Louisville. Half of the subjects had bet on UCLA and half on Louisville. In fact Louisville won by a single point and only after a UCLA player had missed a simple shot in the dying moments of the game. When asked, after the game, which team would they bet on in a rematch, all of the subjects said they would bet on the same team again. Clearly, the victory for Louisville in the current game had no impact on the expectations for the next game. The Louisville supporter can point to the fact that he or she made the correct choice, and the UCLA supporter to the fact that the missed goal in the last moments of the game made all the difference and that that miss was a fluke. Thus, whatever the outcome, the gamblers are able to continue to believe in their first choice. Gilovich was also able to show that gamblers who back the losing team spend more time discussing the result than those who back the winning team. A win does not need discussion since it confirms one's methods, whereas a loss must be explained away if you are to retain confidence in your selection methods. Gilovich and Douglas further investigated biased evaluations in a laboratory game. In the game of bing, two players compete against each other. The game involves filling in a coupon similar to that used in bingo but with only 12 squares. Each player in turn presses a button to have the computer generate a 'random' number, which in turn allows a square to be marked off on the bing coupon. The player who first marks off all of the squares is the winner. The players play two games, and the experimenter takes bets with each player on whether or not that player will win. Of course, the 'random' numbers are not random but are generated in such a way that the winner scores either a clear win in the first game, or scores a 'fluke' win. A fluke win occurs when one player has just one square left in order to win, when the other player has a tremendous run of luck and completes half the coupon in successive turns, thereby winning. The fluke versus clear win takes place on the first trial, and the analysis is based on the bet made on the second trial. Players who scored a clear win on the first game increase their bets for the second game. However, both players who scored a fluke win and players who suffered a fluke loss also increase their bets. Only players who suffered a clear loss decrease their bets. Thus, biased evaluation of the fluke outcome allows both the winners and the losers to maintain their belief in the likelihood that they will win.

THE GAMBLER'S FALLACY

Even though most individuals recognize that games such as roulette, lotteries and keno are entirely a matter of chance (that is, unpredictable) they nevertheless try to pick the winning number or combination. In any casino where roulette is being played, you may observe the roulette players in deep concentration over rows and columns of numbers that represent the previous so many games. From these numbers they hope to derive some purchase on the games to come to be able to eliminate some numbers and combinations, at the very least, and hopefully to zero in on the very next spin of the wheel. Players elaborate strategies, develop confidence in their skills, and interpret both success and failure as significant in the process of predicting the outcome. This point is crucial for understanding the psychology of gambling. Despite the fact that the players concentrate and calculate with diligence, it is all futile (Wagenaar, 1988). But the belief that these stratagems are effective is at the core of the desire to continue gambling. Furthermore, these calculations and expectations are not reserved for roulette alone. For example, blackjack players believe that the probability of winning a hand is increased after three losses, and that the outcome of the hand can be made more or less favourable by the player before the dealer (Wagenaar, 1988).

However, there is perhaps no single belief that is more pervasive than what is known as the gambler's fallacy. The gambler's fallacy is that randomness implies that each number must appear an appropriate number of times. Thus if a coin is tossed 10 times for 10 heads, then tails is very likely on the 11th toss. In roulette, players believe that certain numbers are due, when they have not come up for a long time (Ladouceur and Gaboury, 1988). From the individual's subjective point of view, the chances of different combinations are not perceived as equal. If subjects are asked to pick one of the two following tickets of a 6/49 lottery, either (a) 1, 2, 3, 4, 5, 6 or (b) 7, 13, 22, 43, 41, 47, almost everyone chooses the second combination; the first is viewed as extremely unlikely (Gaboury, Ladouceur and Bussières, 1989; Ladouceur *et al.*, 1987). In casino games, players often prefer to bet on combinations that have not appeared for a relatively long period of time. In an early study, Cohen (1972) demonstrated this bias in favour of the less-frequent alternatives among roulette players. By observing betting on red and black in roulette, Cohen found that the likelihood of betting on the same colour a second time depended on whether that colour won or lost on the previous trial. If a player bets on black, and wins, then he or she is 50% likely to bet on black again. However, if black loses, then the player is 75% likely to bet on black again. Since black did not come up last time, it is more likely to come up this time.

Such studies suggest that many players have a deep-seated misconception of the nature of randomness. In particular, they appear to deny the independence of trials which is fundamental to the notion of randomness. In the following studies, the extent of the erroneous assumptions held by players with respect to randomness are investigated. It is a well-established fact that individuals have great difficulties in either recognizing or generating random sequences of binary events. The main error appears to be that they produce sequences with too many alternations. Despite the variations in procedures used, the results demonstrate that subjects are unable to generate sequences that resemble ones created by a random number generator (Tune, 1964; Wagenaar, 1972). More specifically, subjects tend to avoid repetition of the same events, prefer too many alternations (Bakan, 1960; Neuringer, 1986), and tend to equate randomness with equivalence infrequency of numbers, even in a small sample (Wagenaar, 1972). They associate alternation and a higher number of short sequences of the same events with randomness, and symmetry with non-randomness. Furthermore, they tend to erroneously balance the events in a small sample according to their theoretical probability of appearance in a large sample.

The law of large numbers states that large samples are representative of the populations from which they are drawn. Kahneman and Tversky (1972) characterize the error of local representation as a belief in the so-called law of small numbers, according to which the law of large numbers applies equally to small samples. According to Kahneman and Tversky, this belief underlies erroneous intuitions concerning chance. In analyzing the production of sequences of numbers by subjects, it is difficult to apply statistical criteria of randomness (Ayton, Hunt and Wright, 1989). But one thing is clear: 'contemporary psychology is well aware of the fact that human subjects are bad randomizers' (Wagenaar, 1970, p. 348). In order to understand the ways in which subjects fail in the task of generating random numbers, we studied the cognitive activities of individuals while they judged, recognized or generate simple random sequences of binary events. Previous research has centered on the ways in which sequences of numbers generated by subjects are non-random, but not on the subjects' biases or beliefs when asked to generate or identify sequences of random events. Ladouceur and his colleagues utilized the thinking aloud method, to study how subjects perceive randomness while they are engaged in the task of generating random sequences. The studies described earlier in this chapter demonstrate how this method has proven to be useful in the study of cognitive activities during gambling. By using the same thinking-aloud method in the present study, an idea can be obtained of the cognitions and conceptual biases operating during the production of randomness.

It was hypothesized that a large proportion of the perceptions reported by the subjects while generating sequences of heads and tails would be erroneous and mainly based on the failure to apply the principle of independence between events. Four studies were conducted, involving the recognition, construction and identification of random sequences of binary events. Subjects were asked to produce a sequence of 100 heads and tails, 'as if it was the result of flipping a coin 100 times'. They typed their sequences of H and T on a personal computor which stored the events. In order to identify their misconceptions, they were first trained in the thinking aloud method. Verbalizations were recorded and later rated as accurate or erroneous. The erroneous verbalizations were further classified as follows: (a) equilibration of the number of heads and tails (subject chooses each event such that the total sequence is balanced according to the theoretical proportion of appearance of events (50:50); (b) avoidance of long sequences of the same event (subject chooses each event in order to avoid the long repetition of the same event); (c) breaking patterns in order to avoid regularity (subjects generate either H or T specifically to avoid regularity in the alternations, or to avoid any sequence which seems to have a logical order; and (d) other (content that could not be placed in the foregoing categories. Results showed that, as found in previous research using the thinking aloud method with slot machine and roulette players, erroneous perceptions outnumbered accurate perceptions. Closer analysis revealed that the main error was the inability (or unwillingness) to apply the principle of independence among events. Subjects continuously made reference to their past production in order to avoid three common biases: equilibration, the most prevalent misconception, breaking patterns and avoidance of long sequences. The majority of accurate verbalizations make direct reference to the idea of chance in which there is no mention of previous or future events in determining H or T. However, overall, the fundamental problem for subjects seemed to be the incapacity to process or generate an event which was independent of the foregoing events. Rather, the subjects believe that a 0.5 probability of appearance implies dependency among events, with sequence of heads building pressure for tails, and vice versa.

In order to evaluate how strong this belief is, Ladouceur and Dubé (1996) designed the following study. Subjects were again asked to generate a sequence of heads and tails on the computer. However, as a subject generated a sequence, a screen covered the event chosen as soon as it was typed. Subjects were able to uncover the screen in order to examine the sequence of heads and tails. The number of times they uncovered the sequence, and the numbers of events uncovered where used as the dependent variables reflecting the subjects' incapacity (or unwillingness) to apply the principle of independence. The results showed that all subjects uncovered some elements during the study. Subjects uncovered the sequence an average of four times during the session to view an average number of 12 events. It appears that although individuals know that the probability of appearance of each binary event is 0.5 and that previous events are irrelevant in choosing the next event, they cannot resist the temptation to look at the previous sequence, and to take it into account.

Why do individuals hold this erroneous belief that objectively independent events are linked? One explanation may be that the physical proximity of the events can induce the perception that they are interdependent. When asked to produce sequences of random events, subjects link together events close in time and space. Analysis of the verbal reports sheds light on this erroneous view of randomness. The majority of subjects use the immediate past events in a supposedly random sequence to decide which next event should follow. Specifically, subjects constructing a random sequence check that there are equal numbers of each event, that logical order (characteristic of non-random sequences) is absent, and that there are no long sequences of the same event. Thus, the human judgement, based on cause and effect, is applied erroneously to this task. Ironically, situations in which events are based on randomness, such as gambling, are the only situations in the individual's life where he or she should not use past experience, information or learning. In all other area of our life, we learn from past experiences, and we constantly refer to past performance to modify our current behavior and to plan for the future. Paradoxically, as stated by Weiss (1964) more than three decades ago: 'In order to be random, subjects must actively inhibit other modes of responding: one must pay attention not to pay attention!' (p. 940).

EVALUATION OF THE COGNITIVE PERSPECTIVE ON GAMBLING

It is important to be aware of the limitations as well as the advances made by taking a cognitive perspective on gambling involvement. The central argument of the cognitive perspective is that it is cognitive biases associated with gambling that maintain heavy gambling involvement which sometimes leads to gambling problems. What has been demonstrated is that a number of cognitive biases are present among gamblers and that some of these, such as erroneous perceptions and illusions of control, increase with increasing gambling involvement. However, since most, if not all, of these biases can be demonstrated in non-gamblers as well as gamblers, the cognitive biases by themselves cannot be regarded as a complete explanation of why people gamble or why they gamble to excess. At this stage of research it appears that the cognitive biases of the kind used by gamblers are widespread in the community, and thus constitute a potential for persistence with gambling. It is not that some people have these cognitive biases and go on to become gamblers, whereas others think more rationally and do not become gamblers, but rather that once involved with gambling, these biases can become the basis for persistence despite losses. A full explanation of gambling must explain much more than can be explained by cognitive bias alone. Such a general theory of gambling must explain: (1) how gamblers become involved in gambling in the first place; (2) why some gamblers see a challenge in gambling that others do not; (3) how it is that most regular gamblers maintain control over their gambling, whereas a minority continue until too much has been staked and lost.

The most important perspective which the cognitive perspective does not include is a motivational component for gambling. The status of money (or greed) as the motivational component is strongly debated. Surveys of slot machine players suggest that these gamblers play for amusement rather than money (Caldwell, 1974; Dickerson, Fabre and Bayliss, 1986; Walker, 1988). However, these reasons given by the gamblers themselves are unlikely to be the full explanation. The fact that there is widespread possessiveness about particular machines cannot be explained by claiming that one machine is more amusing than another. When slot machine players must leave 'their' machine for a few minutes, the machine is reserved, and disrespect for reservation is not tolerated. Since in any bank of slot machines, there are machines equivalent to the one that the gambler is using, and since an accurate perception of these machines is that they are equivalent, some erroneous perception of the value of the machine must be present. We have seen that the thinking aloud method gives an insight into the nature of that erroneous perception. Players do not regard each play of the machine as independent, but, by contrast, regard the play of the machine as an ongoing contest in which their skills and luck are pitted against the contrary nature of the machine. And what is the measure of the player's luck and skill? Whether or not money is won. However, despite such arguments, and centrality of money as the motivation for gambling is denied by many, especially those who are associated with the treatment of pathological gambling (see Custer and Milt, 1985, for example).

Finally, research within the cognitive perspective is at its beginning. The research thus far has generated an amount of evidence suggesting that cognitive biases are present among gamblers. However, confirmation of hypotheses constitutes limited evidence. Ultimately, the cognitive perspective must be tested against rival perspectives. Experiments must be designed which test rival hypotheses generated by the arousal perspective, the behavioral perspective and the cognitive perspective. According to the arousal perspective, it is the excitement of gambling and the vulnerability of the gambler to that excitement that is central to explaining heavy gambling involvement. According to the behavioral perspective, it is the schedule of monetary reinforcements that is central. Both of these rival perspectives rule out any major role for cognitions. The challenge to the cognitive perspective is to provide the empirical research which will test these rival perspectives and ultimately allow rejection of the inadequate theories.

TREATMENT OF PATHOLOGICAL GAMBLING

From Table 6.1, it is clear that large numbers of people gamble to such an extent that their gambling causes severe financial problems. In this respect, excessive gambling is a major social problem in many countries, and treatment strategies to help people control their gambling should have a high priority. Unfortunately, many of the treatment programs that have been tried have not proven successful. Where the goal of treatment is that the gambler bring his or her gambling within certain limits (which may include complete cessation), the overall effectiveness of the various treatments tried drops off markedly from 72% controlled gambling after 6 months, to 27% after 2 years (Walker, 1992b). The effectiveness of programs where the goal is the complete cessation of gambling is considerably lower (15% after 2 years). These programs include personal, group and conjoint psychotherapy, psychoanalysis, self-help manuals, and a range of behavioral techniques such as aversive conditioning and imaginal desensitization. Unfortunately, these techniques were not based on an in-depth compehensive approach of the complexity of the cognitive and behavioral activities of the gamblers as discussed in the above sections. This may explain the relatively mediocre results found in previous treatment studies. Interestingly there have been very few attempts to apply cognitive methods to the treatment of gambling problems, even though there are good reasons to expect such methods to be successful.

Baucum (1985) pointed out that, 'Much of what passes for pathology in gambling is relatively straightforward, mistaken belief that it is possible to win consistently even in games of pure chance' (p. 201). The foregoing discussion has focused on some of the cognitive processes that support and maintain such an erroneous view. Given that gamblers hold a range of erroneous beliefs, and that it is these beliefs that maintain the gambling despite financial losses, an effective therapy is likely to be one which attacks, undermines and replaces the erroneous beliefs by accurate beliefs. Thus, cognitive restructuring is an obvious but untried candidate for the treatment of pathological gambling. Currently, several programs have begun in which cognitive methods are being applied. Foremost among these is the program instituted by Ladouceur in Quebec, Canada.

THE QUEBEC PROGRAM (LADOUCEUR)

Initially Ladouceur attempted to correct gambling misconceptions among regular but non-pathological gamblers. By different procedures such as role-playing, stimulated gambling, playback and correction of erroneous perceptions, subjects' verbalizations were modified. One interesting result of this approach is that once the subjects become aware of their misconceptions, and realize the importance of not taking into account previous events, there appears to be a decreased motivation to continue playing (Sylvain and Ladouceur, 1992). Subjects reported that the game was now boring. This result is consistent with previous research which has shown that level of arousal (as measured by heart rate) is correlated with the frequency of erroneous perceptions (Coulombe et al., 1992).

Ladouceur's research involves clinical intervention with pathological gamblers, where the correction of the basic dysfunctional assumptions is the central step and pre-requisite for other therapeutic techniques. Our clinical experience showed that without successful correction of the misconceptions held by the pathological gambler, any further therapeutic intervention is useless! The program includes the following elements and should be applied in this chronological order:

Information about Gambling

Basic information on gambling is provided: (1) examples of the range of gambling activities available; (2) distinctions between games of chance and games of skill; (3) characteristics of legal and illegal gambling; (4) descriptions of, and distinctions between, social and pathological gamblers.

Cognitive Interventions

This component is based on research demonstrating that gamblers forget, deny or are unwilling to consider that the outcome of the game is chance. The first step consists of increasing the patient's awareness of erroneous verbalizations. Subjects listen to their verbalizations recorded during a pre-treatment imaginal or simulated gambling session. They are instructed to signal and identify each erroneous verbalization. The therapist stops the tape and asks subjects to replace each erroneous verbalization with an accurate one. Illusions of control over the game are discussed. The therapist also illustrates erroneous thinking according to what was discussed in the above sections, and gives examples of high-risk behaviors [increasing bets as the game progresses, returning to play to get back money they had lost (chasing), playing more than they had planned, etc.].

Problem Solving Training

This component consists of learning five steps: (1) defining the problem; (2) collecting information about a problem; (3) generating different solutions; (4) listing advantages and disadvantages for each solution; (5) implementing and evaluating a solution (D'Zurilla, 1986; Goldstein, 1988). The method is applied to typical problems encountered by the subjects. For example, in order to have better control over spending, they are instructed to pay their debts, make a budget and to carry only the money they need. Also, social activities such as sports, music and work are suggested and encouraged during the weekend.

Social Skills Training

The goal of social skills training is to develop skills for communicating with peers, parents, superiors (teachers or employers) and friends, if found to be deficient in the pathological gambler. The therapist provides an operational definition of assertive behavior and a rationale for its use. For example, some subjects have difficulties in making demands and giving their opinion in the presence of authority figures, and are unassertive at school and at work.

Relapse Prevention

The goal of this component is to develop skills to cope with potential relapses (Marlatt and Gordon, 1985). Relapses are not seen as treatment failures but as a problem to be solved. Patients learn to become aware of high-risk situations and the reasons for returning to gambling. Therapist and patients identify high-risk situations. For example, a subject may return to gambling because he or she wants to make money quickly, or is alone, or frustrated, or stressed. Examples of high-risk situations include: having money in the pocket, being stressed, having to make oral presentations, free time, loneliness and lack of social activities.

Results of two single case studies have showed positive outcomes for this treatment procedure and more importantly, the maintenance of the therapeutic gains (Bujold et al., 1994; Ladouceur, Boisvert and Dumont, 1994). Currently a large controlled group study, including over 30 pathological gamblers, is in its third year of operation. The preliminary results of this program confirm the positive results obtained in the single case designs (Sylvain, Ladouceur and Baivert, 1995).

THE SYDNEY PROGRAM (ALLCOCK)

One of the main treatment centres in Sydney, Australia, for gambling problems is located in the Cumberland Hospital, a state-run operation. For more than 20 years, the treatment of problem gambling has been carried out in that hospital by Dr Clive Allcock. Although Allcock has used a variety of treatment procedures, his most recent work has emphasized the cognitive perspective in understanding and treating gambling problems (Allcock, 1994). Allcock asked 27 of his most recent patients to rate on a scale from 0 (none) to 10 (certain), the extent to which they expected to win when they were actively gambling, and to assess, now that the gambling had had to stop, how often they did in fact win. The mean rating of actually winning, in retrospect, was 1.77, compared with the mean expectation of winning of 6.99 when they were actually gambling. Furthermore, where skill is applicable, as in horse-racing betting, these gamblers typically rate themselves as similar to or more skillful than the average punter. And when skill is not involved, as in slot machine play, these gamblers typically rate their luck as above average.

In helping gamblers to curb the desire to gamble, Allcock uses cognitive prompts. The gambler carries a card in his or her wallet which makes three accurate statements about the gambling. For example the card may read (Allcock, 1994):

> I lost $6000 in the last six months
>
> I only win on 10% of occasions
>
> Gambling is affecting my marriage.

Thus, whenever the gambler needs money, the card is visible, and accurate statements about gambling can be read. Allcock uses this method in conjunction with supportive psychotherapy. Although, no data are available on the effectiveness of this treatment, Allcock states that this cognitive intervention together with supportive psychotherapy is sufficient for some gamblers to succeed in bringing their gambling under control.

It is clear that this intervention has a common assumption with the Quebec program: that an accurate assessment of gambling expectations will deflate the urge to gamble. The central goal of cognitive therapeutic intervention is to increase patient awareness of their misconceptions about gambling and the predictability of gambling events, and to replace them with accurate, functional and adaptive perceptions. If and when the patients reach a point where they recognize that they are not more skillful or lucky than the odds permit, then changes in gambling would be expected. Allcock has used more extensive cognitive restructuring with some of his clients and believes that this procedure is successful in the treatment of some gambling problems. The extent to which it is successful, and limitations on its use, require more systematic evaluation.

FUTURE DIRECTIONS

Although the last decade has seen a large increase in research conducted within the cognitive perspective, there is much that remains to be done in order to provide a coherent theory of gambling. Further research on the cognitive mechanisms underpinning gambling is urgently needed; clinical trials applying cognitive methods must be encouraged; the arduous task of comparing different treatment strategies must begin; and, finally, a fully fledged theory of gambling involvement based on these cognitive insights must be constructed.

FURTHER RESEARCH ON THE COGNITIVE PERSPECTIVE OF GAMBLING

Since gambling games are based (or mostly based) on chance and the notion of randomness, research on perceptions of randomness is likely to be an area of fruitful investigation for cognitive psychologists. The evidence, thus far, suggests that most perceptions and strategies are erroneous when individuals are gambling on games of chance. An obvious next step involves conducting a fine-grained analysis of these false perceptions in order to identify the basic mechanism or common denominator. Our hunch is that the basic misconception is the failure of the individual to understand or apply the notion of independence between randomly generated events. One way to explore this notion is to use the task designed by Ladouceur described above where subjects were asked to generate a sequence of random events (heads and tails) on a personal computer. As the subject generated a sequence, a screen covered the event chosen as soon as it was typed. Subjects were able to uncover the screen in order to examine the sequence of heads and tails. The number of times they uncovered the sequence, and the numbers of events uncovered, were used as the dependent variables reflecting the subjects' incapacity (or unwillingness) to apply the principle of independence. This procedure could be taken one step further by there being a cost associated with uncovering and viewing the sequence to date. The amount of money spent on reviewing the sequence would measure the strength of the erroneous belief that the sequence so far determines what must or must not come next.

Apart from the further investigation of the perception and misperception of randomness, other erroneous beliefs must be sought and investigated. One such erroneous belief is involved in the situation labelled 'entrapment'. Entrapment refers to a situation in which a person commits further resources to a proposition which is already known to be a failure (Brockner and Rubin, 1985). In the world of gambling, perhaps the clearest example of entrapment involves the avid slot machine player who has already sunk more funds into the machine than can be recouped if the jackpot is won, in order to win the jackpot. It is likely that the slot machine player finds it increasingly difficult to end a session until all of his or her money is gone, because of the erroneous belief that the money invested so far has brought the event of the jackpot much closer. It is the thought that the very next coin may be the one to bring about the jackpot that makes ending the session so difficult. However, these ideas of entrapment have not been investigated in the context of gambling.

Walker (1985) pointed to the core beliefs of gamblers which may be erroneous. An example would be the belief that you are more skilful than the average gambler. However, erroneous beliefs may be specific as well as general. Wagenaar (1988) has investigated the erroneous beliefs commonly held by blackjack players which are specific to blackjack. For example, many blackjack players believe that the decision to hit or stand by the last player influences the expectation for the game. Thus a player in the last position, who correctly decides to hit 15 against a 10, influences the chances of all players positively, whereas a player who stands on 15 incorrectly increases the dealer's chance of winning, for example. It may well be the case that each gambling game induces both specific and general erroneous beliefs, but apart from blackjack and slot machines, it appears that the content of these specific erroneous beliefs has not been investigated.

From a clinical viewpoint, the different ways to correct these false beliefs held by gamblers need to be investigated. Various methods have been used thus far: thought stopping procedures (Maurer, 1985); practice at making accurate statements (Sylvain & Ladouceur, 1992); cognitive restructuring (Allcock, 1994); and win therapy (Sartin, 1988). Each of these methods has been successful in a limited context: thought stopping has not been applied widely and has been unsuccessful in other contexts (see Ladouceur et al., 1995); practice at accuracy has been assessed, thus far, only with slot machine players; cognitive restructuring is still being given its initial trials; and win therapy has only been applied in the context of betting on horses. Comprehensive tools to adequately assess erroneous perceptions that are commonly espoused by gamblers are urgently required. Only when the false beliefs are fully identified can various forms of cognitive therapy be applied across the wide range of gamblers who seek treatment.

Understanding gambling is increasingly hampered by the absence of overarching theories of gambling behavior. Psychoanalytic theory provides one perspective (Bergler, 1957; Maze, 1987), but focuses on excessive gambling behavior. Arousal theory provides a heavily used explanatory notion, but relatively weak attempts have been made to build a theory based on this concept (see Custer and Milt, 1985, for example). Sociocognitive theory (Walker, 1992b) provides the most comprehensive framework now available for understanding levels of gambling involvement, but leaves the question of underlying motivation unanswered. It is not clear whether the empirical evidence is sufficient to build a theory of gambling at this time, but without such a theory, research initiatives are flying blind, and much of the effort expended may prove worthless. By contrast, the development of a comprehensive model of gambling behavior (occasional, frequent and pathological gambler) would provide a basis for a coherent integration of empirical data, suggest innovative treatment strategies and stimulate new and creative research.

NOTE

This paper was written while Robert Ladouceur received grants from Loto-Québec, CQRS and CRSH.

REFERENCES

Abbott, M. and Volberg, R. (1992). *Frequent Gamblers and Problem Gamblers in New Zealand*, New Zealand Department of Internal Affairs, Wellington.
Allcock, C. (1994). The cognitive perspective in the treatment of gambling problems, paper presented at the Ninth International Conference on Gambling and Commercial Gaming, Las Vegas, May.
Ayton, P., Hunt, A.J. and Wright, G. (1989). Psychological conceptions of randomness, *Journal of Behavioral Decision Making*, **2**, 221–238.
Bakan, P. (1960). Response-tendencies in attempts to generate random binary series, *American Journal of Psychology*, **73**, 127–131.
Baucum, D. (1985). Arguments for self-controlled gambling as an alternative to abstention, in Eadington, W.R. (ed.), *Proceedings of the Sixth National Conference on Gambling and Risk Taking*, vol. 5, (pp. 199–204), University of Nevada, Reno.
Becona, E. (1994). Prevalence surveys of problem and pathological gambling in Europe: The cases of Germany, Holland and Spain, paper presented at the Ninth International Conference on Gambling and Commercial Gaming, Las Vegas, May.
Bergler, E. (1957). *The Psychology of Gambling*, Hill and Wang, New York.
Brockner, J. and Rubin, J.Z. (1985). *Entrapment in Escalating Conflicts: A Social Psychological Analysis*, Springer, New York.
Buhringer, G. and Konstanty, R. (1992). Intensive gamblers on German-style slot machines, *Journal of Gambling Studies*, **8**, 21–38.
Bujold, A., Ladouceur, R., Sylvain, C. and Boisvert, J.-M. (1994). Cognitive behavioral treatment of pathological gamblers, *Journal of Behavior Therapy and Experimental Psychiatry*, **25**, 275–282.
Caldwell, G. (1974). The gambling Australian, in Edgar D.E. (ed.), *Social Change in Australia*, pp. 12–28, Cheshire, Melbourne.
Cayuela, R. (1990). Characteristics and situation of gambling in Spain: Epidemiological and clinical aspects, paper presented at the Eighth International Conference on Gambling and Commercial Gaming, London, August.
Christiansen, E.M. (1993). Income 1992 gross annual wager of the U.S. Part 1: Handle, *Gaming and Wagering Business*, **14**(7), 12–35.
Cohen, J. (1972). *Psychological Probability*, George Allen and Unwin, London.
Coulombe, A., Ladouceur, R., Desharnais, R. and Jobin, J. (1992). Erroneous perceptions and arousal among regular and occasional video poker players, *Journal of Gambling Studies*, **8**, 235–244.

Custer, R.L. and Milt, H. (1985). *When Luck Runs Out*, Warner Books, New York.

Dickerson, M.G. (1993). A preliminary exploration of a two-stage methodology in the assessment of the extent and degree of gambling related problems in the Australian population, in Eadington, W.R. and Cornelius, J.A. (eds), *Gambling Behavior and Problem Gambling*, pp. 347–364, Institute for the Study of Gambling and Commercial Gaming, Reno, NV.

Dickerson, M., Baron, E., Hong, S.M. and Cottrel, D. (1994). Estimating the extent and degree of gambling-related problems in the Australian population: A national survey, paper presented at the Ninth International Conference on Gambling and Commercial Gaming, Las Vegas, May.

Dickerson, M.G., Fabre, J. and Bayliss, D. (1986). A comparison of TAB customers and poker-machine players, in McMillen, J. (ed.), *Gambling in the 80s*, Griffith University, Brisbane.

D'Zurilla, T.J. (1986). *Problem-Solving Therapy: A Social Competence Approach to Clinical Interventions*, Springer, New York.

Fisher, S. (1993). The use of slot machines by young people in the UK: The present evidence, in Eadington, W.R. and Cornelius, J.A. (eds), *Gambling Behavior and Problem Gambling*, pp. 405–430, Institute for the Study of Gambling and Commercial Gaming, Reno, NV.

Gaboury, A. and Ladouceur, R. (1989). Erroneous perceptions and gambling, *Journal of Social Behavior and Personality*, **4**, 411–420.

Gaboury, A., Ladouceur, R. and Bussières, O. (1989). Structures des loteries et comportements des joueurs, *Revue de Psychologie Appliquée*, **39**, 197–207.

Gilovich, T. (1983). Biased evaluation and persistence in gambling, *Journal of Personality and Social Psychology*, **44**, 1110–1126.

Gilovich, T. and Douglas, C. (1986). Biased evaluations of randomly determined gambling outcomes. *Journal of Experimental Social Psychology*, **22**, 228–241.

Goldstein, A.P. (1988). Problem-solving training, in Kanfer, F.H. (ed.), *The Prepare Curriculum: Teaching Prosocial Competencies*, pp. 11–65, Research Press, Champaign, IL.

Griffiths, M. (1993). A study of the cognitive activity of fruit machine players, in Eadington, W.R. and Cornelius, J.A. (eds), *Gambling Behavior and Problem Gambling*, pp. 85–110, Institute for the Study of Gambling and Commercial Gaming, Reno, NV.

Griffiths, M.D. (1994). The role of cognitive bias and skill in fruit machine gambling, *British Journal of Psychology*, **85**, 1–19.

Haig, B. (1985). Expenditure on legal gambling, in Caldwell, G., Haig, B., Dickerson, M.G. and Sylvan, L. (eds), *Gambling in Australia*, pp. 71–77, Croom Helm, Sydney.

Hand, I. (1992). Editor's introduction to special issue on gambling in Germany, *Journal of Gambling Studies*, **8**, 3–10.

Henslin, J.M. (1967). Craps and magic, *American Journal of Sociology*, **73**, 316–330.

Jacobs, D.F. (1989). Illegal and undocumented: A review of teenabe gambling and the plight of children of problem gamblers in America, in Shaffer, H.J., Stein, S.A., Gambino, B. and Cummings, T.N. (eds), *Compulsive Gambling: Theory, Research and Practice*, pp. 249–292, Lexington Books, Lexington, MA.

Kahneman, D. and Tversky, A. (1972). Subjective probability: A judgment of representativeness, *Cognitive Psychology*, **3**, 430–454.

Ladouceur, R. (1991). Prevalence estimates of pathological gamblers in Québec, Canada, *Canadian Journal of Psychiatry*, **36**, 732–734.

Ladouceur, R., Boisvert, J.–M. and Dumont, J. (1994). Cognitive behavioral treatment of adolescent pathological gamblers, *Behavior Modification*, **18**, 230–242.

Ladouceur, R., Boisvert, J.–M., Pépin, M., Loranger, M. and Sylvain, C. (1994). Social costs of pathological gambling, *Journal of Gambling Studies*, **10**, 399–409.

Ladouceur, R. and Dubé, D. (1996). Erroneous perceptions in generating random sequences: identification and strength of a basic misconception. (Submitted for publication).

Ladouceur, R., Dubé, D. and Bujold, A. (1994a). Gambling among primary school students, *Journal of Gambling Studies*, **10**, 363–370.

Ladouceur, R., Dubé, D. and Bujold, A. (1994b). Prevalence of pathological gambling and related problems among college students in the Quebec metropolitain area, *Canadian Journal of Psychiatry*, **39**, 289–293.

Ladouceur, R., Freeston, M.H., Gagnon, F., Thibodeau, N. and Dumont, N. (1995). Treatment of obsessional ruminations. *Behavior Modification*, **19**, 247–257.

Ladouceur, R. and Gaboury, A. (1988). Effects of limited and unlimited stakes on gambling behavior, *Journal of Gambling Behavior*, **4**, 119–126.

Ladouceur, R. and Mayrand, M. (1984). Evaluation of the 'Illusion of control": Type of feedback, outcome of sequence and number of trials among occasional and regular players, *Journal of Psychology*, **117**, 37–46.

Ladouceur, R. and Mayrand, M. (1987). The level of involvement and the timing of betting in gambling, *Journal of Psychology*, **121**, 169–175.

Ladouceur, R., Mayrand, M., Dussault, R., Letarte, A. and Tremblay, J. (1984). Illusion of control: Effects of subject's participation and implication, *Journal of Psychology*, **117**, 147–152.

Ladouceur, R., Mayrand, M., Gaboury, A., and St-Onge, M. (1987). Comportements des acheteurs de billets de loteries passives et pseudo-actives: Etude comparative, *Revue Canadienne des Sciences du Comportement*, **19**, 266–274.

Ladouceur, R., Mayrand, M. and Tourigny, Y. (1987). Risk-taking behavior in gamblers and non-gamblers during prolonged exposure, *Journal of Gambling Behavior*, **3**, 115–122.

Ladouceur, R., Tourigny, M. and Mayrand, M. (1986). Familiarity, group exposure and risk taking behavior in gambling, *Journal of Psychology*, **120**, 45–49.

Langer, E.J. (1975). The illusion of control. *Journal of Personality and Social Psychology*, **32**, 311–328.

Lesieur, H.R. (1992). Compulsive gambling. *Society*, **29**, 43–50.

Marlatt, G.A. and Gordon, J.R. (1985). *Relapse Prevention: Maintenance Strategies in the Treatment of Addictive Behaviors*, Guilford Books, New York.

Maurer, C.D. (1985). An outpatient approach to the treatment of pathological gambling, in W.R. Eadington (ed.), *The Gambling Studies: Proceedings of the Sixth National Conference on gambling and Risk Taking*, pp. 205–217, Institute for the Study of Gambling and Commercial Gaming, Reno, NV.

Maze, J.M. (1987). Lady Luck is gambler's mother, in Walker, M.B. (ed.), *Faces of gambling*, pp. 209–214, National Association for Gambling Studies, Sydney.

Neuringer, A. (1986). Can people behave randomly? The role of feedback, *Journal of Experimental Psychology: General*, **115**, 62–75.

Sartin, H.G. (1988). Win therapy: An alternative diagnostic and treatment procedure for problem gambling, in Eadington, W.R. (Ed.), *Gambling Research: Proceedings of the Seventh International Conference on gambling and Risk Taking*, Vol. 5, pp. 365–391, University of Nevada–Reno, Reno, NV.

Sylvain, C. and Ladouceur, R. (1992). Correction cognitive et habitudes de jeu chez les joueurs de poker vidéo, *Revue Canadienne des Sciences du Comportement*, **24**, 479–489.

Sylvain, C., Ladouceur, R. and Boisvert, J.M. (1995). Treatment of pathological gambling: analysis and outcomes. Paper presented at the First European Conference on Gambling Studies and Policy Issues, Cambridge, England, August 1995.

Thorp, E.O. (1984). *The Mathematics of Gambling*, Gambling Times, Secaucus, NJ.

Tune, G.S. (1964). A brief survey of variables that influence randomness-generation, *Perceptual and Motor Skills*, **18**, 705–710.

Volberg, R. and Steadman, H.J. (1988). Refining prevalence estimates of pathological gambling, *America Journal of Psychiatry*, **14**, 502–505.

Volberg, R. and Steadman, H.J. (1989). Prevalence estimates of pathological gambling in New Jersey and Maryland, *America Journal of Psychiatry*, **146**, 1618–1619.

Wagenaar, W.A. (1970). Subjective randomness and the capacity to generate information, *Acta Psychologica*, **33**, 233–242.

Wagenaar, W.A. (1972). Generation of random sequences by human subjects: a critical survey of literature, *Psychological Bulletin*, **77**, 65–72.

Wagenaar, W.A. (1988). *Paradoxes of Gambling Behaviour*, Lawrence Erlbaum, London.

Walker, M.B. (1985). Explanations for gambling, in Caldwell, G.T., Dickerson, M.G., Haig, B. and Sylvan, L. (eds), *Gambling in Australia*, pp. 146–162, Croom Helm, Sydney.

Walker, M.B. (1988). Betting shops and slot machines: comparisons among gamblers, in Eadington, W.R. (ed.), *Gambling Research: Gamblers and Gambling Behavior*, pp. 66–83, University of Nevada–Reno, Reno, NV.

Walker, M.B. (1992a). Irrational thinking among slot machine players, *Journal of Gambling Studies*, **8**, 245–262.

Walker, M.B. (1992b). *The Psychology of Gambling*, Pergamon Press, Oxford.

Walker, M.B. (1994). The role of superstitious behaviour in maintaining slot machine play, paper presented at the Ninth International Conference on Gambling and Commercial Gaming, Las Vegas, May.

Weiss, R.L. (1964). On producing random responses, *Psychological Reports*, **14**, 931–941.

Chapter Seven

JEREMY D. SAFRAN

Emotion in Cognitive-Behavioral Theory and Treatment

BACKGROUND AND CURRENT STATE OF THE ART

Prior to the 1980s, emotion was treated by the cognitive behavioral tradition primarily as a post-cognitive phenomenon. It was assumed that undesirable emotions were produced by faulty thinking processes and that the focus of intervention should consist of reducing these emotions through modifying dysfunctional cognitive processes or through behavioral interventions. The role of more positive emotions in human functioning was for the most part neglected and the general emphasis was on controlling emotions rather than facilitating their experience. Another commonly accepted assumption was that rationality is the hallmark of mental health and that change is brought about either by thinking about things in a more rational way or through the use of hypothesis testing procedures.

Two developments in the field of general experimental psychology set the stage for reconsidering the standard assumptions about the relationship between emotion and cognition. First, Zajonc's (1980) provocative article in *American Psychologist* led to a lively debate about whether it is reasonable to assume that cognition proceeds emotion. Then, Bower's (1981) research on mood and memory pointed to the potential importance of evoking specific emotions in therapy in order to access underlying cognitions.

Trends in Cognitive and Behavioural Therapies. Edited by P.M. Salkovskis.
© 1996 John Wiley & Sons Ltd.

Mahoney (1980) was probably one of the first to draw cognitive therapists' attention to the fact that they were subscribing to an overly restrictive conceptualization of the role of emotion in human functioning. Les Greenberg and I (Greenberg and Safran 1984, 1986, 1987; Safran and Greenberg, 1982, 1986, 1991) followed Mahoney in arguing for the importance of broadening our conceptualization of the role of emotion in the change process. Influenced by the experiential approaches (Gestalt therapy and client-centered therapy), we argued that patients are often all too good at coming up with rational re-evaluations of their experience and that the therapeutic task is often one of accessing hidden appraisals that are occurring at a more affective level.

We also attempted to integrate theory and research in the area of emotion theory with cognitive information processing theory in order to articulate a framework for dealing with emotion in a more comprehensive fashion. Bower's (1981) research on mood and memory and Zajonc's (1980) review of research on the primacy of emotion were used to provide theoretical justification for the clinical practice of accessing automatic thoughts in an emotional lively way, or accessing 'hot cognitions' [a term borrowed from Ableson (1963)]. Additional theoretical scaffolding was provided by Leventhal's (Levanthal, 1979) concept of the emotion schema.

Over the last decade or so my impression has been that the importance of accessing 'hot cognitions' has gained a reasonably large acceptance amongst cognitive behavioral therapists. A second set of principles, however, has been slower to be absorbed into cognitive behavioral theory and practice. These involve the recognition of the adaptive role of emotion in human functioning and the potential value of interventions that access emotional experience because of its adaptive nature. Here we based our thinking on the work of a number of different theorists, including Arnold (1960), Eckman and Friesen (1972), Leventhal (1979), Tompkins (1980) and Izard (1977). These ideas, while grounded in contemporary emotion theory, were anticipated by early analytic theorists such as Rank (1936) and Reich (1942), and by experiential therapists (Perls, 1973; Rogers, 1961). It is interesting to speculate about the reasons that these principles and related interventions have been slower to catch on with cognitive therapists.

One reason may be that the modification of theory to accommodate this broader conceptualization of the role of human functioning necessitates some fundamental revision of metatheoretical assumptions. An important distinction between cognitive behavioral theory and experiential theory is that cognitive behavioral interventions are grounded within a metatheoretical framework that sees change as resulting from a willful attempt to modify the self (self-control). In contrast, experiential interventions are grounded within a paradoxical world view which holds that change takes place when one stops trying to change. The emphasis is thus on accepting or 'letting go' rather than on self-control. A second related issue is that the ability to work with interventions that evoke intense emotions requires therapists to develop a certain acceptance of emotional experience that can only arise out of having gone through and witnessed related therapeutic processes themselves.

A third is that many affectively oriented interventions are difficult to implement properly without extensive training. The recent development of a manual on experiential approaches by Greenberg, Rice and Elliott (1994) may somewhat remedy the situation, but it is still the case that many of these interventions are difficult to acquire without proper training at an experiential level.

There are a number of recent developments that may create a more receptive climate amongst cognitive therapists to interventions that recognize the adaptive role of emotions in human functioning. First, some mainstream cognitive therapists have recently advocated shifting towards a more paradoxical view of human change that emphasizes the role of acceptance (Jacobson, 1994; Linehan, 1993). Second, many cognitive therapists are becoming interested in exploring the potential contributions of other therapeutic traditions to cognitive therapy (e.g. Goldfried and Davison, 1994). Third, research evidence has accumulated regarding the efficacy of certain interventions derived from the experiential tradition (Greenberg, Elliot and Lietaer, 1994).

I will now summarize some of the central assumptions about emotion in human functioning that are common to a variety of contemporary theories of emotion (e.g. Izard, 1977; Leventhal, 1979; Plutchik, 1980; Tomkins, 1980) and outline some of the implications for psychotherapy.

EMOTIONS PLAY AN ADAPTIVE ROLE IN HUMAN FUNCTIONING

Emotions are wired into the human organism through an evolutionary process because of their adpative nature. In order to have a full understanding of the way in which to work with emotional experience therapeutically it is important to have an understanding of the role that emotions play in healthy human functioning.

Emotions safeguard the various goals and the sub-goals of the biological organism. Some of these goals are innate and some of them are learned.

Fundamental goals are wired into the biological system (e.g. self-protection, attachment, procreation). Other goals are derivatives of more basic goals and they develop as a result of learning. For example, the specific beliefs one develops about the way one needs to be in order to maintain relatedness or maintain proximity to the attachment figure are learned.

Emotions provide action disposition information. They provide information about the readiness of the biological system to act in certain ways. Cognition provides information about the environment but emotion provides information about the self in interaction with the environment. For example, anger provides information regarding the readiness of the system to protect itself in an aggressive fashion. Love provides information regarding the readiness of the systems to act in an affiliative fashion.

Psychological problems often arise from a failure to fully process adaptive emotional experience. Emotion can provide people with the conviction that a certain course of action is right for them and with the motivation to pursue that course of action. For example, a person in an abusive relationship may begin the process of ending it when he or she accesses his or her feelings of anger. A socially isolated individual may begin to face their anxiety and make social contact when they fully process and experience their sadness and pain.

EMOTIONS ORGANIZE SYSTEMIC PRIORITIES THROUGH THEIR SALIENCE

Because emotions play a role in safeguarding important systemic goals they have a compelling quality about them that can override the entire system and move it in a certain direction. For example, anger may override a rational decision to act in a more cautious fashion. Attraction may override a rational evaluation regarding the risks of becoming emotionally involved. This compelling quality is important to survival. For example, if one is in a life threatening situation (for example, being attacked by a predator) it is adaptive for the mobilization of the system toward flight to take precedence over other goals such as eating. For this reason, emotions are activated and continue to colour one's perception of the situation until they are processed and dealt with in some way. For example, feeling angry at someone will predispose one to look at that person critically even if one is not fully aware of the anger. Therapeutic interventions designed to rationally re-evaluate situations may not always be effective.

AFFECTIVE RESPONSES ARE MEDIATED BY THE PERCEPTION OF INTERPERSONAL CONSEQUENCES

A person's ability to experience a particular emotion is shaped both by the history of his or her interpersonal learning experiences and by his or her anticipation and perception of current interpersonal consequences. For example, an individual who has learned that the experience of sadness will alienate other people will have difficulty fully experiencing and expressing such feelings. Learning experiences of this type will tend to shape the perception of current interpersonal situations.

In therapy, an important part of helping patients to access emotional experience consists of exploring and challenging dysfunctional beliefs regarding the experience of various emotions. Moreover, the therapist's spontaneous response to a patient's emotional experience will mediate his or her ability to access it. For example, a therapist who fears his or her patient's sadness will have difficulty helping him or her to access it.

EMOTIONS HAVE A SOMATIC COMPONENT TO THEM

Different emotions are associated with different somatic experiences. For example, the emotion of love is associated with somatic correlates of softness and vulnerability (decreased muscular tension). Anger is associated with muscular tension and somatic correlates of aggression.

This has important significance from a therapeutic perspective. Emotional experience which people have not fully articulated to themselves may nevertheless be implicit as a bodily felt sense (Gendlin, 1962). Thus an important intervention consists of directing patients' attention to their bodily felt sense experience in order to promote the construction of emotional experience.

EMOTION IS A PRIMARY COMMUNICATION SYSTEM

Emotion plays a primary role in human communication. Human beings are biologically wired to make sense of and respond to the emotional expressions of others. From a therapeutic perspective this has important implications. People may be communicating things to other people without being fully aware that they are doing so. For example, somebody may communicate hostility towards others through his or her voice tone, body posture or facial gesture without being fully aware this anger. Providing patients with feedback

about the emotions they evoke in others can be an important form of therapeutic feedback (Kiesler, 1988; Safran and Segal, 1990).

EMOTION IS A FORM OF TACIT MEANING

Since emotion provides us with information regarding how well we are pro-
gressing towards the goals and sub-goals of the overall system, they also
implicitly provide us with information about what these goals and sub-goals
are. For example, the fact that a child becomes frightened when the attachment figure leaves, reflects the fact that maintaining proximity to the attachment figure is an important goal of the system. Many of the goals we develop
through learning are tacit rather than explicit. Since much of this learning
takes place at an early, pre-verbal stage of development many of these attitudes are implicit in the functioning of the system rather than verbally explicit.
For this reason, attending to the nuances of one's emotional experiences can
provide one with important information about what one's goals are.

AFFECTIVE ASSESSMENT

A question that often comes up for cognitive therapists who are learning to
work in a more emotion focused fashion is when to deepen the intensity of
the patient's emotional experience and when not to. Here it is important to
differentiate between different types of emotional experience. Les Greenberg and I (Greenberg and Safran, 1987) have articulated a clinical heuristic
that distinguishes between three types of emotional expression: primary
emotion, secondary emotion and instrumental emotion. *Primary emotion*
consists of the individual's initial affective appraisal of the situation prior to
more complex conceptual activity. This is a biologically adaptive signal that
provides information about the individual's action dispositions, motivates
adaptive behavior and provides implicit information about the meaning of
events for the individual. The therapist may wish to help the patient to
access primary emotions as an end towards a number of therapeutic goals
such as motivating adaptive behavior or obtaining information about the
individual's tacit values.

A *secondary emotion* consists of the emotional expression that results from
the individual's secondary internal response to their primary emotional appraisal. For example, an individual feels angry and then begins to feel self-
critical because of his or her anger. This leads to feelings of sadness and
hopelessness. Another example is the individual who begins to feel needy and
vulnerable and then responds with anger because of his or her anticipation of

being abandoned. In this situation the anger is a secondary emotional reaction to an underlying feeling of vulnerability. The therapist's task here is to help the patient ultimately access the underlying primary emotion rather than the secondary emotion. For example, a patient tended to react to others in an angry, defensive and self-protective fashion whenever he felt vulnerable. This alienated others and made it difficult for them to respond to his needs in a nurturing fashion. By helping the patient to access underlying feelings of vulnerability the therapist was able to help him function in a more adaptive fashion. Rather than lash out at people when he was angry he was able to acknowledge his vulnerability in a way that brought people closer to him.

Instrumental emotions are emotional patterns that people have learned in order to influence others. For example, the individual cries in order to evoke sympathy or expresses anger as a way of controlling people. As with secondary emotions it would be a mistake for the therapist to attempt to deepen the patient's experience of instrumental emotions. Instead the task is to illuminate the nature of the underlying emotional experience. Distinguishing between these different types of emotional experience, while critical, is a complex clinical task that requires experience. Many of the cues are subtle and difficult to articulate. A key source of information consists of the therapist's own emotional reaction to the patient. If the patient is expressing a primary emotion the therapist is more likely to feel attuned to and empathically connected to him or her than if he or she is expressing a secondary or instrumental emotion. To the extent that patients are in contact with and expressing their own primary emotional experience the clinician is more likely to feel affectively engaged.

If the clinician does not feel engaged with his or her patient's emotional experience it can be a cue that the patient is alienated from his or her primary emotion. Of course the therapist must always seriously consider the possibility that the lack of engagement may be attributable to a lack of empathy resulting from his or her own issues.

Another source of information can emerge from putting one's self in the patient's shoes and imagining how one would feel in the situation and then contrasting the patient's expressed emotional experience with one's own anticipated feelings. For example, a patient was describing a situation in which her boyfriend was mistreating her and then burst into tears. The therapist, through an act of identification with the patient, experienced anger rather than sadness. This discrepancy in reactions alerted him to the possibility that the sadness might be a secondary emotion. When the situation was explored more carefully it emerged that the patient had a habitual style of responding to her own feelings of anger with self-criticism, fears of abandonment and helplessness. By becoming aware of this process she was able to experience her anger more fully and ultimately was motivated to leave the situation.

The therapist has no choice ultimately but to rely on his or her own emotional experience during therapy as an important therapeutic tool. This notion can be distressing to those who see psychotherapy as more of a science than an art or who are mistrustful of emotion as an important source of information. There is always an affective component to our appraisals, however, even if we are unaware of it, and the best safeguard against making therapeutic mistakes involves becoming fully aware of our emotional experience rather than trying to ignore it. There is an inevitable element of subjectivity to our perceptions and it is safer to make use of and acknowledge this subjectivity rather than to delude ourselves into believing that our judgements are made on purely rational grounds.

AFFECTIVE PROCESSING DYSFUNCTIONS

In this final section I will describe a number of specific dysfunctions in emotional processing and briefly outline some of the relevant interventions.

ANXIETY AS A SECONDARY RESPONSE TO PRIMARY EMOTION

In this situation the patient presents clinically with anxiety-related problems. This anxiety is a secondary response to an underlying primary feeling that the individual anticipates will be threatening to interpersonal relatedness. For example, a patient who has difficulty fully processing and experiencing anger because she perceives it as threatening to interpersonal relatedness presents with diffuse anxiety symptoms. The therapeutic task is to work with the patient to help her attend more fully to a bodily felt sense associated with anger that is currently not being fully processed. An important piece of the work may involve exploring and challenging automatic thoughts and dysfunctional beliefs related to the prohibition of anger.

MULTIPLE ANXIETY CONCERNS SECONDARY TO AVOIDANCE

In this syndrome the focus of the patient's attention shifts from one anxiety concern to another in rapid succession. A presentation of this type can be rather overwhelming to the therapist who has not yet begun to get a grasp of one problem before the patient moves on to another. In addition, the patient's feeling of being overwhelmed is communicated to the therapist. Multiple anxiety-related concerns of this sort can often be the reflection of a patient's difficulty in experiencing one particular situation and the painful feelings associated with it more fully. An important therapeutic intervention here consists of directing the patient's attention to avoided feelings more fully and helping him or her to become aware of ways in which those feelings are avoided.

DEPRESSION RESULTING FROM DEACTIVATION OF BEHAVIORAL SYSTEMS

In this syndrome the client experiences a sense of hopelessness and depression because his or her primary emotions are not being attended to. As Bowlby (1980) suggests, depression is an organismic response constellation that in one way or another involves a deactivation of behavioral systems. When an individual feels that exertion of further effort is futile or dangerous, the normal link between emotional processing and actions can be broken through a failure to fully attend to and synthesize relevant emotional information. For example, a depressed patient who experiences a pervasive sense of numbness may in fact be failing to fully attend to underlying feelings of sadness. This blockage may result from a belief that he or she may be abandoned if he or she expresses this sadness or that nobody will be there. In a situation of this type, therapeutic interventions aimed at helping the patient to fully experience the underlying sadness can be a powerful experience which helps him or her regain contact both with the self and with the rest of the world. Feelings of numbness and deadness can be replaced with yearning and a desire for nurturance and can lead to interpersonal contact and support, if expressed.

COGNITIVE DISCONNECTION OF RESPONSE FROM SITUATION

This form of dysfunctional affective information processing, also identified by Bowlby (1980), involves a failure to make the connection between a particular emotion and the environmental stimulus that elicits it. For example, rather than feeling anger in response to a particular person in a specific situation, the individual walks around with a diffuse sense of anger and bitterness that is not attached to anything and that cannot be worked with. This affective information processing dysfunction serves a defensive or avoidance function in that it helps the individual to avoid exploring and expressing feelings in a particular interpersonal situation which may seem too dangerous or threatening. An important therapeutic intervention here consists of working with the patient to help him to continue to attend to a relevant interpersonal situation that evokes a response rather than to experience things in a more diffuse fashion. In this respect it is useful to focus on the here and now of the therapeutic relationship as an interpersonal laboratory in which emotions are constantly evoked and to help the patient become aware of the way he or she may avoid experiencing certain feelings in the relationship.

UNRESOLVED GRIEF OR INCOMPLETE MOURNING

The normal grieving or mourning process is one that has been observed and described by a number of theorists and researchers. An important part of the grieving process typically involves the experience of intrusive thoughts about the person being grieved for and alternations between feelings of sadness, pain and anger.

Although it is not fully understood how the normal process of mourning operates, one commonly accepted hypothesis is that the intrusive images of the loved one permits the individual to gradually change his internal represen- tation of the interpersonal world in order to accommodate to the new reality. In this process both sadness and anger are natural responses to the loss of a loved one. The sadness motivates the individual to attempt to recover the loved one while the anger is associated with the severing of the connection to the loved one when one's goal of recovery cannot be attained. Both emotions can be extremely painful and defensively avoided. In the natural grieving process, however, the oscillation back and forth between periods of sadness and anger in response to the intrusive images ultimately functions to sever emotional connection to the loved one and to modify the individual's cogni- tive representations of the interpersonal world. (Horowitz, 1979).

CONCLUSION

There has been an explosion of interest amongst academic psychologists in the topic of emotion since the early 1980s. Cognitive therapists have been influenced in certain respects by these developments, but their potential im- pact on the field has yet to be fully realized. In this chapter I have summarized a number of theoretical and technical principles relevant to the adoption of a broader range of approaches towards affective experience. It is probably more accurate to think of these principles as generic in nature rather than specific to cognitive therapy. As cognitive therapists become more familiar with these principles, however, the possibility of a distinctive cognitive- behavioral approach to emotion emerges.

REFERENCES

Ableson, R.P. (1963). Computer simulation of 'hot cognitions', in Tomkins, S. and Messick, S. (eds), *Computer Simulations of Personality*, John Wiley & Sons, New York.

Arnold, M.B. (1960). *Emotion and Personality*, Columbia University, New York.

Bower, G.H. (1981). Mood and memory, *Psychological Bulletin*, **99**, 229–148.

Bowlby, J. (1980). *Attachment and Loss*: Vol. 3. *Loss: Sadness and Depression*, Hogarth Press, London.

Ekman, P. and Friesen, W.V. (1975). *Unmasking the Face*, Prentice-Hall, Englewood Cliffs, NJ.

Gendlin, E.T. (1962). *Experiencing and the Creation of Meaning*, Free Press, New York.

Goldfried, M.R. and Davison, G.C. (1994). *Clinical Behavior Therapy*. John Wiley & Sons, New York.

Greenberg, L.S., Elliott, R.K. and Lietaer, G. (1994). Research on experiential psycho-therapies, in Bergin, A. and Garfield, S. (eds), *Handbook of Psychotherapy and Behavior Change*, John Wiley & Sons, New York.

Greenberg, L.S., Rice, L.N. and Elliott, R. (1994). *Process-Experiential Therapy: Facilitating Emotional Change*, Guilford Press, New York.

Greenberg, L.S. and Safran, J.D. (1984). Integrating affect and cognition: A perspective on the process of therapeutic change, *Cognitive Therapy and Research*, **8**, 559–578.

Greenberg, L.S. and Safran, J.D. (1986). Hot cognition and psychotherapy process: An information-processing/ecological perspective, in Kendall, P.C. (ed.), *Advances in Cognitive-Behavioral Research and Therapy*, Vol. 5, pp. 143–177, Academic Press, New York.

Greenberg, L.S. and Safran, J.D. (1987). *Emotion in Psychotherapy Affect, Cognition, and the Process of Change*, Guilford Press, New York.

Horowitz, M.H. (1979). *States of Mind*, Plenum Press, New York.

Izard, C.E. (1977). *Human Emotions*, Plenum Press, New York.

Jacobson, N.S. (1994). Behavior therapy and psychotherapy integration, *Journal of Psychotherapy Integration*, **4**, 105–119.

Kiesler, D.J. (1988). *Therapeutic Metacommunication: Therapist Impact Disclosure as Feedback in Psychotherapy*, Consulting Psychologists Press, Palo Alto, CA.

Leventhal, H. (1979). A perceptual–motor theory of emotion, in Pliner, P., Blankenstein, K. and Spigel, I. (eds), *Advances in the Study of Communication and Affect*, Plenum Press, New York.

Linehan, M. (1993). *Cognitive Behavioral Treatment of Borderline Personality Disorder*, Guilford Press, New York.

Mahoney, M.J. (1980). Psychotherapy and the structure of personal revolutions, in Mahoney, M.J. (ed.), *Psychotherapy Process: Current Issues and Future Directions*, Plenum Press, New York.

Perls, F. (1973). *The Gestalt Approach and Eye Witness Therapy*. Science and Behavior Books, Bantam edn, Palo Alto, CA.

Plutchik, R. (1980). *Emotion: A Psychoevolutionary Synthesis*, Harper, New York.

Rank, O. (1936). *Truth and Reality: The Central Statement of Rank's Ideas*, W.W. Norton, New York.

Reich, W. (1942). *The Function of the Orgasm*, Orgone Institute, New York.

Rogers, C.R. (1961). *Client-Centered Therapy*, Houghton Mifflin, Boston.

Safran, J.D. and Greenberg, L.S. (1982). Cognitive appraisal and reappraisal: Implications for clinical practice, *Cognitive Therapy and Research*, **6**, 251–258.

Safran, J.D. and Greenberg, L.S. (1986). Hot cognition and psychotherapy process: An information-processing/ecological perspective, in Kendall, P.C. (ed.), *Advances in Cognitive-Behavioral Research and Therapy*, Vol. 5, pp. 143–177, Academic Press, New York.

Safran, J.D. and Greenberg, L.S. (eds) (1991). *Emotion, Psychotherapy and Change*, Guilford Press, New York.

Safran, J.D. and Segal, Z.V. (1990). *Interpersonal Process in Cognitive Therapy*, Basic Books, New York.

Tomkins, S.S. (1980). Affect as amplification: Some modifications in theory, In Plutchik, R. and Kellerman, H. (eds), *Emotion: Theory, Research and Experience*, Vol. 1, Academic Press, New York.

Zajonc, R.B. (1980). Feeling and thinking: Preferences need no inferences, *American Psychologist*, **35**, 171–175.

Chapter Eight

LAWRENCE YUSUPOFF, GILLIAN HADDOCK, WILLIAM SELLWOOD AND NICHOLAS TARRIER

Cognitive-Behavioural Therapy for Hallucinations and Delusions: Current Practices and Future Trends

INTRODUCTION

Cognitive-behavioural therapies for persistent hallucinations and delusions have now been developed and recent outcomes support their continued refinement. What appears to be commonly appreciated by clinicians investigating these approaches is that psychotic phenomena do not exist in isolation from an individual's psychological and emotional functioning and are thus amenable to psychological manipulation. This chapter begins with a brief description of previous psychological treatments and the more recent cognitive-behavioural therapies for hallucinations and delusions; some common themes are extracted. Cognitive remediation training is the current alternative to cognitive-behavioural methods and some comments are offered about this therapeutic option. The extent to which research findings are generalizable to the broader population of individuals with persistent hallucinations and delusions is discussed. If consistently favourable outcomes can be achieved using psychological approaches with this population, there will be much interest in developing informative psychological models of psychosis

Trends in Cognitive and Behavioural Therapies. Edited by P.M. Salkovskis.
© 1996 John Wiley & Sons Ltd.

and associated symptoms; some potential pitfalls are noted. Finally, other long-term implications of recent advances and current research are considered.

PSYCHOLOGICAL TREATMENTS FOR POSITIVE PSYCHOTIC SYMPTOMS

Much of the literature concerning psychological treatment of positive psychotic symptoms involves single case studies or case series (see Slade and Bentall, 1988; Tarrier et al., 1990). The approaches used have varied from operant procedures designed to provide reinforcement when the patient is engaged in non-psychotic behaviour or speech (Lindsley, 1959; Nydegger, 1972; Wincze, Leitenberg and Agras, 1972); distraction techniques designed to reduce auditory hallucinations (Margo, Hemsley and Slade, 1981; Nelson, Thrasher and Barnes, 1991); belief modification approaches designed to alter the characteristics of delusions (Chadwick and Lowe, 1990; Milton, Patwa and Hafner, 1978; Watts, Powell and Austin, 1973) and systematic desensitization (Slade, 1972). Many authors have focused on single behavioural or cognitive techniques in order to alter the severity of the psychotic symptoms. Alternatively, a number of researchers have attempted to use a range of techniques which have been shown to be effective in the management of individual symptoms and combined them to produce comprehensive management packages for individuals who have a diagnosis of schizophrenia (Fowler, 1992; Tarrier et al., 1993). These studies have confirmed that psychological approaches have a useful role in the management of psychotic symptoms. More recently, authors have noted the need for controlled studies with larger numbers of subjects (Kuipers, Garety and Fowler, 1996; Tarrier et al., 1993) in order to demonstrate the efficacy of psychological approaches. Randomized controlled trials should ideally involve an epidemiological-based sample to avoid selection bias in the treated sample.

Although recent research has developed in a number of different research centres and from different models accounting for the cause and maintenance of psychotic symptoms and schizophrenia, the main cognitive-behavioural approaches have evolved with some common themes. Over the last 50 years there has been a common myth that psychotherapy conducted with people who were psychotic was contra-indicated; this position developed from the influences of both psychoanalytic and operant schools of thought. Avoiding direct discussion of psychotic symptoms continues to be part of the management strategy which is recommended to mental health professionals in many training programmes. There are no data which suggest that symptoms worsen as a result of cognitive-behavioural therapy; indeed, recent studies suggest that psychological intervention even during acute episodes may facilitate coping (Allen and Bass, 1992) and rate of recovery (Drury, 1994). Contrary to previous practice, the majority of researchers are now advocating discussion of symptom content and related feelings and thoughts as essential elements of treatment (Bentall, Haddock and Slade, 1993; Chadwick and Birchwood, 1996). The prevailing theme in current approaches appears to be that the content of patient's voices and other types of psychotic symptoms are meaningful and are important variables to consider in treatment. The content of voices, for example, may reflect unpleasant worries or concerns; the specific details of delusional beliefs may not be arbitrary and may begin to make psychological sense for the patient once they are assessed in the context of the individual's current life and history. In addition, there is some suggestion that techniques which solely encourage the person to distract or suppress their hallucinations are associated with coping badly with psychotic symptoms (Romme and Escher, 1993) and may result in decreased self-esteem (Haddock, Bentall and Slade, 1996). This is consistent with the finding that suppression of intrusive thoughts increases their occurrence (Salkovskis and Campbell, 1994). It should be noted that distraction techniques in the management of auditory hallucinations have been shown to have some value, although they may not generalize well or produce long-lasting benefits.

The current trend of attempting to make psychological sense of psychotic symptoms for the patient appears to be a major clinical advance and offers a potentially far more credible account for patients rather than just to re-label their experiences in pathophysiological terms.

It has also been noted by a number of researchers (Kingdon, Turkington and John, 1994; Kuipers, Garety and Fowler, in press) that psychotic patients experience high levels of depression and have low self-esteem. This may be due to a range of factors, from the stigma attached to experiencing psychotic symptoms, the poor community services offered to psychiatric patients, the insistence by mental health professionals on labelling their experiences as 'unreal' and their poor financial and social situation. Many patients experiencing psychotic symptoms will experience secondary disability and handicap, such as having poor social networks and finding it difficult to find and maintain full-time employment. As a result of this, some authors are suggesting that treatments should be directed not only towards reducing the frequency of or distress associated with symptoms, but also towards the symptoms of depression and low self-esteem. These observations and therapeutic conclusions may appear obvious and mundane, however, crediting schizophrenic patients with ordinary psychological reactions, such as depression in response to tragic life circumstances, is a recent development.

A further theme that has emerged is that a number of authors have described the potentially complex motivational factors associated with patients' attitudes to symptom loss or change. For example, Miller, O'Connor and DiPasquale (1993) observed that a good proportion of their hallucinated psychiatric inpatients perceived their symptom as being beneficial in some way (even in cases where the symptom was also associated with disadvantages). A positive attitude at pre-treatment predicted continuing hallucinations following a combination of drug and psychosocial therapies. Roberts (1991) observed that patients with chronic systematized delusions preferred their present lives to times prior to delusional development and were largely threatened by and negatively predisposed to the prospect of belief loss. Grandiose delusions and positive erotic delusions were over-represented in the chronically deluded group. The potential ethical and practical implications for psychological intervention with this sub-group of patients whose reconstructed realities are preferred to their pre-morbid ones, are clear.

THE CONTEXT OF SYMPTOMATIC CHANGE

There is an assumption that intervening with positive psychotic symptoms is clinically desirable. There is much justification for this, but there is some danger that well-documented successes may result in an over-emphasis on symptomatic change as a clinical priority. Quality of life changes may not automatically follow reductions in positive symptomatology. For a sub-group of individuals, reduction in positive psychotic symptoms may appear trivial compared with their overall level of disability. Furthermore, improvements may be short-lived, or even result in negative consequences. For example, the duration of symptoms may be such that a wide range of important social competencies may never have fully developed, especially where the symptoms have interfered directly with functioning and resulted in marked avoidance behaviour. Symptom loss or reduction may be an inherently threatening prospect. The patient may now be faced with a social world that they are ill-equipped to deal with. An increase in the patient's expectations of their role and competency without addressing the potential deficit in their skills and resources to meet these new demands may result in a return of symptoms.

Thus, apparently good outcomes may be successful only from a technical point of view. The clinical and social needs of patients are often complex, and chronic social functioning deficits may represent the combined effects of both positive and negative symptomatology, the long-term social response of others, medication side-effects, secondary psychological reactions and material poverty. Patients themselves may welcome an opportunity to change their symptoms, whilst they attribute the source of their distress to them, only to discover at the end of therapy that their attributions were only partially correct and that they remain considerably unhappy.

One context of symptom change worthy of further research is the immediate social environment of the patient. The social responses of others may provide powerful influences which support or undermine clinical changes. This is perhaps not surprising considering the large body of evidence demonstrating the influence of the family environment on the course of schizophrenia. Carers' adaptation of role in response to the chronic social debilitation of the patient may be such that an improvement in symptoms may be perceived as inconsequential or indeed threatening where a change in that role may occur. Conversely, the social response may be overly enthusiastic and expectations of a 'cure' may be reactivated along with increased pressure to improve functioning to the pre-morbid level.

Furthermore, an improvement in positive symptoms may inadvertently increase critical communications by reinforcing relatives' attributions that illness variables are internal to the patient and indeed controllable; there is some evidence that such an attributional style is more powerfully predictive of relapse than expressed emotion status (Barrowclough, Johnston and Tarrier, 1994). The implication here is that some form of family intervention may need to be introduced to support positive symptom changes. It is as yet unclear whether this should be offered in parallel to individual work or sequentially, or perhaps symptom-focused therapies should be conducted in the family context using carers as co-therapists. A similar logic might be applied to staffed establishments, caring for patients in lieu of family support.

The more general point is that simplistic accounts which emphasize the reduction of positive symptoms, without considering the interpersonal and intrapersonal contexts in which these changes are to occur, should be avoided (Kuipers, Garety and Fowler, in press). Acknowledging the complexity of the needs of this population, with regard to future service provision, need not undermine current researchers, who are attempting to evaluate 'pure' versions of their therapies.

MECHANISMS OF CHANGE

The development of cognitive-behavioural approaches to the treatment of hallucinations and delusions has taken place independently in different centres. There are a number of similarities and overlaps between these approaches, which is perhaps not surprising, as they originate from a common paradigm; but they also originate from conceptualizations that do differ even if they share basic assumptions. It is helpful in developing testable hypotheses, to distil each conceptualization and associated clinical method down to its raw form. For example, the Coping Strategy Enhancement (CSE) approach (Tarrier et al., 1990) is based on an antecedent and consequence formulation in which biological and contextual (i.e. environmental and psychological) antecedents result in the experience of positive symptoms through a common pathway of elevated or dysfunctional arousal (see Barrowclough and Tarrier, 1992, p. 161). A feedback mechanism is postulated in which the consequences of experiencing the symptom, such as distress, anxiety, inactivity, results in the increased probability of the symptom recurring. In its pure and restricted form CSE would aim to break the feedback cycle by attempting to alleviate the toxic action of the symptom's consequences. On the other hand, a more traditional cognitive model would postulate that symptoms were maintained by misattributions and maladaptive beliefs. Hence, the treatment would focus on these and not on the distress or associated behaviours. As such it should be possible to generate opposing hypotheses to test the accuracy of these conceptualizations and the limited treatments they suggest.

NEUROPSYCHOLOGY AND TREATMENT

Despite cognitive-behavioural therapy advances, much of the schizophrenia research continues to be biologically based. The neuropsychological study of schizophrenia offers a link between the biological and social aspects of the disorder (Strauss, 1993). There are two main reasons for studying the neuropsychological deficits which underlie schizophrenia. First, it is important to understand the nature of schizophrenia, and second, so that relevant psychological therapies or compensatory tactics can be developed in order to overcome some of the problems associated with this illness. Patients with schizophrenia perform poorly on a wide variety of neuropsychological tests, but it is unclear which deficits are specific to this disorder, which occur commonly in schizophrenia but are not related to symptomatology, and which are diffuse effects and secondary disabilities resulting from the disorder and its pharmacological treatment.

As a result of developments in neuropsychology, Green (1993) has argued that the time is ripe for the clinical exploitation of cognitive remediation, despite there being no clear conclusions as to the nature of the deficits associated with schizophrenia or its symptoms. He divides remediation tactics into general stimulation, substitution transfer, and behavioural. General stimulation involves the repetition of relevant cognitive tasks. Studies where this approach has been used with head-injured patients have shown that it is not effective (see Green, 1993). Substitution transfer involves training patients to use intact parts of the brain to overcome deficits caused by damage to other areas. Green cites studies of normal elderly subjects where memory for various types of material was improved. He states that this group is a good comparison group for schizophrenic patients in terms of memory rehabilitation. This can be discounted for two reasons. First, the main deficits seen in schizophrenic patients concern neuropsychological abnormalities other than impaired memory, which are of more concern in the expression of symptoms and poor social functioning. Second, schizophrenic patients are likely to have greater problems in applying this technique if other neuropsychological abnormalities interfere with it.

Behavioural approaches are useful in the enhancement of desirable behaviours and the reduction of undesirable ones in both the head-injured and schizophrenic patient groups. Behavioural interventions are successfully used, for example, in social skills training, but it is unusual for therapists to base their intervention on some aspect of patients' specific neuropsychological profiles. It is most usual for sessions to be frequent and repetitive, making some compensation for general problems in information processing.

In spite of the above problems there have been attempts to develop therapy for schizophrenic symptoms based on what are acknowledged information processing and cognitive deficits seen in patients with schizophrenia. Integrated Psychological Therapy (Brenner et al., 1992) is such an approach. Patients undergo a programme of training which at first involves the acquisition of basic cognitive skills. Then patients are trained to use more complex social skills which are assumed to be dependent on the more basic skills learned earlier. Patients do learn the specific skills in which they are trained, however, there is little evidence that these generalize to 'real life' or that the skills learned are especially relevant. Is learning how to successfully complete a card sorting task really going to lead to improved quality of life for the patient? Moreover, social skills training can be successfully applied without preliminary cognitive training (Bellack and Mueser, 1993), although it should be noted that the evidence for generalization as a result of social skills training is also limited (Halford and Hayes, 1991). A further problem in the assumptions underlying the Brenner et al. study is that training in more complex social skills tasks can lead to improvement on more fundamental cognitive tasks (see Green, 1993).

In conclusion, research has yet to establish the contribution of the neuropsychological literature to the development of independent therapeutic paradigms which are as effective as cognitive-behavioural therapies. It is likely, however, that cognitive-behavioural practices might be modified or adapted in the light of continuing neuropsychological investigations.

RESEARCH STRATEGIES

Despite the optimism generated by recent research outcomes, the parameters and limitations of cognitive-behavioural therapies for hallucinations and delusions remain ill-defined and we are not yet in a position to accurately profile the characteristics of individuals for whom these interventions are suitable or effective. The first problem relates to the strict exclusion criteria usually adopted in studies, thus possibly rejecting a sizeable number of subjects who constitute a significant part of the 'psychiatric population'; examples include patients with current alcohol and substance abuse histories and patients who fall between diagnostic categories, which include those with a schizo-affective disorder and patients over the age of 65 years. Second, it has been argued that good outcomes have been obtained with self-selected samples, who survive the typically high attrition rates at the assessment stage and during treatment. Tarrier et al. (1993) reported that there was a large drop out (45%) from their study and Haddock, Bentall and Slade (in press) found that more than half of the subjects referred to their auditory hallucinations treatment study were not able to be included.

A solution for the first issue regarding exclusion criteria might be to target these individuals in separate controlled trials. An example here is a research programme currently underway in the USA (S. Gingerich, 1994, personal communication) which aims to establish the impact of cognitive-behavioural therapy for individuals with psychotic symptoms who have a concurrent alcohol or substance abuse diagnosis; one question is whether successful reductions in symptoms or an increase in psychological coping strategy effectiveness results in changes in the use of alcohol or drugs.

The second problem regarding treatment refusers and drop outs is reflective of the heterogeneity of the psychotic population. Patients may not have specific incentive to achieve therapeutic changes; symptoms may be valued or not perceived as distressing, or the content may be so aversive that the prospect of discussing them in therapy is too anxiety provoking. Also, cognitive-behavioural therapies are based on structured verbal communication, which may automatically exclude patients who are so verbally incoherent or disorganized in their speech that symptom severity cannot be measured accurately at pre-treatment assessment. Regular attendance and therapeutic compliance may also be compromised by the amotivational state characteristic of the negative symptoms of schizophrenia. The very least that is required is that researchers accurately detail the characteristics of treatment refusers and the reasons for drop out (including subjective accounts elicited using drop-out questionnaires).

In terms of treatment acceptors, large-scale, controlled trials are required to confirm or disconfirm putative predictors of outcome which have been described elsewhere (Sellwood et al., 1994) and to determine whether cognitive-behavioural therapies improve outcome compared with standard psychiatric care alone and non-specific therapist contact conditions.

Clinical researchers are becoming more aware that the nature of the therapeutic relationship and the interest shown in the patient is of great importance in the treatment of psychotic patients. It has yet to be established that the active elements in cognitive-behavioural treatments are necessary to produce the reported positive benefits of such treatments. The non-specific aspects of treatment have yet to be ruled out as the sole requirements for positive outcomes. We are currently examining this question in a large randomized controlled trial of cognitive-behavioural therapy based on CSE which is being compared with supportive psychotherapy and routine care. The long-term effects of treatment and the potential for relapse prevention are further questions being investigated in this study funded by The Wellcome Trust.

There has been an implicit assumption that cognitive-behavioural therapy should be targeted on the chronic patient who experiences persistent symptoms. However, recent exciting results reported by Birchwood's group in Birmingham have indicated that inpatient programmes with acutely ill patients can be effective in decreasing recovery time and reducing the time spent in hospital (Drury, 1994). The possibility that cognitive-behavioural therapy could be a front-line treatment for florid episodes of psychosis is therefore suggested. In Manchester we are currently running a pilot trial to replicate and extend the Birmingham study.

THE CONCEPT OF SELF-ESTEEM IN SCHIZOPHRENIA

The finding that psychological interventions can reduce the occurrence of psychotic symptoms as opposed to just the distress associated with them, is strongly suggestive of the role of psychological factors in their maintenance. A more tentative inference would be that psychological factors are also aetiologically implicated.

There has been renewed interest in the psychological construct of self-esteem in relation to the psychoses and psychotic symptoms. Self-esteem is most obviously relevant in terms of the social consequences of psychosis. It has also been proposed as a key factor in the development and maintenance of specific psychotic symptoms; a good example here is recent experimental research on persecutory delusions. Kaney and Bentall (1989) demonstrated that patients with persecutory delusions exhibited more global and stable attributions concerning events than normal subjects and that when these events were negative they were more likely to be externally attributed. When events were positive they were internally attributed. In addition, Bentall, Kaney and Dewey (1991) found that deluded subjects were more likely to attribute other people's negative actions to their general disposition rather than as a result of the specific context of the behaviour involved. A recent study (Bentall, Kinderman and Kaney, 1994) suggests that this tendency to attribute negative outcomes externally is more likely to occur when self-ideal discrepancies are explicitly activated, i.e. when self-esteem is overtly threatened. Given that these individuals also have been noted to have a selective bias for threat-related stimuli (Bentall and Kaney, 1989), the development of a delusional state characterized by persecutory concerns may be explicable.

More speculatively, it has been suggested that low self-esteem has an aetiological role in the development of symptoms. Proponents of this model typically reject the concept of schizophrenia on the basis of its poor scientific validity (Boyle, 1990). The mechanism proposed is that specific symptoms are a result of a dramatic attempt to protect low self-esteem made fragile as a result of poor bonding early in life. This account is solely psychogenic and the development of a fragile self-esteen does not require an underlying vulnerability. One implication of this is that maternal behaviour has a causative role in dysfunctional bonding, which potentially means the return of the concept of the schizophrenegenic mother. Any explanation exclusively locating the centre of pathology in the individual, as also does an organic medical model, risks ignoring the wider social and environmental context and hence negates social changes as legitimate interventions. It also centres blame on the mother, a hypothesis viewed with considerable scepticism by the women's movement. It is perhaps ironic that those arguing for the rejection of one model on scientific grounds propose instead another explanation which is vague and potentially without substance.

LONG-TERM IMPLICATIONS

Cognitive-behavioural treatments are now available to change hallucinations and delusions. It is anticipated that on-going research will, in time, identify the circumstances and characteristics of individuals for whom these approaches are suitable or appropriate and the therapeutic modifications which will be required to maximize meaningful outcomes for a heterogeneous group of patients with complex needs.

Historically, the development of neuroleptics in the 1950s in the management of schizophrenia is often cited as a major mental health breakthrough, for example, in reducing symptoms during acute episodes and in the prophylactic benefit they confer (Davis and Andriukaitis, 1986; Vaughn and Leff, 1976). Recent advances in the cognitive-behavioural treatment of psychotic symptoms have occurred in response to the realization that neuroleptics offer only a partial solution, some studies indicating that positive psychotic symptoms persist in nearly half of patients (Curson, Patel and Liddle, 1988; Silverstein and Harrow, 1978).

The impact of psychosocial factors on outcome in schizophrenia is now well established. A stress-vulnerability model of psychosis (Neuchterlein and Dawson, 1984) may be a powerful heuristic, but our models of psychotic onset and relapse remain unsophisticated; for example, critical comments made by families are stressful, and because of schizophrenics' reduced threshold for stress they then relapse. This account offers little explanation of the internal psychological mechanisms mediating psychotic breakdown; this is very much a 'black box' account. Attempts have been made to explain this relationship through hypothetical mediators such as arousal (Tarrier and Turpin, 1992) but these are not entirely satisfactory.

It has been assumed that psychotic symptoms, which are frequently bizarre, are by definition discontinuous with reality and hence meaningless, from a psychological point of view. Cognitive behavioural advances in the field of hallucinations and delusions now represent a challenge to this position. Perhaps by acknowledging that the subjective aspects of the experience of psychotic symptoms are valuable and facilitate clinical success, this may revolutionize our conceptualizations of 'madness' and the often de-humanizing consequences of being diagnosed psychotic.

Cognitive-behavioural therapies for psychotic symptoms have been developed as adjuncts to neuroleptics, where the latter have failed in their desired antipsychotic effects. As yet, no trials of cognitive-behavioural therapy have been conducted with psychotic patients who are not receiving medication, although a case study by Morrison (1994) indicates that this may be a feasible option, for at least some patients. The availability of a viable alternative to medication, would indeed constitute a breakthrough.

The translation of research findings to actual service provision on a wide scale, will be the final strategic challenge. The dissemination of other psychosocial treatments that have demonstrated efficacy, such as family management, has been disappointing. It has been argued that the number of clinical psychologists is limited and that treatments should be carried out by other trained staff and supervised by psychologists and other cognitive-behavioural therapists. Skills training modules have been produced to improve the quality of care in day hospitals (Liberman and Eckman, 1989). Training programmes for family management (see Barrowclough and Tarrier, 1992) which include both didactic teaching and clinical supervision have been carried out with social workers (Tarrier, Barrowclough and D'Ambrosio, 1988) and community psychiatric nurses (CPNs) (Brooker et al., 1992). Two of us (NT and GH) are currently involved with colleagues from the Universities of Manchester and London in producing and evaluating a comprehensive training programme for CPNs in problem-oriented and psychosocial management of schizophrenia, funded by the Sir Jules Thorn Trust. This project includes a module on treatment of individual positive symptoms. The aim is to provide the necessary skills for professionals who have responsibility for the continuing care of sufferers of schizophrenia and update them with the innovations and developments in research.

Will cognitive behaviour therapy become a major option for managing psychosis? The answer will depend on a number of factors, not the least being the demonstrated efficacy through randomized controlled trials. Also important will be the availability of skilled therapists and of high-quality training courses. Perhaps of equal importance will be the capacity of mental health services and professionals to accept psychological methods which may lie uncomfortably with a prevalent philosophy to treatment still largely dominated by a psychiatric medical model. At present the jury is still out!

REFERENCES

Allen, H. and Bass, C. (1992). Coping tactics and the management of acutely distressed schizophrenic patients, *Behavioural Psychotherapy*, **20**, 61–72.
Barrowclough, C., Johnston, M. and Tarrier, N. (1994). Attributions, expressed emotion and patient relapse: An attributional model of relatives' response to schizophrenic illness, *Behaviour Therapy*, **25**, 67–88.
Barrowclough, C. and Tarrier, N. (1992). *Families of Schizophrenic Patients: Cognitive-Behavioural Intervention*, Chapman and Hall, London.
Bellack, A.S. and Mueser, K.T. (1993). Psychosocial treatment for schizophrenia, *Schizophrenia Bulletin*, **19**, 317–336.
Bentall, R.P., Haddock, G. and Slade, P.D. (1994). Psychological treatment for auditory hallucinations: From theory to therapy, *Behavior Therapy*, **25**, 51–66.
Bentall, R.P. and Kaney, S. (1989). Content-specific processing and persecutory delusions: An investigation using the emotional Stroop test, *British Journal of Medical Psychology*, **62**, 355–364.
Bentall, R.P., Kaney, S. and Dewey, M.E. (1991). Paranoia and social reasoning: An attribution theory analysis, *British Journal of Clinical Psychology*, **30**, 13–23.
Bentall, R.P., Kinderman, P. and Kaney, S. (1994). The self, attributional processes and abnormal beliefs: Towards a model of persecutory delusions, *Behaviour Research and Therapy*, **32**, 331–341.
Boyle, M. (1990). *Schizophrenia: A Scientific Delusion?*, Routledge, London.
Brenner, H.D., Hodel, B., Roder, V. and Corrigan, P. (1992). Treatment of cognitive dysfunctions and behavioural deficits in schizophrenia, *Schizophrenia Bulletin*, **18**, 21–26.

Brooker, C., Tarrier, N., Barrowclough, C., Butterworth, A. and Goldberg, D. (1992). Training community psychiatric nurses for psychosocial intervention, *British Journal of Psychiatry*, **160**, 836–844.

Chadwick, P. and Birchwood, M. (1996). Cognitive behaviour therapy with voices, in Haddock, G. and Slade, P.D. (eds), *Cognitive Behavioural Interventions for Psychotic Disorders*, Routledge, London.

Chadwick, P. and Lowe, C.F. (1990). The measurement and modification of delusional beliefs. *Journal of Consulting and Clinical Psychology*, **58**, 225–232.

Curson, D.A., Patel, M. and Liddle, P.F. (1988). Psychiatric morbidity of a long stay hospital population with chronic schizophrenia and implications for future community care, *British Medical Journal*, **297**, 819–822.

Davis, J.M. and Andriukaitis, S. (1986). The natural course of schizophrenia and effective maintenance drug treatment, *Journal of Clinical Psychopharmacology*, **6**, (supplement), 2s–10s.

Drury, V. (1994). Cognitive therapy for psychotic symptoms: A trial in acute psychosis, paper presented at the Psychological Approaches to the Management of Psychosis Conference, Manchester University, Manchester, UK, 3 June.

Fowler, D. (1992). Cognitive behaviour therapy in the management of patients with schizophrenia: Preliminary studies, in Werbart, A. and Cullberg, J. (eds), *Psychotherapy of Schizophrenia: Facilitating and Obstructive Factors*, Scandinavian University Press, Oslo.

Green, M.F. (1993). Cognitive remediation in schizophrenia: is it time yet? *American Journal of Psychiatry*, **150**, 178–187.

Haddock, G., Bentall, R.P. and Slade, P.D. (1996). Focusing versus distraction in the psychological treatment of auditory hallucinations, in Haddock, G. and Slade, P.D. (eds), *Cognitive-Behavioural Interventions with Psychotic Disorders*, Routledge, London.

Halford, W.K. and Hayes, R. (1991). Psychological rehabilitation of chronic schizophrenic patients: recent findings on social skills training and family psychoeducation, *Clinical Psychology Review*, **11**, 23–44.

Kaney, S. and Bentall, R.P. (1989). Persecutory delusions and attributional style, *British Journal of Medical Psychology*, **62**, 191–198.

Kingdon, D.G., Turkington, D. and John, C. (1994). Cognitive-behaviour therapy of schizophrenia: The amenability of delusions and hallucinations to reasoning, *British Journal of Psychiatry*, **164**, 581–587.

Kuipers, L., Garety, P., and Fowler, D. (1966). An outcome study of cognitive behavioural treatment for psychosis, in Haddock, G. and Slade, P.D. (eds), *Cognitive Behavioural Interventions with Psychotic Disorders*, Routledge, London.

Liberman, R.P. and Eckman, T.A. (1989). Dissemination of skills training modules to psychiatric facilities, *British Journal of Psychiatry*, **155** (supplement 5), 117–122.

Lindsley, O.R. (1959). Reduction in rate of vocal psychotic symptoms by differential positive reinforcement, *Journal of the Experimental Analysis of Behaviour*, **2**, 269.

Margo, A., Hemsley, D.R. and Slade, P.D. (1981). The effects of varying auditory input on schizophrenic hallucinations, *British Journal of Psychiatry*, **139**, 122–127.

Miller, L.J., O'Connor, E. and DiPasquale, T. (1993). Patients' attitudes toward hallucinations, *American Journal of Psychiatry*, **150**, 584–588.

Milton, F., Patwa, V.K. and Hafner, R.J. (1978). Confrontation vs. belief modification in persistently deluded patients, *British Journal of Medical Psychology*, **51**, 127–130.

Morrison, A.P. (1994). Cognitive behaviour therapy for auditory hallucinations without concurrent medication: A single case, *Behavioural and Cognitive Psychotherapy*, **22**, 259–264.

Nelson, H.E., Thrasher, S. and Barnes, T.R.E. (1991). Practical ways of alleviating auditory hallucinations, *British Medical Journal*, **302**, 327.

Neuchterlein, K.H. and Dawson, M. (1984). A heuristic vulnerability-stress model of schizophrenic episodes, *Schizophrenia Bulletin*, **10**, 300–312.

Nydegger, R.V. (1972). The elimination of hallucinatory and delusional behaviour by verbal conditioning and assertive training: A case study. *Journal of Behaviour Therapy and Experimental Psychiatry*, **3**, 225–227.

Roberts, G. (1991). Delusional belief systems and meaning in life: A preferred reality? *British Journal of Psychiatry*, **159**, (supplement 14), 19–28.

Romme, M.A.R. and Escher, A.M.A.C. (1993). The new approach: A Dutch experiment, in Romme, M.A.R. and Escher, A.D.M.A.C. (eds) *Accepting Voices*, Mind, London.

Salkovskis, P.M. and Campbell, P. (1994). Thought suppression induces intrusions in naturally occurring negative intrusive thoughts, *Behaviour Research and Therapy*, **32**, 1–8.

Sellwood, W., Haddock, G., Tarrier, N. and Yusupoff (1994). Advances in the psychological management of psychotic symptoms, *International Review of Psychiatry*, **6**, 201–215.

Silverstein, M.L. and Harrow, M. (1978). First rank symptoms in the post-acute schizophrenic: A follow-up study, *American Journal of Psychiatry*, **135**, 1481–1486.

Slade, P.D. (1972). The effects of systematic desensitisation on auditory halucinations, *Behaviour Research and Therapy*, **10**, 85–91.

Slade, P.D. and Bentall, R.P. (1988). *Sensory Deception: A Scientific Analysis of Hallucination*, Croom Helm, London.

Strauss, M.E. (1993). Relations of symptoms to cognitive deficits in schizophrenia, *Schizophrenia Bulletin*, **19**, 215–231.

Tarrier, N. and Turpin, G. (1992). Psychosocial factors, arousal and schizophrenic relapse: The psychophysiological data, *British Journal of Psychiatry*, **161**, 3–11.

Tarrier, N., Barrowclough, C. and D'Ambrosio, P. (1988). A training programme in psychosocial intervention with families with a schizophrenic member, *The Behavioural Psychotherapist*, **27**, 2–4.

Tarrier, N., Beckett, R., Harwood, S., Baker, A., Yusupoff, L. and Ugarteburu, I. (1993). A trial of two cognitive-behavioural methods of treating drug-resistant residual psychotic symptoms in schizophrenic patients: I. Outcome, *British Journal of Psychiatry*, **162**, 524–532.

Tarrier, N., Harwood, S., Yusupoff, L., Beckett, R. and Baker, A. (1990). Coping strategy enhancement (CSE): A method of treating residual schizophrenic symptoms, *Behavioural Psychotherapy*, **18**, 283–293.

Vaughn, C.E. and Leff, J.P. (1976). The influence of family and social factors on the course of psychiatric illness: A comparison of schizophrenic and depressed neurotic patients, *British Journal of Psychiatry*, **129**, 125–137.

Watts, F.N., Powell, E.G. and Austin, S.V. (1973). The modification of abnormal beliefs, *British Journal of Medical Psychology*, **46**, 359–363.

Wincze, J.P., Leitenberg, H. and Agras, W.S. (1972). The effects of token reinforcement on the delusional verbal behaviour of chronic paranoid schizophrenics, *Journal of Applied Behaviour Analysis*, **5**, 247–262.

Chapter Nine

WILLIAM YULE

Post-Traumatic Stress Disorder in Children

Children have experienced traumatic, life-threatening events since the dawn of time. They have been upset by such experiences, but adults have been slow to recognize that sometimes children and adolescents suffer both acute and chronic distress. It was widely believed that children are very resilient, so that even when they experienced an acutely stressful event, they would develop at worst some sort of transient reaction disorder (Garmczy and Rutter, 1985).

It is right to direct clinicians' and researchers' attention to the fact that many children do act in a resilient way in the face of adversity, thereby focusing enquiry on healthy reactions rather than on pathology. However, it is also important to acknowledge that children can, and do, develop debilitating and distressing reactions following some acute and chronic traumas. This has been the achievement of the past decade and this chapter will summarize these developments, draw attention to some of the many gaps in our understanding, and point out the need for further studies.

POST-TRAUMATIC STRESS DISORDER IN CHILDREN AND ADOLESCENTS

As recently as 1994, Pynoos (1994) described post-traumatic stress disorder (PTSD) as a controversial diagnosis. The two major classifactory systems in psychiatry, ICD and DSM, are predominantly phenomenological, but PTSD

Trends in Cognitive and Behavioural Therapies. Edited by P.M. Salkovskis.
© 1996 John Wiley & Sons Ltd.

identifies not only an aetiological agent, the traumatic event, but also draws attention to the adverse personal consequences of certain personal experiences. A number of concerns follow from this. What sort of personal experiences should be considered? Do different types of adverse personal experiences lead to different types of distress? Before examining these questions, let us look at the phenomenology of PTSD as described in the 'official' classifications and how it presents in real life.

Following many years of work with Vietnam veterans returning to an indifferent, embarrassed and at times hostile society, the pioneering work of Horowitz (1976) and others recognized that these traumatized soldiers often presented with three groups of symptoms – persistent re-experiencing of the traumatic event; avoidance of aspects of the trauma or numbing of responsiveness; and increased physiological arousal – that hung together to form a syndrome. This was further codified in DSM III (American Psychiatric Association, 1980), revised in 1987 as DSM IIIR (American Psychiatric Association, 1987) and further revised in 1994 in DSM IV (American Psychiatric Association, 1994). The official classificatory system of the World Health Organization recognized PTSD in the 10th revision of the International Classification of Diseases (ICD 10, World Health Organization, 1992). There are a number of points to be made about this process of recognition of the disorder. Clearly it is not the case that suddenly a new disorder emerged from new stresses at the end of the twentieth century. Rather, stress disorders that had been associated mainly with combat and later with civilian disasters at the turn of the century were seen as manifestations of the same process of reacting to major stress. However, there were not many studies that could clarify which symptoms regularly went together and so expert committees had to reach consensus on incomplete data. This is presumably why 'survivor guilt' appears as one criterion symptom in DSM III but is not mentioned in DSM IIIR. It is not that survivors of disasters no longer experience survivor guilt – far from it – but rather that a second committee gave it less prominence. In a similar fashion, APA emphasized the emotional numbing as part of the diagnosis, whereas ICD sees that as a frequent but not necessary concomitant of PTSD.

In relation to children, DSM IIIR first made a specific mention of PTSD as occurring in children, and the past decade has seen an upsurge of studies in this area. However, inadequate attention has so far been paid to the developmental aspects of PTSD and whether it manifests itself differently in children of different ages and abilities. From my own clinical and research experience over the past decade, it has proven a very useful framework for describing and understanding children and adolescents' reactions to a wide range of life threatening experiences. Even so, the way that the syndrome manifests does seem to alter with age. For example, many workers have found it difficult to elicit evidence of emotional numbing in children (Frederick, 1985). They do at times report that in the first few hours they felt numb, and at times they even report that the whole incident seemed like a dream and that they cannot believe that it really happened. However, the younger the child, the more difficult it is to ask about feelings of detachment or estrangement from others, let alone about a restricted range of affect.

Much has been made of the idea of 'a sense of foreshortened future', which in part was discussed in the context of Terr's studies of the effects of the Chowchilla kidnapping on children (Terr, 1979). I certainly find it difficult to ask children about their plans for the future and whether they think these plans have been changed by their experiences if for no other reason than that many children do not really have much idea of what they want to do 10 years on. Rather, I find that what does seem to change is the children's and adolescents' ideas of their own invulnerability. They develop a premature sense of their own mortality. They have experienced in a road traffic accident or other disaster that people with them were alive one moment and dead the next. Life can be snuffed out in a second. Their reactions to this vary, but two stand out: some feel that since their lives have been spared, they should put every minute to good use, and they become very altruistic; others feel that if they could die at any second, then they should take every opportunity that presents itself. Experiences that they might otherwise have deferred until they were older, they try out because they may never have another chance. The resulting behaviour may have a driven and impulsive quality, but the force behind it is of a knowledge of their own mortality.

As I have written elsewhere (Yule, 1994), the common reactions observed after a number of major disasters affecting children and adolescents seem to be wider than the narrow confines described in either DSM or ICD. Most children were troubled by repetitive, intrusive thoughts about the accident. Such thoughts could occur at any time, but particularly when the children were otherwise quiet, as when they were trying to drop off to sleep. At other times, the thoughts and vivid recollections were triggered off by reminders in their environment. Vivid flashbacks were not uncommon. Sleep disturbances were very common, particularly in the first few weeks. Fears of the dark, bad dreams, nightmares and waking through the night were widespread. Separation difficulties were frequent, even among teenagers. For the first few days, children often did not want to let their parents out of their sight, even reverting to sleeping in the parental bed. Many children became much more irritable and angry than previously, both with parents and peers. Although child survivors experienced a presure to talk about their experiences, paradoxically they also found it very difficult to talk with their parents and peers. Often they did not want to upset the adults, and so many parents were unaware of the full extent of their children's suffering. Peers sometimes held back from asking what happened in case they upset the child further: the survivor often felt this as a rejection.

Children reported a number of cognitive changes. Many experienced difficulties in concentration, especially in school work. Others reported memory problems, both in mastering new material and in remembering old skills such as reading music. They became very alert to danger in their environment, being adversely affected by reports of other disasters. Survivors learned that life is very fragile. Many developed fears associated with specific aspects of their experiences. They avoided situations that they associated with the disaster. Many experienced 'survivor guilt' – about surviving when others died; about thinking they should have done more to help others; and about what they themselves did to survive.

Adolescent survivors reported significantly high rates of depression, some becoming clinically depressed, having suicidal thoughts and taking overdoses in the year after the disaster. A significant number became very anxious after accidents, although the appearance of panic attacks was sometimes considerably delayed. When children had been bereaved, they sometimes needed bereavement counselling.

Much younger children showed clear evidence of changes in their adjustment and characteristic behaviour, but did not always show the full range of symptoms detailed above. They were more likely to show all sorts of regressive behaviour or antisocial behaviour. It was often the case that parents said (or hoped) that the very young children did not remember what had happened. My experience was that it is possible to get children as young as 4 to 6 years to describe very vividly what they had experienced. This fits in with Terr's (1988) experience of the vividness of young children's memories for trauma.

Young children do describe bad dreams, nightmares and other re-experiencing phenomena, but they also show repetitive play and drawing involving themes related to the traumatic event. Misch et al. (1993) describe the play and drawings of nursery children who witnessed a workman incinerated in an electrical accident outside their school. An interesting developmental question is whether this sort of repetitive behaviour serves the same function for children as the re-experiencing serves for adults. It is also not yet established at what age the child-like reaction takes on the adult form.

SINGLE VERSUS REPEATED OR CHRONIC STRESSORS

Both DSM and ICD in different, and changing, ways discuss the nature of the event that gives rise to the stress reaction. Each concentrates on single, acute stressors such as an unexpected disaster or a violent attack, each of which occurs in the context of ongoing normality. Gradually, the nature of the stressor is being discussed more and more as one in which the 'victim' felt that their life was under threat or in which such a threat was perceived in relation to a loved one. This is a difference from the earlier formulations in which the stressor was seen as one that would cause significant distress to almost anyone.

Thus, it is increasingly recognized that the stressor cannot be fully defined in objective terms. There is a very important element of subjective evaluation which goes some way towards explaining individual differences in reactions to extreme stressors. Rachman (1980) examined the objective and subjective factors which he saw as being related to continuing difficulties in processing the emotions that arose from life threatening experiences.

OBJECTIVE FACTORS

Rachman's (1980) list included the suddenness with which a disaster strikes, the severity in the sense of the numbers killed or maimed, and the extent to which the incident involved 'prepared fears'. This way of considering the stimulus properties of a disaster opens the way for emergency services to develop a profile of potential scenarios indicating which are most likely to give rise to high proportions of people with severe psychopathology. As researchers are increasingly using standard assessments in their studies, so it is becoming clearer that there are differences which tend to follow Rachman's model. Thus, the level of reported distress was greater following the capsize of the *Herald of Free Enterprise*, in which many people were killed, compared with that following the sinking of the cruise ship *Jupiter*, in which only one pupil, one teacher and two rescuers were killed. In both cases, the level of distress reported in teenagers was greater in these shipping disasters than recorded after a school bus crash in which no one was killed (Stallard and Law, 1993). Children who survived the Lockerbie air disaster (Parry Jones, 1992) and those who survived Hurricane Hugo (Lonigan et al., 1991) presented with intermediate levels of distress on standard measures.

Within particular disasters there is evidence of a dose–response – or more specifically an exposure–response – relationship. Pynoos et al. (1987) reported the effects of a sniper attack on children in a Californian school. There was a clear relationship between the distance from the sniper (and hence the objective, personal danger) and later psychopathology, with some individual differences such as a boy who had left early to play football, leaving his sister in the line of fire. Although he was in a safe area when the firing started, he experienced considerable post-traumatic stress.

In a systematic follow-up study, Nader et al. (1991) reported that 74% of the most severely exposed children in the playground still reported moderate to severe levels of PTSD, whereas only 19% of the unexposed children reported any PTSD. It is of note that in this study the lower the objective level of threat, the more did other subjective factors enter the equation to produce stress reactions. Pynoos et al. (1993) studies three large groups of children following the Armenian earthquake – one from a town at the epicentre where buildings were totally destroyed: one from a town on the periphery; and one from a city outside the affected area. Again, a very clear exposure–effect relationship was demonstrated.

A further consensus is appearing in the published literature to the effect that greater psychopathology follows the witnessing of death and mutilation, as well as the feeling that the child's own life was under threat.

SUBJECTIVE FACTORS

In PTSD work in general, there has been an increasing interest in cognitive appraisal, coping strategies and attributional processes (Joseph et al., 1991, 1993). Yule, Udwin and Murdoch (1990) presented some evidence that there was a subjective exposure–effect relationship in so far as children who had experienced a school trip disaster were much more badly affected than children in the same school who had wanted to go on the cruise but had not obtained places, compared with even less distress among children who had never wanted to go. In another study of a larger group of adolescents who survived that same ship disaster, Joseph et al., (1993) reported on the attributions of 16 adolescent survivors of the *Jupiter* sinking and found that more internal and controllable attributions were related to intrusive thoughts and feelings of depression one year after the accident.

SINGLE VERSUS MULTIPLE TRAUMAS

Naturally, as work on PTSD in children and adolescents began to appear, so people tried to extend the paradigm to help understand other experiences that affect children's development. Wolfe, Gentile and Wolfe (1989) were among the first to try to formulate the effects of child sexual abuse within a PTSD framework, and this certainly helped to focus attention on aspects of the whole experience that were perhaps more amenable to intervention. Thus, by drawing attention to many of the avoidance behaviours, it was possible to think of desensitization and exposure treatments that might help alleviate some of the distress.

However, there are important differences between child sexual abuse and a one-off civilian disaster. In the first place, the latter happens in the context of ongoing normality. The threat comes out of the blue and the event is public. Thus the therapist or researcher can quickly gain a reasonably clear picture of what each survivor must have encountered during the event and so can guide the survivor in remembering what happened. By contrast, sexual abuse takes place in conditions of secrecy and shame, often with threats of violence should the child ever tell anyone else about it. Important details surrounding the violations are therefore private and not readily accessible to the investigator. Moreover, the abuse often occurs on many occasions over many years, and so it is very difficult to focus on one particular incident when investigating cause–effect relationships in research on trying to help the victim relive the experiences in therapy.

Two other sorts of chronic stressors that affect children have been discussed in recent years, and each brings yet more variables into play. Worldwide concern was focused on the psychological effects on children following the Chernobyl nuclear disaster in 1986. The World Health Organization has co-ordinated a number of studies of the health effects on children in Ukraine, Byelarus and Russia, and a number of local studies have also tried to assess the effects on psychological adjustment. The problem here is that while the acute stage of the disaster can be pinpointed, there has been continuing concern about the delayed effects of radiation to the extent that nine years later people in the affected areas still restrict children from playing outdoors and avoid eating mushrooms and other foods that are thought to be contaminated. Thus, there is a continuing, chronic level of stress and the symptoms displayed by the population affected appear to be expressed somatically much more than is found in classic PTSD.

The other chronic stressor being investigated is that which occurs in war situations. UNICEF has been at the forefront of stimulating research into the effects of war on children, particularly the dreadful war in former Yugoslavia. Stuvland et al. (1994) used a version of the War Trauma Questionnaire and showed that children in Sarajevo had experienced very high levels of stressful events such as sniping and shooting. Over 50% of their large sample had seen dead people and in half the cases they had actually witnessed the killings. The level of exposure to war-related stress correlated highly with symptoms of PTSD reported on the Impact of Events Scale and with levels of depression reported on the Birleson Scale. But again, it is difficult to disentangle the effects of the many other things that happen during a bloody war – the ethnic cleansing, the break-up of families, the forced move from home and school, the loss of parents, and so on. Children take on adult roles prematurely and then find it difficult to adjust to more normal, more age-appropriate demands when they return to school after hostilities cease.

While I am here arguing strongly that the context in which stressors occur has to be taken in to account in understanding the effects produced, sadly I have also to realize that these dreadful events will continue to occur and so will continue to provide natural laboratories for the study of the effects of stressors on children.

DESNOS

The debate about the different effects of single versus repeated stressors continues and the need to agree on a classification of stressors is clearly identified. Terr (1991) argued the need to distinguish what she termed Type I and Type II stressors – with greater dissociative symptoms being associated with the Type II, repeated stressors. Others, working with adults have argued the need to recognize a category called DESNOS – disorders of extreme stress not otherwise specified (Herman, 1992). As noted above, it is highly likely that different types of stressor will be associated with different psycho-logical reactions, both in terms of severity and content. A better understand-ing of these links will lead to better assessment and intervention.

RISK AND PROTECTIVE FACTORS

AGE

Age has been thought to be a factor in the development of PTSD. Indeed, DSM cited children as being at a high risk of psychopathology following a trauma. This seems to owe more to a particular theoretical view of child development than to any hard evidence. Age was not found to be related to Stress Reaction Index scores within the Armenian earthquake group (Pynoos et al., 1993). Indeed, it can be argued that developmental age in the sense of cognitive understanding could act in different ways – younger children may not fully appreciate the dangers they faced and so may be protected from strong emotional reactions (Keppel-Benson and Ollendick, 1993). This would imply that brighter children would be at an increased risk, and this does not appear to be the case by teenage years.

GENDER

It is generally found that girls score higher than boys on self-report measures of anxiety, depression and stress reactions following a trauma (Gibbs, 1989; Lonigan et al., 1991; Pynoos et al., 1993; Yule, 1992a). There are only a few unexplained exceptions to this pattern of findings and, as always, it is far from clear whether these are culturally or biologically determined differences.

ABILITY AND ATTAINMENT

In general, higher ability is seen as a protective factor against developing psychopathology. The developmental concern around appraisal of the threat noted earlier complicates the issue. Early studies of *Jupiter* survivors indicated that high risk was associated with prior *low* pre-accident attainment (Yule and Udwin, 1991). There are now many individual case examples of children's educational careers being thrown off course by the after-effects of traumas happening at crucial times, and there is also evidence that in general academic attainment falls for a while after a major trauma (Tsui, Dagwell and Yule, 1993).

FAMILY FACTORS

It has already been noted that children often try to protect their parents from learning about their reactions to a trauma for fear of upsetting the parents. Where parents have difficulty processing their own emotional reactions, they are less successful in helping their children (McFarlane, 1987). Families who had difficulty sharing immediate reactions had more problems later. While some authors argue that all of children's reactions to trauma are mediated by parental reactions, in my clinical and research experience this is far from the case. The evidence for there being direct effects on the children is overwhelming.

ASSESSING PTSD IN CHILDREN

I have said enough to make the case that while childhood PTSD can be very similar to the manifestation of PTSD in adults, it differs sufficiently to warrant separate assessment tools that are more relevant to their developmental level.

There are now many measures suitable for establishing post-traumatic reactions in children (Finch and Daugherty, 1993). The Children's Post Traumatic Stress Reaction Index (Frederick and Pynoos, 1988) has been widely used in a number of major studies (Nader et al., 1990; Pynoos et al., 1987, 1993; Pynoos and Nader, 1988) and has been shown to have good internal consistency and to relate well to clinical judgement of severity of PTSD (Yule, Bolton and Udwin, 1992). Saigh's (1989) Children's Posttraumatic Stress Disorder Inventory also has good psychometric properties. The Impact of Events Scale (Horowitz et al., 1979) has been found useful with children aged 8 and over (Yule and Udwin, 1991; Yule and Williams, 1990), especially when used in conjunction with measures of anxiety and depression (Stallard and Law, 1993; Yule and Udwin, 1991). However, factor analyses of the IES indicate that some items are misunderstood by children and should be replaced (Yule, ten Bruggencatte and Joseph, 1993).

There has been a rush to develop semi-structured interviews to elicit and quantify PTSD in children. It is laudable that at last children are being asked to give their own accounts of internal distress direct to professionals, but a number of the attempts at developing suitable interviews are misguided as they only rephrase DSM criteria into question format. Since some of the criteria are irrelevant to children, the exercise seems doomed. Far better to consider Pynoos and Eth's (1986) suggestions on conducting a good clinical interview.

There is a dearth of standardized approaches to assess stress reactions in children under the age of 8, although at least those in the age range 3 to 8 can give adequate verbal responses. There is a need to develop additional measures for younger children.

TREATMENT OF PTSD

While there have been a number of single case reports of treatment of children suffering PTSD, as yet there are no accounts of randomized controlled studies. For the most part, treatment approaches are predominantly cognitive-behavioural and appear to consist of adaptations of approaches used with adults (Yule, 1991).

CRITICAL INCIDENT STRESS DEBRIEFING

Critical incident stress debriefing techniques have been adapted for use with groups of children following a variety of traumas (Dyregrov, 1991). Such a structured crisis intervention approach was used with some children following the *Jupiter* sinking, with good effects on lowering the levels of intrusion and of fears (Yule and Udwin, 1991). Stallard and Law (1993) used two debriefing sessions to reduce distress in girls who survived a school bus crash.

GROUP TREATMENTS

Group treatments are obviously to be preferred as a first line of intervention when large numbers are involved. Gillis (1993) suggests that groups of six to eight are optimum, and advises that separate groups should be run for boys and girls. However, different types of incident surely require different responses from professionals (Galante and Foa, 1986; Yule and Williams, 1990) and it is too soon to pontificate on what should be a standard approach.

INDIVIDUAL TREATMENT

Individual treatment centres mainly on cognitive-behavioural therapies that aim both to help the survivor make sense of what happened and to master their feelings of anxiety and helplessness. Drug treatments, as in the rest of child psychopathology, have little place. Asking children to draw their experiences can be useful in helping them recall both the event and the emotions associated with it (Blom, 1986; Galante and Foa, 1986; Newman, 1976; Pynoos and Eth, 1986) but merely drawing the trauma is not a sufficient therapy. A recent study from former Yugoslavia where great emphasis was placed on getting children to express their emotions through drawing found that six months after having had very structured sessions on drawing and other expressive techniques, there was no measurable change in children's adjustment on a whole range of self-report measures of stress reactions (Bunjevac and Kuterovac, 1994).

Saigh (1986) was one of the first to provide clinical evidence that, as Rachman (1980) had predicted, there were dangers in using standard systematic desensitization approaches as the length of exposure sessions may be too short to permit adequate habituation of anxiety. It should also be remembered that where children are frightened by the vividness of their memories then relaxation may only serve to intensify the vividness. The theoretical aspects of exposure therapy in treating PTSD in children are discussed elsewhere (Saigh, Yule and Inamdar, 1995) and other suggestions of techniques to promote emotional processing are described in Rachman (1980), Yule (1991), Richards and Lovell (1990) and Saigh (1992).

There is considerable interest and scepticism in Eye Movement and Desensitization and Reprocessing (EMDR) treatment (Shapiro, 1991). To date there are no published accounts of its use with children and adolescents, although claims for its value are being made on the conference circuit! As with all techniques that have no clear rationale, caution has to be exercised. However, if symptomatic relief can really be attained in a few brief sessions, then the approach needs to be carefully evaluated. Since there does seem to be a different quality to the memories of a trauma that appear at the same time to be locked in, vivid and unchangeable by merely talking about them, then any technique that will allow emotional processing to proceed must be examined.

CONTINGENCY PLANNING

When trauma affects a large number of children at once, as in an accident at school, then a public health approach to dealing with the emergency is required (Pynoos, Goenjian and Steinberg, 1995). Schools need to plan ahead not only to deal with large-scale disasters, but also to respond to the needs of children after threatening incidents that affect only a few of them. Thus, there are now a number of texts written especially for schools to help them develop contingency plans to deal with the effects of a disaster (Johnson, 1993; Klingman, 1993; Yule and Gold, 1993).

CURRENT ISSUES AND FUTURE TRENDS

Gradually, the research and clinical communities are recognizing that major stressors produce stress reactions in children and adolescents that are not merely transient. A great deal of misery is caused by assuming that children are totally resilient. Now, the need is to understand more about the effects of single and repeated trauma on the short- and long-term adjustment of children.

The most elaborated model of a developmental approach to understanding the effects of trauma has been articulated by Pynoos and his colleagues (Pynoos, 1993; Pynoos, Steinberg and Wraith, 1995). The point is strongly argued that trauma may disrupt development and so the effects must be looked at within a developmental perspective. There may be immediate and distal effects. Pynoos pays particular attention to the potential retraumatizing effects of children being repeatedly exposed to reminders of the original trauma. Such a model highlights the need for different types of study that can help improve our interventions.

The issue of vividness of memory looms large in trying to help traumatized children. There is a need to integrate the clinical interventions with work in the mainstream of experimental cognitive and developmental psychology. Conway (1995) discusses the parameters associated with 'flashbulb memories' – namely that they tend to be associated with experiences that are both very surprising and very emotionally relevant to the individual. Van der Kolk (1994) produced evidence from a PET scan study to show that traumatic memories are indeed encoded non-verbally on the right temporal lobe, a further indication that such memories are less accessible to verbally mediated processing. As yet there are few studies of any psychophysiological, neurochemical or neurphysiological aspects of PTSD in children or adolescents and the time is approaching when these will be done to shed light on the developmental aspects of the condition.

We have begun to study the cognitive processing of emotions in children with PTSD, anxiety and depression using a modified Stroop paradigm and other tests of memory processing (Moradi et al., 1995). The preliminary results indicate that children and adolescents aged 9 to 16 respond to the Stroop very similarly to adults (Thrasher, Dalgliesh and Yule, 1994), in that they show more interference when trauma-related words as opposed to emotionally neutral or positive words are displayed. Having developed a paradigm that appears to work with much younger subjects than have been investigated previously, a whole new line of investigations is possible.

But above all, the time has come to institute proper treatment studies with children. The pioneering single-case studies of Saigh (1986) were vital in establishing that cognitive behavioural treatments work in individual cases. In the following decade, little progress has been made in extending this work and no randomized controlled studies have been published. There are uncontrolled studies of large-scale interventions by rapidly trained therapeutic aides in times of disaster and war, and these are certainly very promising. But we now need to develop a much more rigorous approach to evaluating alternative treatments, as well as to dissecting treatment packages to identify the necessary elements. The children are out there needing help. Ways of identifying them and assessing changes during treatment are sufficiently well developed as to be of clinical value. What is needed is the resolve to undertake proper evaluations. But, of course, the same can be said for the whole of applied child psychology!

REFERENCES

American Psychiatric Association (1980). *Diagnostic and Statistical Manual of Mental Disorders* (3rd edn), APA, Washington, DC.
American Psychiatric Association (1987). *Diagnostic and Statistical Manual of Mental Disorders* (third edn – revised), APA, Washington, DC.

American Psychiatric Association (1994). *Diagnostic and Statistical Manual of Mental Disorders* (4th edn), APA, Washington, DC.

Blom, G.E. (1986). A school disaster – intervention and research aspects, *Journal of the American Academy of Child Psychiatry*, **25**, 336–345.

Bunjevac, T. and Kuterovac, G. (1994). Report on the results of psychological evaluation of the art therapy program in schools in Hercegovina, UNICEF, Zagreb.

Conway, M. (1995). *Flashbulb Memories*, Lawrence Erlbaum, Hove.

Dyregrov, A. (1991). *Grief in Children: A Handbook for Adults*, Jessica Kingsley, London.

Finch, A.J. and Daugherty, T.K. (1993). Issues in the assessment of posttraumatic stress disorder in children, in Saylor, C.F. (ed.), *Children and Disasters*, ch. 3. pp. 45–66, Plenum Press, New York.

Frederick, C.J. (1985). Children traumatized by catastrophic situations, in Eth, S. and Pynoos, R. (eds) *Post-Traumatic Stress Disorder in Children*, ch. 4, pp. 73–99, American Psychiatric Press, Washington, DC.

Frederick, C.J. and Pynoos, R.S. (1988). *The Child Post-Traumatic Stress Disorder (PTSD) Reaction Index*, University of California, Los Angeles.

Galante, R. and Foa, D. (1986). An epidemiological study of psychic trauma and treatment effectiveness after a natural disaster, *Journal of the American Academy of Child Psychiatry*, **25**, 357–363.

Garmezy, N. and Rutter, M. (1985). Acute reactions to stress, in Rutter, M. and Hersov, L. (eds), *Child and Adolescent Psychiatry: Modern Approaches* (2nd edn), pp. 152–176, Blackwell, Oxford.

Gibbs, M.S. (1989). Factors in the victim that mediate between disaster and psychopathology: A review, *Journal of Traumatic Stress*, **2**, 489–514.

Gillis, H.M. (1993). Individual and small-group psychotherapy for children involved in trauma and disaster, in Saylor C.F. (ed.), *Children and Disasters*, ch. 9, pp. 165–186, Plenum Press, New York.

Herman, J.L. (1992). Complex PTSD: A syndrome in survivors of prolonged and repeated trauma, *Journal of Traumatic Stress*, **5**, 377–391.

Horowitz, M.J. (1976). *Stress-response syndromes*, Jason Aronson, New York.

Horowitz, M.J., Wilner, N. and Alvarez, W. (1979). Impact of event scale: A measure of subjective stress, *Psychosomatic Medicine*, **41**, 209–218.

Johnson, K. (1993) *School Crisis Management: A Team Training Guide*, Hunter House, Alameda, CA.

Joseph, S.A., Brewin, C.R., Yule, W. and Williams, R. (1991). Causal attributions and psychiatric symptoms in survivors of the *Herald of Free Enterprise* disaster, *British Journal of Psychiatry*, **159**, 542–546.

Joseph, S., Brewin, C., Yule, W. and Williams, R. (1993). Causal attributions and psychiatric symptoms in adolescent survivors of disaster, *Journal of Child Psychology and Psychiatry*, **34**, 247–253.

Keppel-Benson, J.M. and Ollendick, T.H. (1993). Posttraumatic stress disorders in children and adolescents in Saylor, C.F. (ed.), *Children and Disasters*, ch. 2, pp. 29–43, Plenum Press, New York.

Klingman, A. (1993). School-based intervention following a disaster, in Saylor, C.F. (ed.), *Children and Disasters*, ch. 10, pp. 187–210, Plenum Press, New York.

Lonigan, C.J., Shannon, M.P., Finch, A.J., Daugherty, T.K. and Saylor, C.M. (1991). Children's reactions to a natural disaster: Symptom severity and degree of exposure, *Advances in Behaviour Research and Therapy*, **13**, 135–154.

McFarlane, A.C. (1987). Family functioning and overprotection following a natural disaster: The longitudinal effects of post-traumatic morbidity, *Australia and New Zealand Journal of Psychiatry*, **21**, 210–218.

Misch, P., Phillips, M., Evans, P. and Berelowitz, M. (1993). Trauma in pre-school children: A clinical account, in Forrest, G. (ed.) *Trauma and Crisis Management*, ACPP Occasional Paper.

Moradi, A., Taghavi, R., Doost, H.N. and Yule, W. (1995). The performance of children with PTSD on the Stroop colour interference task, poster presented at the Fourth European Conference on Traumatic Stress, Paris, May.

Nader, K., Pynoos, R.S., Fairbanks, L. and Frederick, C. (1990). Childhood PTSD reactions one year after a sniper attack, *American Journal of Psychiatry*, **147**, 1526–1530.

Newman, C.J. (1976). Children of disaster: Clinical observation at Buffalo Creek, *American Journal of Psychiatry*, **133**, 306–312.

Parry Jones, W. (1992). Children of Lockerbie, paper presented at Guy's Hospital meeting.

Pynoos, R.S. (1993). Traumatic stress and developmental psychopathology in children and adolescents, *American Psychiatric Press Review of Psychiatry*, **12**, 205–238.

Pynoos, R.S. (1994). Preface, in Pynoos, R.S. (ed.), *Posttraumatic Stress Disorder: A Clinical Review*, Sidran Press, Lutherville, MD.

Pynoos, R.S. and Eth, S. (1986). Witness to violence: The child interview, *Journal of the American Academy of Child Psychiatry*, **25**, 306–319.

Pynoos, R.S., Frederick, C., Nader, K., Arroyo, W., Steinberg, A., Eth, S., Nunez, F., and Fairbanks, L. (1987). Life threat and posttraumatic stress in school-age children, *Archives of General Psychiatry*, **44**, 1057–1063.

Pynoos, R.S., Goenjian, A., Karakashian, M., Tashjian, M., Manjikian, R., Manoukian, G., Steinberg, A.M. and Fairbanks, L.A. (1993). Posttraumatic stress reactions in children after the 1988 Armenian earthquake, *British Journal of Psychiatry*, **163**, 239–247.

Pynoos, R.S., Goenjian, A. and Steinberg, A.M. (1995). Strategies of disaster interventions for children and adolescents, in Hobfoll, S.E. and de Vries, M. (eds), *Extreme Stress and Communities: Impact and Intervention*, Kluwer, Dordrecht.

Pynoos, R.S. and Nader, K. (1988). Psychological first aid and treatment approach for children exposed to community violence: research implications, *Journal of Traumatic Stress*, **1**, 243–267.

Pynoos, R.S., Steinberg, A.M. and Wraith, R. (1995 in press). A developmental model of childhood traumatic stress, in Cicchetti, D. and Cohen, D. (eds) *Manual of Developmental Psychopathology*, John Wiley & Sons, New York.

Rachman, S. (1980). Emotional processing, *Behaviour Research and Therapy*, **18**, 51–60.

Richards, D. and Lovell, K. (1990). Imaginal and in-vivo exposure in the treatment of PTSD, paper read at the Second European Conference on Traumatic Stress, Netherlands, September.

Saigh, P.A. (1986). In vitro flooding in the treatment of a 6-yr-old boy's posttraumatic stress disorder, *Behaviour Research and Therapy*, **24**, 685–688.

Saigh, P.A. (1989). The development and validation of the Children's Posttraumatic Stress Disorder Inventory, *International Journal of Special Education*, **4**, 75–84.

Saigh, P.A. (1992). The behavioral treatment of child and adolescent posttraumatic stress disorder, *Advances in Behavioiur Research and Therapy*, **14**, 247–275.

Saigh, P.A., Yule, W. and Inamdar, S.C. (1995 in press) Imaginal flooding of traumatized children and adolescents, *Journal of School Psychology*.

Shapiro, F. (1991). Eye movement desensitization and reprocessing procedure: From EMD to EMD/R – a new treatment model for anxiety and related traumas, *Behavior Therapist*, **14**, 133–135.

Stallard, P. and Law, F. (1993). Screening and psychological debriefing of adolescent survivors of life-threatening events, *British Journal of Psychiatry*, **163**, 660–665.

Stuvland et al. (1994). A UNICEF report on war trauma among children in Sarajevo, Zagreb, UNICEF.

Terr, L.C. (1979). The children of Chowchilla, *Psychoanalytic Study of the Child*, **34**, 547–623.

Terr, L.C. (1988). What happens to early memories of trauma? A study of twenty children under age five at the time of documented traumatic events, *Journal of the American Academy of Child and Adolescent Psychiatry*, **27**, 96–104.

Terr, L.C. (1991). Childhood traumas – An outline and overview, *American Journal of Psychiatry*, **148**, 10–20.

Thrasher, S., Dalgliesh, T. and Yule, W. (1994). Information processing in post-traumatic stress disorder, *Behaviour Research and Therapy*, **32**, 247–254.

Tsui, E., Dagwell, K. and Yule, W. (1993). Effect of a disaster on children's academic attainment. (in preparation).

van der Kolk, B. (1994). Plenary presentation at 'Trauma, Memory and Dissociation', the 10th Annual Meeting of the International Society for Traumatic Stress Studies, Chicago, 5–9 November.

Wolfe, V., Gentile, C. and Wolfe, D.A. (1989). The impact of sexual abuse on children: A PTSD formulation. *Behavior Therapy*, **20**, 215–228.

World Health Organization (1992) *International Classification of Diseases: 10th Edition (ICD 10)*, WHO, Geneva.

Yule, W. (1991). Work with children following disasters, in Herbert, M. (ed.) *Clinical Child Psychology: Social Learning, Development and Behaviour*, ch. 20, pp. 349–363, John Wiley & Sons, Chichester.

Yule, W. (1992a). Post traumatic stress disorder in child survivors of shipping disasters: The sinking of the 'Jupiter'. *Psychotherapy and Psychosomatics*, **57**, 200–205.

Yule, W. (1992b). Resilience and vulnerability in child survivors of disasters, in Tizard, B. and Varma, V. (eds), *Vulnerability and Resilience: A festschrift for Ann and Alan Clarke*, pp. 82–98, Jessica Kingsley, London.

Yule, W. (1994). Post traumatic stress disorder, in Rutter, M., Taylor, E. and Hersov, L. (eds), *Child and Adolescent Psychiatry: Modern Approaches* (3rd edn), Basil Blackwell, Oxford.

Yule, W., Bolton, D. and Udwin, O. (1992). Objective and subjective predictors of PTSD in adolescents, paper presented at 'Trauma and Tragedy', the World Conference of the International Society for Traumatic Stress Studies, Amsterdam, 21–26 June.

Yule, W. and Gold, A. (1993). *Wise Before the Event: Coping with Crises in Schools*, Calouste Gulbenkian Foundation, London.

Yule, W., ten Bruggencatte, S. and Joseph, S. (1994). Principal components analysis of the Impact of Events Scale in children who survived a shipping disaster, *Personality and Individual Differences*, **16**, 685–691.

Yule, W. and Udwin, O. (1991). Screening child survivors for post-traumatic stress disorders: Experiences from the 'Jupiter' sinking, *British Journal of Clinical Psychology*, **30**, 131–138.

Yule, W., Udwin, O. and Murdoch, K. (1990). The 'Jupiter' sinking: Effects on children's fears, depression and anxiety, *Journal of Child Psychology and Psychiatry*, **31**, 1051–1061.

Yule, W. and Williams, R. (1990). Post traumatic stress reactions in children, *Journal of Traumatic Stress*, **3**(2), 279–295.

INDEX

adolescents, 150
alcohol problems, 77–88
allergy hypothesis of alcoholism, 78–79
avoidant personality disorder, 43–61

bias in evaluation of outcomes, 104–105
biological theory, 2, 138
blood-injury phobia, 27
borderline personality disorder, 63–76

clomipramine, 27
cognitive biases in gambling, 94–109
comorbidity in social phobia, 48, 55, 58
critical cognitions, 13, 15

depression, 10, 58, 129, 135
dialectical behaviour therapy, 73
dogma, 80

economic factors, 1, 90–91
effectiveness of CBT in alcoholism, 83
emotion, 121–132
emotion as communication, 125–126
empathy, 127
exposure principle, 27, 29

gambler's fallacy, 105–109
gambling, 89–99
grief, 130

hallucinations, 69
hypochondriasis, 19

illusion of control, 95–98
instrumental emotions, 127

learning theory, 3

mono-amine oxidase inhibitors, 56
motivation in alcoholism, 83–84

neuropsychology, 65–68, 138–139

obsessive–compulsive disorder, 18–19, 27

panic disorder, 9, 11–16, 31–32
post-traumatic stress disorder, 147–162
preparedness, 31
prevalence of pathological gambling, 90–91
primary emotion, 126
psychological trauma, 70–72
psychotherapy, 3–5

randomness, 106–109
re-experiencing, 150

safety seeking behaviour, 34–38
schizophrenia, 64, 69, 133–146
schizotypal personality disorder, 63–76
secondary emotion, 126–127
self-esteem, 141–142
sexual abuse, 153
social phobia, 43–61
social skills deficits, 57, 139
suicidal behaviour, 63
superstitions, 98–99
systematic desensitization, 6–7, 27

two-process theory, 29–31

Related titles of interest from Wiley...

Cognitive Therapy for Delusions, Voices and Paranoia
Paul Chadwick, Max Birchwood and Peter Trower

Provides a description of cognitive therapy and its application to the management of severe mental illness.

0-471-93888-2   250pp   1996   Hardback
0-471-96173-6   250pp   1996   Paperback

Obsessive Compulsive Disorder
A Cognitive and Neuropsychological Perspective
Frank Tallis

Reviews the nature and incidence of OCD in the light of the related research on cognitive processes and cognitive neuropsychology, and discusses the treatment of OCD with special reference to behavioural and cognitive therapies.

0-471-95775-5   272pp   1995   Hardback
0-471-95772-0   272pp   1995   Paperback

Cognitive Behaviour Therapy for Psychosis
Theory and Practice
David Fowler, Philippa Garety and Elizabeth Kuipers

Offers a comprehensive approach which focuses on the four main problems presented by people with psychosis: emotional disturbance, psychotic symptoms like delusions and bizarre beliefs, social disabilities and relapse risk.

0-471-93980-3   224pp   1995   Hardback
0-471-95618-X   224pp   1995   Paperback

Psychological Management of Schizophrenia
Edited by Max Birchwood and Nicholas Tarrier

Offers a practical guide for mental health professionals wanting to develop and enhance their skills in new treatment approaches.

0-471-95056-4   176pp   1994   Paperback